Books by William H. Gass

The World Within the Word

The World Within the Word

Essays by

William H. Gass

BASIC
BOOKS

A Member of the Perseus Books Group

The World Within the Word was originally published
in hardcover by Alfred A. Knopf Publishers in 1978.
The Basic Books edition is published by arrangement
with Alfred A. Knopf.

Copyright © 1971, 1972, 1973, 1974, 1975, 1976
by William H. Gass
Published by Basic Books,
A Member of the Perseus Books Group

Library of Congress Cataloging-in-Publication Data
Gass, William H. 1924–
    The world within the word.
    Reprint of the 1st ed. Published in 1978 by Knopf,
New York.
Includes bibliographical references.
    1. Literature, Modern—History and Criticism—
Addresses, essays, lectures.   I. Title.
[PM710.G33   1979]   809   79-52364

ISBN 0-465-02625-7

00 01 02 / 10 9 8 7 6 5 4 3 2 1

For

Robert Silvers

who made me write

most of these essays

and

to

Mary

who had to endure

their doing

Contents

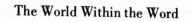

The World Within the Word

The Doomed
in Their Sinking

Crane went sudden as a springboard. The Gulf gave nothing back. My mother, I remember, took her time. She held the house around her as she held her bathrobe, safely doorpinned down its floorlength, the metal threads glinting like those gay gold loops which close the coat of a grenadier, though there were gaps of course . . . unseemly as sometimes a door is on a chain . . . so that to urinate she had to hoist the whole thing like a skirt, collecting the cloth in fat pleats with her fingers, wads which soon out-oozed her fists and sprang slowly away . . . one consequence . . . so that she felt she had to hover above the hole, the seat (clouds don't care about *their* aim), unsteadily . . . necessarily . . . more and more so as the nighttime days drew on, so that the robe grew damp the way the sweater on a long drink grows, soggy from edge to center, until I found I cared with what success she peed when what she swallowed was herself and what streamed out of her in consequence seemed me.

Though Hart shed his bathrobe frugally before he jumped, my mother, also saving, would have worn hers like the medal on a hussar straight through living room and loony bin, every nursing home and needle house we put her in, if those points hadn't had to come out (they confiscate your pins, belts, buckles, jewelry, teeth, and they'd take the air, too, if it had an edge, because the crazy can garrote themselves with a length of breath, their thoughts are open razors, their eyes go off like guns), though there was naturally no danger in these baubles to herself, for my mother was living the long death, her whole life passing before her as she went, the way those who drown themselves are said to have theirs pass . . . a consequence, yes . . . her own ocean like a message in a bottle, so that she sank slowly somewhere as a stone sill sinks beneath the shoes of pilgrims and tourists, not like Plath with pills, or Crane or Woolf with water, Plath again by gas, or Berryman from a bridge, but, I now believe, in the best way possible, because the long death is much more painful and punishing than even disembowelment or bleach, and it inflicts your dying on those you are blaming for it better than burning or blowing up—during an exquisitely extended stretch—since the same substance which both poisons you, preserves, you both have and eat, enjoy and suffer your revenges together, as well as the illusion that you can always change your mind.

Yet my mother wasn't what we call a suicide, even though she died as though she'd cut her throat when the vessels burst there finally, and my father, who clenched his teeth till neither knees nor elbows would unfist, dying of his own murderous wishes like the scorpion who's supposed to sting itself to death—no—he wasn't one either: both had a terribly tenacious grip on life . . . so that some suicides will survive anything, and many who court death have no desire to wed her . . . it mixes us up . . .

Should a suicide be regarded as the last stage of a series of small acts against the self, since the murderer who arsenics his wife little by little is still a murderer though she takes a decade dying; or does this confuse kinds of hostility in a serious way, because harsh words aren't the same as blows or their bruises, desire isn't adultery whatever Jesus preached, not even a degree of it? Cigarettes shorten our life, but the alcoholic's fuddle mimics death (the loss of control, the departure of the soul) in a way the smoker's never does. What can we make of that? We shall manage something.

My mother managed. She was what we call a dedicated passive . . . liquidly acquiescent . . . supinely on the go. Still, she went in her own way—the way, for instance, her robe was fastened.

Socrates acquiesced in his own execution, others demand theirs. The Kamikaze pilot intends his death, but does not desire it. Malcolm Lowry, who choked on his vomit, evidently desired his, but did not intend it. Soldiers charging the guns at Verdun neither wished for death nor were bent on it, though death was what they expected. My mother accepted.

I used to think my father was the actively aggressive one because while he sat, temporized, bided and brooded and considered and consolidated, he growled, swore, and made horrible faces.

During the decline of Christian morals, few groups have risen so rapidly in the overall estimation of society. It was dangerous for Donne to suggest that suicide was sometimes not a sin. It was still daring for Hume to reason that it was sometimes not a crime. Later one had to point out that it was sometimes not simply a sickness of the soul. Now it seems necessary to argue that it is sometimes not a virtue.

To paraphrase Freud, what does a suicide want? Not what he gets, surely.

Some simply think of death as the absence of their present state, a state which pursues them like a malignant disease and which cannot be otherwise escaped. Others consider it quite positively, as though to die were to get on in the world. Seventh Heaven, after all, is a most desirable address. Still others spend their life like money, purchasing this or that, but their aim is to buy, not to go broke. Are we to say to them (all and every kind) what we often say to children? no, Freddie, you don't want a pet boa, you wouldn't like the way it swallows mice.

It doesn't follow at all that because it is easy enough to kill yourself, it is easy enough to get, in that case, what you want. Can you really be said to want what you cannot possibly understand? or what you are in abysmal confusion about? or what is provenly contrary to your interests? or is plainly impossible? Is "I'd rather be dead" anything like: "I want to be a chewed-up marshmallow"; or: "I want 6 and 3 to make 10"; or: "I want to be a Fiji princess"; or: "I want a foot-long dong"; or: "I want that seventh scotch-on-the-rocks"; or "I would love to make it with Lena Horne"?

It's been said that suicide is a crime of status. Poverty limits it, as it virtuously inhibits so many other vices. It occurs, we are also told, when its victim is not properly folded into the general batter of society, and when external constraints upon one's behavior are weak. (The superego, however, can come down on conscience like a hammer.) So suicide is a disease of singularity and selfhood, because as we are elevated in the social system, and authorities "over" us are removed, as we wobble out on our own, the question of whether it is better to be or not to be arises with real relevance for the first time, since the burden of being is felt most fully by the self-determining self.

In a sense, society has already rejected the prospective suicide, hurled him overboard as Jonah was. His beliefs, all that was beloved, have forsaken him. He is a jinx. Once in the water, is it his fault he drowns? Hamlet, of course, has too many motives. Death and adultery have parted him from his family—murder and adultery from his king—imbecility from his love. He's in the firmly impalpable grip of guilt. Above all, he is too fine a spirit for this wormy world. Don't we often think so?

The logic of misery hides its premises to forget its fallacies: Hamlet's a prison; Hamlet's a Dane; Denmark's a prison; then is the world one.

On the other hand, if I were to commit suicide, I am sure

it would be from a surfeit of family and society, in a desperate effort to escape its selfish swallowing hug; yet to feel that way may already signify the absence of the necessary melodic relation. To be ruled by Reason, rather than by Father, Nature, King, or God, is an antisocial resolve. The autonomous self listens only to its own voice, unaffected by the grate of force, the lure of bribes, or the temptations of love.

Anyway, men have been killing themselves, we may suppose, as long as life has afforded them the opportunity, but to be sick of life is not the same as having a painful illness or suffering a shame so denobling life is no longer endurable. The presence everywhere of decay, disease, coarseness, brutality, and death—the flow of value into a blank abyss—this death-in-life that made living like the aftertaste of drunken vomit—was the black center of the plague of melancholy which afflicted the Elizabethans.

Hamlet's question, indeed, throws everything in doubt. The doubt becomes a commonplace, and a century later Pope defends the self-slaughter of an unfortunate lady in an elegant poem which takes for granted what continually shocked the Elizabethans—the democracy of death.

> *Poets themselves must fall, like those they sung;*
> *Deaf the prais'd ear, and mute the tuneful tongue.*
> *Ev'n he, whose soul now melts in mournful lays,*
> *Shall shortly want the gen'rous tear he pays;*
> *Then from his closing eyes thy form shall part,*
> *And the last pang shall tear thee from his heart,*
> *Life's idle business at one gasp be o'er,*
> *The Muse forgot, and thou belov'd no more!*

Definitions of suicide, like definitions of adultery, are invariably normative, and frequently do little more than reflect the shallowest social attitudes, embody the most parochial perspectives. Above all, these attitudes are for the most part deeply irrational. Failures may be executed, for example, while the corpses of successes are assaulted. Studies of suicide, including those of Alvarez and Choron,[1] are soon elaborately confused about desire, intention, deed, and consequence, ownership and responsibility (whether we belong to ourselves, society, or God); neglect the difference between act and action, refuse to decide whether to include deaths of soul (Rimbaud?) as well as deaths of body, since holy living may indeed be holy dying, so that physical and metaphysical murders become hopelessly intertwined; and they are content to record, with a tourist's widened eyes, the sweet, sour, wise, or benighted opinions of nearly everyone.

If we are to call suicide every self-taken way out of the world, then even the Platonic pursuit of knowledge, involving as it does the separation of reason from passion and appetite, is suicidal . . . as are, of course, the search for ecstatic states, and longings for mystical union. It is the habit of such examinations to mess up these matters as if they were so many paints whose purpose was purely to give pleasure to the fingers.

Nowadays the significance of a suicide for the suicide and the significance of that suicide for society are seldom the same. If, according to the social workers' comforting cliché, they are often a cry for help, they're just as frequently a solemn vow of silence. Nevertheless, it is easy to imagine circumstances under which some of our conventional kinds of suicide would be impossible—impossible because we would simply refuse to recognize them. The liver fails. The veins collapse. Sleep seizes the wheel. No suicides there. Suppose that starving yourself were a "going-home-to-God" (no suicide there), while slashing your wrists were a "cowardly-copping-out." In order to speak your piece properly you might have to shoot, hang, or poison yourself. Sprott records the case of "one that hang'd himself, upon his Knees, with a Bible on a Stool open

---

[1] A. Alvarez, *The Savage God* (New York: Random House, 1972), and Jacques Choron, *Suicide* (New York: Scribner's, 1972).

before him, and a Paper to signifie that he had repented."[2]
The liberated woman must do something manly, shotgun herself at the very least, avoid sleeping pills like the devil—that
soothing syrup of the oppressed sex. If you don't want the manner of your dying to be a message to mankind, if your aim is
just to get the hell out, then you will have to be as clever at
disarming symbols as Mallarmé. Alas, the way we think and
write about suicides would provide many with still another motive, an additional despair, were they alive again and merci-
lessly aware.

Breeding is not out of place even here. Petronius, the critics say, had class. Cato has consistently had a good press. And
we write cheery loving thank-you notes; we put our affairs in
order; we do not leap on top of people, run in front of cars
owned by innocent strangers, bleed in public, allow the least
hint of indecision, ambiguity, or failure to spoil our aim, and
avoid every form of vulgar display. The ledge-huggers want to
be coaxed, for instance. That's a suicide for shopgirls. On the
other hand, if you are, like Mishima, too stylish, your actions
risk being thought incomprehensible. My favorites are rather
theatrical, though. Choron tells us how Arria, the wife of a Roman senator who'd been caught plotting, in order to stimulate
her husband to his duty, plunged a sword into her breast and
then handed it to him with the words: *Paete, non dolet* (It does
not hurt). Others seek the third rail and interrupt the service;
swallow combs, crosses, safety pins, fountain pens, needles,
nails; they blow up the planes they are riding in, smother themselves in plastic Baggies, or simply find a wall and dash out
their brains. Sprott says that by 1600

> Suicidal types had become traditional: the epicure, the
> disappointed lover, the great spirit, the melancholiac, the
> jealous man, the frightened child, the debauched appren-

---

[2] S. E. Sprott, *The English Debate on Suicide from Donne to Hume* (La Salle, Illinois:
Open Court, 1961).

tice, the unfortunate merchant, the bloody murderer des-
pairing of God's pardon, the desperate zealot, the "tender
Conscience't Despairer" . . . (p. 36)

Though methods, motives, meanings differ ("Whose head is
hanging from the swollen strap?" asked Crane), most can be
expected to mess up their deaths exactly as they've messed up
their lives. Poor folks. Poor ways.

Never mind. If you pay with your life you get a ticket to
the tent: martyrs, daredevils, the accident-prone, those who
cheat "justice" as Hannibal did, or are condemned by it as
Seneca was; those who would die rather than surrender, even
en masse, as the Jews died at Massada; those too poor, too
rich, too proud, too ineffably wicked; all addicts, Cleopatras,
all desolate Didos, mystics, faddists, young sorrowful Wer-
thers; the fundamentally frigid, who cannot allow life to give
them any pleasure; the incurably ill, the mad, the metaphysically gloomy; widows who go up with the rest of the property,
and all those who from disgust or rage protest this life with em-
blematic ignitions and ritual sacrifice . . . it's like cataloguing
books according to the color of their covers . . . the mourners,
the divided selves (not just Cartesians, severed into bum and
bicycle as Beckett's men are, but those who are cut up into
competing personalities as vicious as sisters in some *Cin-
derella*); then the downright stupid, the inept and careless, the
sublimely heroic, the totally disgraced . . . the color may be
significant (the blue cover of *Ulysses* is), but it is scarcely a
mode of classification which carves reality at the joints . . .
those whom guilt feeds on as if they were already carrion; the
Virginia Woolfs, too, who enter their own imagery, and the
ones for whom death is a deer park, a convent, a place in
outer space; also the impotent, ugly, acned, lonely; the inadvertently pregnant, and otherwise those who embrace their as-
sassins, or who have felt only the hold of their own hand, thus
to come and go finally in the same way . . . from little death
to large . . . everyone's welcome.

Lost in lists, in the surveyor's sweepings, borne along on conjecture like gutter water, the same act can signify anything you like, depending on the system—even the mood or the line of the eye—which gives it meaning: I cock my head one way and it appears to me that my mother was murdered; I cock it another and she seems a specially vindictive suicide; while if I face firmly forward as one in military ranks she seems to have been overcome by a rather complex illness, a chronic and progressively worsening disease. Simply examining "suicides" is like trying to establish a science of—let's say—*sallescape*, which we can imagine contains the whys and wherefores of room-leaving. The word confers a fictitious unity upon a rabble of factors, and the ironic thing about suicide itself, intrinsically considered (and what my little litanies have been designed to demonstrate), is that it is a wholly empty act. It is—more than Rigaut, the Dada hero, was—an empty suitcase.

And if the suicide believes his final gesture, like the last line of an obscure poem, will unite, clarify, and give meaning to all that has gone before; or if actual poems have held offhand hints—

The news from Spain got worse. The President of my Form
at South Kent turned up at Clare, one of the last let out of Madrid.
He designed the Chapel the School later built
& killed himself, I never heard why
or just how, it was something to do with a bridge.
(Berryman: "Transit")

or seemed like chilling scenarios—

> *We have come so far, it is over.*
>
> *Each dead child coiled, a white serpent,*
> *One at each little*
>
> *Pitcher of milk, now empty.*
> (Plath: "Edge")

so that the line between literature and life appears underdrawn (before she killed herself, Sylvia Plath put out two mugs of milk for her children); or if he has fallen for a romantic comparison like Camus's "An act like this is prepared within the silence of the heart, as is a great work of art," then at least he will suffer no further disappointment dead, because, of course, acts aren't language, and there's no poetry at all in suicide, only in some accounts of it . . . significance, value *in this sense*, belongs solely to sentences. Actions, and other similar events, have meaning only secondarily, as we impute it to them, and so may mean many things to many people. Words are acts only secondarily. They principally exist in the systems which establish and define them (as numbers do in mathematics), so while feasting may mean one thing to a Jew and quite another to a Samoan, the word *"Traum,"* uttered anywhere by anybody, remains irrevocably German.

Death will not fill up an empty life and in a line of verse it occupies only five letters of space.

Choron's readable little handbook, with its capsule summaries of speculation, its few tables of statistics, brief histories of opinions, merely provokes its questions, instead of asking them, and touches so lightly on all its subjects, they never feel it. Totally porous, the data are simply slowed down a trifle in seeping through. It resembles Choron's earlier *Death and Modern Man* in being a kind of easy introductory text.

Alvarez, observing the immense diversity of his material, wisely offers no solutions. Yet because he does not rigorously differentiate sorts, define terms, regulate interpretations, exclude kinds, but is content to report, reflect, admonish, and look on, his "study" turns out to be gossipy and anecdotal, though sometimes splendidly so, as his account of the suicide of Sylvia Plath is, because Alvarez is sensitive and sympathetic, knows how to handle a text, and writes with conscience and skill about a subject which is close enough to his own personal concerns (he is himself a "failed" suicide) that one could reasonably expect it to shake both skill and conscience as though they were rags in a gale.

It must have seemed like a good idea to sandwich his historical and literary studies of suicide between two kinds of direct acquaintance with it, all the more so when Alvarez's dissatisfaction with most theoretical investigations lies in their natural lack of contact with inner feeling, although much the same might be said of the physical laws for falling bodies, especially when the falling body is your own. The result of this division has not been entirely happy, however. Natural reticence, moral restraint, and simple lack of knowledge make his accounts of suicide from the inside-side seriously deficient in essential data, and therefore reduce them to sensitively told and frequently moving *stories*, although with less excuse Choron manages to make even the expounding of a theory sound like gossip (in effect: "Do you know what Plato said? Well—you won't believe this—but *he* said . . .").

Throughout *The Savage God*, too, again because it has no ruling principle, details fly out like sparks from every point that's struck, to fade without a purpose. The conditions surrounding Chatterton's suicide, for example, are certainly interesting, and Alvarez recites them nicely enough, but which ones really count, and which ones don't, and how do they count if they do, and if they do by how much? Vivid details, picturesque circumstances . . . my mother's copterlike bathroom posture, her gap-pinned robe, miscolored toes . . . well, their relevance isn't clear. Perhaps they have mainly a vaudeville function—to enliven without enlightening. Throughout, my mention of my mother merely mimics the problem.

The value of *The Savage God*, and it is high, lies mainly in the humanity of the mind which composed it, in the literary excellence of its composition, and the suggestiveness of many of its passages—the moment-by-moment thoughtfulness of its author as a reader.

The world of the suicidal is, in a certain sense (for all its familiar elements: pain, grief, confusion, failure, loss . . .), a private and impenetrable one, hence the frustration of those who are trying to help, and whose offers to do so, as raps on the glass disturb fish, often simply insult the suicide immersed in his situation. It is a consciousness trapped, enclosed by a bell jar, in the image which encloses Plath's novel, and Alvarez's book should do a great deal to correct the sentimentalist's happy thought that art is a kind of therapy for the sick, trapped, homeless, and world-weary, and that through it, deep personal problems get worked benignly out.

Poetry is cathartic only for the unserious, for in front of the rush of expressive need stands the barrier of form, and when the hurdler's scissored legs and outstretched arms carry him over the bars, the limp in his life, the headache in his heart, the emptiness he's full of, are as absent as his streetshoes, which will pinch and scrape his feet in all the old leathery ways once the race is over and he has to walk through the front door of his future like a brushman with some feckless patter and a chintzy plastic prize.

Rilke sometimes took this therapeutic attitude toward the writing of *Malte Laurids Brigge*, but if writing kept him sane, as he thought, it was one of the chief sources of his misery as well. If life is hard, art is harder. Plath's last poems, considered in this way, are announcements and warnings; they are promises; and their very excellence was a threat to the existence of their author, a woman whom success had always vanquished, and who was certainly defeated without it. Not only does the effort of creation often cultivate our problems at their roots, as Alvarez notes, the rich eloquence of their eventual formulation may give to some "solutions" an allure that is abnormal, one that art confers, not life. And if we have tried often enough, warned, performed and promised, must we not sometime keep that promise, if only to ensure that our sufferings have not been mockeries and showoffs, and succeed at failure one final time?

Malcolm Lowry, that eminent drunk, perhaps put Plath's particular case best when he wrote:

> *When the doomed are most eloquent in their sinking,*
> *It seems that then we are least strong to save.*

Writing. Not writing. Twin terrors. Putting one's mother into words . . . It may have been easier to put her in her grave.

Malcolm Lowry

There is no o'clock in a cantina. They are dim as a church is dim, often candle-lit or momentarily illuminated by sudden dusts of light from slits in dirty unscheduled walls, and there is the frequent murmur of the priests at service or the worshippers who attend even at odd hours the shrine of this or that outlandish saint—the Virgin for those who have nobody with, for instance—sanctuaries with strange yet significant names: El Bosque or the Bella Vista Bar, the Salón Ofélia, El Petate, El Farolito (Lowry once shuffled up a book of poems called *The Lighthouse Invites the Storm*); and indeed one is drawn in out of the Mexican light or the English or Canadian, out of Paris, from dockside or the railroad station, out of a light like a fall of hail, in Haiti, in Vancouver, at the bus depot with its daystorms, the endless sterile walkwells of airports, neon nighttimes in New York, and there is a mirror—*absolutamente necesario*—behind the bar which reflects the door, a chloroformed square, the street beyond, and there are bottles which it multiplies, their labels too, like the face of the drinker, names which, on the Day of the Dead in Mexico, and the day of his own demise, Malcolm Lowry's alcoholic hero reads as one reads scripture: Tenampa, perhaps, and Barreteago, certainly the beautiful Oaxaqueñan gourd of *mescal de olla* from which the same British consul's drink is measured, a flask of peppermint cordial, Tequila Añejo, Anís doble de Mallorca, a violet decanter of Henry Mallet's *delicioso licor*, and that tall voluted column of Anís del Mono on which a devil brandishes a pitchfork like a poster on a pillar, while in back of the bar there's a barman called The Elephant, though in the Mexico of Lowry's novel *Under the Volcano*, it may be a boy with an equally absurd name like A Few Fleas, or possibly it is a young man who is borrowing a puff of your cigarette while you stumble aloud after the slowing train of your thought; then there will usually be saucers of toothpicks laid about, salt, chilis, lemons, a tumblerful of straws, and crossed spoons in a glass tankard on the counter, or in the USA, soggy with bottle spill and the sweat of highballs, cash register receipts in a smear of purple print.

Cantina means cellar, means cave, but it sounds like a song, and it is Lowry's favorite playground, with its teeters, slides, and roundabouts, its sandbox and its swings, although the Consul sits there like a bum on a bench, the beautiful ruin of a man, now as splendidly incompetent and out of place as a john in a junkyard. He shakes too badly to shave or to sign his name. He misplaces his Plymouth. He neglects to pull socks on his nephritic feet. His penis cannot stand, and he likewise falls down in the street.

The drunk returns to childhood—in this case, babyboyhood. Innocence reclaims him. Since there is no o'clock in a cantina, he escapes his age. Lowry, like the Consul, drank himself back through his life: from the squatter he became, the failure he was, the writer, sailor, talker, Cantabrigian and momentary master of the uke, the unwilling English publicschoolboy he had been, to that rich man's fourth and quite unnecessary son where he began; not quite to recover the past, part of which was painful as a burn, but to go over it again and get it right, and to reach the desired condition of helplessness. The alcoholic trance is not just a haze, as though the eyes were also unshaven. It is not a mere buzzing in the ears, a dizziness or disturbance of balance. One arrives in the garden again, at nursery time, when the gentle animals are fed and in all the world there are only toys.

In such a state, like Lear's fool, he has a license to speak the truth, let impulse loose, and not be blamed. He can lie, too, and not be blamed. He can play, can act—playact—and not be blamed. He is excused. Unable to fend—to eat, to dress, conduct affairs—unable to fuck: he is excused. If pleased, he laughs; if offended, he sulks; if disappointed, he throws himself wailing on the world like a mourner on a grave. Of course, he'll be accused of being intoxicated, and of that charge it is absolutely necessary for him to be guilty, but he can't be blamed for being impotent or ugly, for failing to face up, for losing heart or job or love or money, for fecklessness, for rage: that is the main thing, and he will happily accept this lesser charge in the place of all the others, since it is also true that he is, in the moment of deepest fuddle, mad, inhabited, possessed of prophetic powers, so *perfectamente borracho* that like the most naïve children of Christ, the fools of God, he makes with his dirty lying toper's tongue the inspired speech of the Spirit, and on that ground, too, he is excused . . . excused.

Let out. Let off. Excused. Not for long, though. Not for nearly long enough. Eventually the body fails. The chemical has forced it to concoct a consciousness it cannot care for or continue; it cannot support this basin of puke or endure the ringing of these poisonous bells, the reverberations of their stink. Frequently the victim sweats his pits sore as pain passes away through the pores, and the steel shutters of the cantina come down with a crash. Later, though not enough later, not an eternity after, after only a drugged snooze, the drinker awakes with a conscience ready to be reconsumed, and to a sort of soberness so physically wretched and an awareness so vengeful and spiritually cruel, that another species of hallucination takes possession of him. Kafka could not describe the transformations, or Sabbatai Zevi account for them. Thus rubbed from a bottle, the day begins again, even though it's the moon that's up, and a consciousness must reinvent the world.

For the male . . . ah . . . nightly there advances toward him the body of his presumed beloved, since it will be clock-dark eventually; it will be lovetime; and it was better when he was a baby in his bed and he was hoping not to wet it or pass blood through his nose or be frightened into screaming by shadows representing the self holding a knife or a garrote; it was better then to lie down upon dreams which would be soon shaken by the hooves of dark horses, than it was now to be in bed with a body which expected passion, and his blood to be bottled in his penis simply because there were breasts nearby or viny hair like darkness creeping across a doorway; and so daily toward evening it becomes desperately necessary to have a drink, to sit in the cool of a cantina, the whole of him, as if he had already penetrated the fearful crease as easily as parting strings of fly-beads and was now conversing calmly in the quieting comfort of the cunt . . . warm womb of the world . . . whatever . . . because a cantina signifies the rich enticing inwardness of all things.

The cantina is not, then, a complete calamity; it calms; it protects; it restores. It is the head itself, the container of consciousness too, and the bar which bisects it is the bar of judgment, where cases are argued; and in the cantina everything is beautiful, even when ugly; everything is significant, even when trivial; all is orderly, even when the drinker is deranged; all is known; and even if there are headaches and the eyes fall back in their sockets like stones; even if the saloon pitches like a ship in a storm; even if every word is a groan and sickness begs the stomach for something to flush through its throat the way turds whirl in a toilet, there is always tomorrow; there is always the hope of change, the fresh resolution, and the drink to celebrate it, for didn't I just say that the container of consciousness was the brown pint, the clear quart, and haven't whole cultures worshipped the spirit in the plant, the pulque which preserves, the life in the vine? because wine winters over in the vats, it defies time; and where better to celebrate this miracle than in the cantina? although it may be a morning so awash with moonlight the sidewalks are urine yellow, never mind, we have come round, we rebegin; let's pawn—let's drink —the typewriter, wedding ring, the clock, and have another round, a tick, another round, a tock, another round.

But you see that we really do not lose our grip, we do not really repeat as if we've forgotten already what we've said, it is just that some of our commonest connectives have come undone, we swing back and forth into our thought now like a ball on the end of a string, the body must stumble so the mind may leap, or rather perhaps it would be better to say that we sink down softly into things as though they were laps.

Some matters after all are magnified without alcohol and in the ordinary course of events for example when the sun falls asleep at midday there is a frightful darkness like Guinness in a glass and the bar mirror smears and the bar stool turns of itself with a squeak and we are free finally to let the mind pass into the space of its speaking, mescaleening, you might say, as over water waterskiers—such is the kind of excuse we're seeking when we flip or twist or pull or pry or pop or tap the keg or cork or lid or cap or top—go like spray.

What do you have against me in your files, Lowry asks the sub-chief of Migración. The sub-chief slaps the folder facing him: "*Borracho, borracho, borracho.* Here is your life."

Nightmare and madness fly up and down like shades. Figures emerge from the walls: customs officials, pimps, busdrivers, wives, police. Fear grows the wings of evil birds. What is this semen which runs from our nose? this hot blot on the bedclothes? loaf of red bread? There's a nest of noisy ants in that canister of candy. Anxiety like light leaks—pip—from a pipe. Pip-a-dip. Pip. Flowers flattened in the wall's paper puff like adders, but they're orchid-mouthed, and at last we have someone to talk to, someone who understands the initial pronoun of our speech the way a fine sentence does the design of its writer.

It is ourselves, of course, or one member of that club, with whom we take communion in the cantina (part of us taking your part, perhaps, and playing it better, too, but remaining one of our own crowd still, leaning alone like a broom in a closet, apart from the pail and the mop as we must, because in this spiritless realm of matter, like a bar without booze, no cozy interpenetration of molecules is possible), and Lowry would hold extended conversations with empty corners and vacant chairs, but what is remarkable about that? each of us has seen street-talkers deep in quarrel with invisible companions; or he would, having passed out, nevertheless remember what had been said in the presence of his absent self, so one wonders if he might sometimes have been faking, but there is a fragment of us constantly awake, alert as a lantern, microphone: why should our ear sleep when our eyes close? pip! like insects we breathe with more than our nose; it is simply that the division which occurs when we've taken a sufficiently engrossing drink is almost complete, and we meet all elements as equals: the glass that holds the hand, the hand that is a bottle to the body, the body that wickedly wobbles the world, and the mirror which imagines this immense earthquaking to be merely the sea-crossing of a cloud.

> *El espíritu*
> *Es una invención del cuerpo*
> *El cuerpo*

Es una invención del mundo
El mundo
Es una invención del espíritu
(*Octavio Paz, Blanco*)

In any case it becomes *absolutamente necesario* to have
a drink. Easy for anyone whose entire intelligence and whose
whole energy is bent upon it, because naturally the need has
been foreseen and there is a bottle stashed under the sink or
buried in the window box or hidden in the clothes hamper, and
on the bad odd off chance that they have been emptied already,
one mustn't lose faith, heart, or hope, because there are other
opportunities, some bars open early, there are friends . . .
yes, *con permiso*, just a nip to steady the nerves, calm the
stomach, dispel the demons, only a drop, *amigos*, a spot, a
touch, and in addition . . .

There is a cantina at every corner of the Consul's world.
Sin and innocence, guilt and salvation, shape Lowry's private
square of opposition, and if sanctuary and special knowledge
are its gifts in one guise, and gaiety and relaxation its gifts in
another, catercorner from church and gym are brothel and
prison. Here men are fastened to themselves as though they
were both shackle and chain, their eyes on images: above the
bar to advertise Cafeaspirina a woman wearing a scarlet bras-
siere is depicted reclining on a scrolled divan. Outside the cantina you can see the mountain, alongside runs a deep ravine.
Symbols, surely, but remote and close, steep and frightening,
just the same. El Farolito, with its diminishing inner rooms, the
nesting innercubes of Hell, is the last cantina, sitting in the
shadow of Popocatepetl as though under that volcano. There
the Consul will wad himself into a slut the way we wedge with
cardboard a skinny candle in its holder. There he will be mistaken for an anarchist, a Jew, a thief, a spy. There he will be
murdered by backwoodsy fascists. Who has a hand upon his
penis now?

Wrider? you anticrista. Sí, you anticrista prik . . .
And Juden . . .

Chingar . . .

Cabrón . . .

You are no a de

wrider, you are de espider, and we shoota de espiders
in Méjico . . .

You no wrider . . .

You Al Capón. You a

Jew chingao . . .

You are a spider.

In the road in front of El Farolito the Consul is shot with
a Colt '17. "Christ, what a dingy way to die," the Consul says,
but that is merely his opinion. His body is thrown into a *bar-
ranca*, pariah dog tossed after him. Despite the fact that the
scene is excessively operatic and the writing wails like an endlessly expiring soprano, there is no death in recent literature
with more significance.

> Las Manos de Orlac
> con Peter Lorre

Several leaves from one of Lowry's little notebooks are reproduced in Douglas Day's fine biography,[1] and on one we can
decipher:

The psychology & horror of the shakes. The real horror
is in the hands. All the poison to go down into the hands,
mental and physical. Burning hot. There seems almost a

---

[1] Douglas Day, *Malcolm Lowry: A Biography* (New York: Oxford, 1973).

buzzing *inside* your hands. Fear of coming into dining
room with shakes, especially with captain present.

Eventually he could not hold pen or pencil, not even to sign his
name, and the hands which were so mysteriously stained, not
like Lady Macbeth's or Orlac's were by the blood of murder,
but—who knows?—by the masturbation of the bottle (the crystal phallus, in Berryman's phrase), these hands he placed on
their backs on his desk, his weight standing into them as he
dictated to Margerie, hours at a stretch sometimes and of
course day after day, until the knuckles became callused as an
ape's and the veins in his legs ballooned so badly he entered
a hospital to have them stripped.[2] They were swollen as if he'd
had babies, although by then he'd only engendered *Ultrama-
rine*, and the *Volcano* was still in utero.

These stubby clumsy hands which he hated and hid because they gave his condition away the way rings around the
eyes, I remember, were supposed to, and which shook drunk
or sober, often uncontrollably, were hands with their own
mean will. While absentmindedly fondling a friend's pet rabbit, they somehow break its neck, and for two days Lowry carries the corpse of the rabbit about in a small suitcase wonder-
ing what to do with it. "Look what happens when I try to touch
something beautiful," their owner complains with a self-pity
perfectly misplaced.

Yet Lowry's not a Lenny whose mice cannot survive his
caresses. Yet Lowry's love is as murderous as the simple-
minded. Yet . . .

And before he will agree to enter Cambridge he persuades
his father to let him go like London and O'Neill romantically
to sea, so he is driven to the dock in the family Rolls while reporters watch: RICH BOY AS DECK HAND, they headline him. He
goes aboard shamed and of course finds no romance in the

fo'c'sle. He sleeps in something called "men's quarters" instead. Predictably, he scrubs decks, scrapes paint, polishes brass. He observes the coolie longshoremen coupling with their women in the cargo holds. He paints a bunker black. He is despised and teased. Clumsy. Bored. He carries meals to the seamen. Is often drunk.

Perhaps life was a forest of symbols, as Baudelaire had said, but Lowry was no lumberman. He brought his shaping signs, as *a priori* as the best idealist's, to his dreams, his drunkenness, his ordinary day-to-day concerns and his desires: sex, syph, stoker, bunker, fire . . . hand, shame, seaman. Eventually these hands refuse the vocation offered them. A poisoned brain burns there. Trapped flies buzz. Ashamed, stained, they blush, and terrified, enraged, they shake so violently the threatened air flees through their fingers. And he would live hand to mouth all his life. A cliché. A phrase. Yet associations such as these obsess him, compel him to run in front of his own blows, to fulfil prophecies as though they were threats, and promises as though they were designs against the self, since he will die by his own hand, too . . . by bottle and by pill . . . unsteadily . . . *la petite mort*.

Lowry is a one-book author, everyone says, and the excellence of that book is accidental because he never learned how to write; he continually started and stopped, commenced and abandoned, caught in an endless proliferation of designs, so that the more evident it became that he would never complete his great work, the grander grew his schemes: everything he wrote would enter into them, one vast voyage, long as his life, just as confusing, just as deep, with ups and downs to rival Dante; yet he was wholly absorbed in himself and consequently could not create even an alter ego able to pull on socks ahead of shoes; at the uncork of a bottle he would fall into long dull disquisitions on the powers and bewilderments of alcohol; he hammered home themes like someone angry at the nail, yet buttered his bread on both sides and every edge; then, as if determined to destroy whatever mattered most, left manuscripts about like half-eaten sandwiches, and emptied Margerie of everything except the carton she came in.

However, when one thinks of the general sort of snacky under-earnest writers whose works like wind-chimes rattle in our heads now, it is easier to forgive Lowry his pretentious seriousness, his old-fashioned ambitions, his Proustian plans, his desire to pump into every sentence such significance as a Shelley or a Shakespeare had, to bring together on the page, like fingers in one fist, sense, sensation, impulse, need, and feeling, and finally to replace the reader's consciousness wholly with a lackaday magician's—drunk's—a fraud's—his own.

It was not glory or money, as a writer, Lowry wanted. He simply wanted masterpieces. He had no politics, particularly, no religion, no fastidious monkey-groomed morality, no metaphysics which would fancy up for him a world with more worth and order than a shelf of cheap sale books. It is hard to believe he believed in much, though he read Goethe and Dante, dabbled in the occult, and used the Cabbala as a symbolic scheme (even if its choreography was an afterthought), and to begin with laid down a political plot for his great book like a rug he then swept a mountain over. Attitudes he had, but attitudes aren't philosophy. Redemption through art was his real creed. He was too eager to make use of what he read to be serious about it, and like Joyce he carried back to his books every tinshine thought he came across, the way jackdaws beak bright buttons off one's wash. He was not profoundly acquainted with literature, either, though he was quick to name-drop: Marlowe, Maitland, or Cervantes. His work is certainly contemporary, too, in expecting the most silent creatures of its author's reading to be loud on every tongue. And again like Joyce, like Rilke, Lowry idolized certain irrelevant Scandinavians.

The writers he really took to . . . well, he absorbed Conrad Aiken's books, unabashedly plundered his conversations, copied his life-style, both served and assaulted his person, competed for his women, occupied his home, borrowed his figure for a father. Lowry was sufficiently conscious of this habit often to deny himself any originality, and felt he had stolen from or exploited others when he had not.[3] Still, we must remain suspicious of these exaggerated claims of crime, inflated and misplaced to encourage our discounting or excusing them as so much talk, just as the Consul, about to be shot, hears himself accused:

> Norteamericano, eh?
> Inglés. You Jew.
> What the hell you think you do around here?
> You pelado, eh?
> It's no good for your health. I shoot de twenty people.

and then dying gorges on the accusation as only conscience can:

> Presently the word "pelado" began to fill his whole consciousness. That had been Hugh's word for the thief: now someone had flung the insult at him. And it was as if, for a moment, he had become the pelado, the thief—yes, the pilferer of meaningless muddled ideas out of which his rejection of life had grown, who had worn his two or three little bowler hats, his disguises, over these abstractions: now the realest of them all was close.

And although the account seems to be carried away by itself, as Cyrano was by his nose, it is nevertheless true that the Con-

---

[3] If one is familiar with Aiken, one can indeed feel his presence in Lowry's books. The two authors continually intercross, because of course Lowry figures in Aiken's autofictional biography, *Ushant*, and is the model for a character called Hambo in Aiken's autofactual fiction, *A Heart for the Gods of Mexico*. They borrow one another like roommates steal shirts for an evening out, yet the bodies which wear them remain distinct and the shirts get returned after use.

sul is an exploiter, because an alcoholic, in the best old sense, *depends*: depends from his wives like their drooping breasts, clings to his mistresses, his friends, as moisture trembles at a tumbler's edge; depends upon the mercy of the world . . . relies, requests, requires . . . yet in the devious way the hopeless loser hopes to win by losing big, the thorough soak employs all the brutal ruses of self-righteous helplessness, and by chemically keeping himself confined "in that part used to be call: soul" makes the world seem—so subversive is this stratagem —rather to depend on *him* . . . yes, and this isn't difficult because consciousness is the thief *par excellence*, removing the appearances of things without a trace, replacing the body with the spirit.

Since the cantina is the very image of the head, the world-within which is the single subject of Malcolm Lowry's life and work, all those anxieties and adjectives, verbs of inaction, prepositions, copulations, shadowing names and paranoid suspicions, which obsessed his creator and pursue Geoffrey Firmin—Consul, pelado, and borracho—apply perfectly to the tragedy of the *Volcano*: the progressive loss of consciousness which we call "getting on" and should call simply "passing out," instead.

To his editor, Albert Erskine:

Dear old Albert . . .

I am going steadily & even beautifully downhill: my memory misses beats at every moment, & my mornings are on all fours. Turning the whole business round in a nutshell I am only sober or merry in a whiskey bottle, & since whisky is impossible to procure you can imagine how merry I am, & lucid, & by Christ I am lucid. And merry. But Jesus. The trouble is, apart from Self, that part (which) used to be called: consciousness. I have now reached a position where every night I write 5 novels in imagination, have total recall (whatever that means too) but am unable to write a word. I cannot explain in human terms the incredible effort it has cost me to write even this silly little note, in a Breughel garden with dogs & barrels & vin kegs & chickens & sunsets & morning glory with an approaching storm & bottle of half wine.

And now the rain! Let it come, seated as I am on Brueghel barrel by a dog's grave crowned with dead irises. The wind is rising too, both on the ocean & in the stomach. And I have been kind to in a way I do not deserve . . . A night dove has started to hoot & says incessantly the word "dream, dream." A bright idea.[4]

The bus windows were like mirrors—looking out, one saw in—and Margerie and Malcolm were always on buses, or perhaps a plane, some mode of travel, a ship, a train, and even on foot they window-shopped, the glass passing them, holding its images oddly upright like bottles on a tray, though they were moving, in Lowry's insistently recurring word, "downhill," since the world, for him, was always on edge, the land like his work running up and down, never nicely along, even when they found a path that had taken itself pleasantly through the woods, and every journey was mostly a descent, or rather, descending was a spatial metaphor for "going in."

The sense of speed, of gigantic transition, of going southward, downward, over three countries, the tremendous mountain ranges, the sense at once of descent, tremendous regression, and of moving, not moving, but in another way dropping straight down the world, straight down the map, as of the imminence of something great, phenomenal, and yet the moving shadow of the plane below them, the eternal moving cross, less fleeting and more

[4] Harvey Breit and Margerie Bonner Lowry, *Selected Letters of Malcolm Lowry* (New York: Lippincott, 1965), p. 165.

substantial than the dim shadow of the significance of what they were actually doing that Sigbjørn held in his mind: and yet it was possible only to focus on that shadow, and at that only for short periods: they were enclosed by the thing itself as by the huge bouncing machine with its vast monotonous purring, pouring din, in which they sat none too comfortably, Sigbjørn with his foot up embarrassedly, for he had taken his shoe off, a moving, deafening, continually renewed time-defeating destiny by which they were enclosed but of which they were able only to see the inside, for so to speak of the streamlined platinum-colored object itself they could only glimpse a wing, a propeller, through the small, foolish, narrow oblong windows.[5]

The paragraph encloses us like the fuselage of the plane. We progress down narrow overlapping phrases toward the bottom of the page, pushing our way through adjectives which gather like onlookers at an accident. Though feelings persevere, logic is lost like loose change. We suffer symbolic transformations (soul: shade, window and eye, cross: plane, hellbent); endure sentences which have the qualities they were constructed to account for; our reading eye, as Sigbjørn's and the shadow of the plane, flitting over the ranges the way thought in its sphere, ourselves in our cylinders, pass like ghosts on schedules, wraiths with aims.

Faulkner's rhetoric also reaches for the universal as though its very pawing would create the ledge, secure the handhold. It is a style so desperate to rise, it would burst its own lungs.

And if he had not been born, mistakenly, a Leo, he would have made a perfect Pisces: swimmer, sailor, soak, souse,

---

[5] This is the first paragraph of *Dark as the Grave Wherein My Friend Is Laid* (New York: New American Library, 1968). Douglas Day and Margerie Lowry have edited this posthumous novel. There is an excellent brief introduction by Day.

sponge—all that absorbent—oral, impotent, a victim of un-differentiation and the liquid element, shoreless like his writing, wallowy, encompassing, a suicide by misadventure, bottle broken, drinker, diver, prisoner of self . . .

Thrice doubly indented then, Lowry's books in consequence have no boundaries. They are endless wells down which in a deepening gloom that is its own perverse illumination the reader passes; therefore every effort to give them the shape and normal accelerations of the novel is as futile as flailing air; and you remember how deeply into Tartarus Uranus hurled the rebellious Cyclopes? . . . . . . an anvil and a petal: nine days.

Clínica Dr. Vigil,
Enfermedades Secretas de Ambos Sexos,
Vías Urinarias, Trastornos Sexuales,
Debilidad Sexual, Derrames Nocturnos,
Emisiones Prematuras, Espermatorrea,
Impotencia.

Guilty fears follow him everywhere. He is being watched. Espidered. Are those his father's eyes behind those blackened glasses? In any case, his plans are known in advance. He is awaited at the border. He will be expelled from the country. He will be evicted from his property. He will catch the VD. How? through his hands? He *has* contracted it. He believes. Long ago . . . as a sailor. It is hidden in his blood, this punishment. Any rash bespeaks its presence, since the soul contains the body. And as a child . . .

At one or two or three or four he claims to have been molested by nannies. He is five when his brother takes him to an anatomical museum in Liverpool (on Paradise Street, inevitably) where he sees bleach-pale plaster casts depicting the ravages of venereal disease. In his father's house there was no smoking. While six he suffers a fall from a bike which leaves him with a jagged scar on his knee, a wound he will later say he received when his ship was caught in a Tong war along the Chinese coast. A glass of port at Christmas was indulgence enough. When seven he complains of being bullied by the other Cub Scouts. But cold baths made men—made Englishmen—stiffened the sinews, restrung the nerves. As did tennis, rugger, swimming, shooting, golf, church, long strenuous walks. And Malcolm became good at them. Still he is teased about the size of his penis. Away at the Caldicote School, now nine, he is struck in the eye playing ball. The injury is neglected and an infection sets in which leaves him partially blind for four years. Or so he chooses to believe. He also imagines that his mother, unable to bear the sight of her half-sighted boy, refuses to let him come home on vacations, and that everyone has left him alone.

But he is becoming a touch-me-not. In America, visiting Aiken, he meets a young woman with whom he decides he is in love. He will convince her. "His attempt at this is remarkable," Day judiciously observes, "and possibly unique in the history of erotic correspondence."

I cannot kiss anybody else without wiping my mouth afterwards. There is only you, forever and forever you: in bars and out of bars, in fields and out of fields, in boats and out of boats . . . there is only love and tenderness of everything about you, our comings in and our goings forth, I would rather use your tooth brush than my own: I would wish, when with you on a boat, that you would be sick merely so that I could comfort you. Nor is there one ounce of criticism in this. I do not conceal in my heart the physical repulsion which, not admitted to oneself hardly, exists usually in the filthy male. I would love you the same if you had one ear, or one eye: if you were bald or dumb: if you had syphilis, I would be the same; it is the love that one

stronger algebraic symbol in a bracket has for its multiple
—or complement . . . it cannot live without the other.
(Day, p. 109)

In short, Lowry loves her as he wants to be loved. And he
wants to be loved by his mother.

Thief and exploiter: that's what we're told *pelado* means:
peeled: barefoot, bald. Where in his unconscious did Lowry
deposit what he knew? that *pelada* is a kind of alopecia, which
means, in dictionary speech, a distempered state of the body
leading to a patchy loss of hair, and arising from a venereal
cause.

A resentment psychology is developing rapidly. In college
a young man, presumably in love with Lowry, commits suicide,
and this event, too, becomes one of the crimes which haunt his
heroes. By now every crime which he conceives for himself is
also another injury done him, and he is already drinking more
than much.

Thus eyes, fires, follow him. Disaster. Ashes, ashes, all
fall down. And it is true that he cannot competently manage
his life. He *does* put himself in bad hands, the hands of exploit-
ers (in photos his own are often in his pockets). His squatter's
shack at Dollarton *does* burn; a manuscript, not the first, *is*
lost; he has constantly to fear eviction; he slips from the pier
he's built there, which means so much to him, and thereby in-
jures his back; the cold drives him every winter into travel so
that homelessness can continue his motto, and paradise return
with the spring. He is kicked out of Mexico, in alcoholic horror
held for a time in an Oaxaqueñian gaol where he decides an
unsuccessful attempt to castrate him has been made. He suggests through the mail that he's been mistakenly imprisoned
for spying, and that he must drink furthermore from his pisspot
. . . probably.

The list winds on like a bus on a mountain road. Wounds,
bruises, broken bottles, suicidal gestures, blackouts, falls,

fire: attacking the self he is alone in, he cuts a ridiculous figure, and Douglas Day has difficulty depicting Lowry's redoubt-
able charm, for charm is evanescent and does not lend itself
to anecdote. More than one friend describes Malc as puppy-
like, refers to his infectious disarming grin, his amazing amusing memory, his simple devotion, the bulk of his chest, his
strength, the jokes told on the soul.

Yet in Grenada, his huge head shaded by a great touristy
sombrero, this *borracho inglés*, trailed by mocking children
and eyed by the Guardia Civil, lurches shamefully through the
streets, his trousers held up by a tie. During a friendly drunken
tussle shortly after arriving in America to see Conrad Aiken,
he tosses his new father figure into the fireplace and fractures
his skull. "Look what happens when I try to touch . . ."
Ashes, ashes, all fall . . .

And into every happening there entered, early, imagination like a liar and a thief, arranging reality as it ought and was
felt to be, until sometimes it seemed to Lowry he was himself
a fiction, and that the work he was writing was writing him.
That enmeshment, itself, became a theme.

> . . . the novel is about a character who becomes en-
> meshed in the plot of the novel he has written, as I did in
> Mexico. But now I am becoming enmeshed in the plot of
> a novel I have scarcely begun. Idea is not new, at least so
> far as enmeshment with characters is concerned. Goethe,
> Wilhelm von Scholz, "The Race with a Shadow." Piran-
> dello, etc. But did these people ever have it happen to
> *them*? [6]

---

[6] A quotation from "Through the Panama." This profoundly self-reflexive novella was
written in the fifties, and although its concerns are now a commonplace, the fictional
techniques employed remain in advance of our time. Lowry's collection of short stories, *Hear Us O Lord from Heaven Thy Dwelling Place* (Philadelphia & New York:
Lippincott, 1961), contains another masterpiece, "The Forest Path to the Spring."
Margerie Lowry is apparently gathering another sheaf of shorter pieces, and Lowry's
life as a dead author will soon be longer, as it is already more productive, than his
life as a live one.

It must have begun in the most ordinary way, Malcolm Lowry's habit of making up life as he went along. It must have begun with little elaborations, lies as harmlessly decorative as those sugar flowers whose stony blooms enliven our birthday cakes. We all did it—added frills. We do it still: we penny-candle conversations, ice anecdotes, bake ourselves in pies. When we were maybe a boy with a ball or a worm in a can, there was no entrance easier than of fact to fancy, because we were more likely to be living on the inside of our nature then, where distant skiers safely slid the hazardous slopes of our sheeted beds, and little facts came along like sticks in a stream to be snatched up. The garage's broken window could become a bullet wound, a furtive peerpoint, violent eyecrash. The step seems a small one, but the difference between an imaginary world which flows around the real one and uses it, catch as catch can, and a real world which is hung each way one turns with dreams like evergreens by bagworms, is—

And if at first our daydreams merely close and open softly on reality like a convolvulus, we find it useful later, with our little fabrications, to make life move more centrally around us. Thus do we appoint ourselves a sun, to shine and tan in turn; we compel our inner shapes and outer shadows to coalesce; we speak sternly to experience in romantic German till *der als ob ist*, pointlessness becomes plan, sheer coincidence design, and it is no longer surprising that the wages of sin should be exhibited in plaster of Paris on Paradise Street.

The wormy ubiquitousness of the sign reminds many of *Ulysses*, but the similarity is deceptive because Lowry's feeling for the world is in no way like Joyce's, nor are his literary skills, although both pun. For Stephen Dedalus, walking along Sandymount strand, the world is a series of words which find their final connections in the mind, but for Lowry it is not simply that some grand Master moves each piece of life into a single sentence, it is rather that each piece has its own lungs and legs, and a sign is, for instance, the advertising poster BOX!

which follows the Consul like an urchin uttering itself. ⎢BOX!⎢
It shouts, to be sure, like one of the furies, like a messenger
of the gods. It is itself alive and menacing, as full of private
mischief as any chief of Rostrums or sub-chief of Migración.

Lowry could not invent at the level of language, only at the
level of life, so that having lied life into a condition suitable for
fiction, he would then faithfully and truthfully record it. No
wonder he felt enmeshed. No wonder, too, that he had to re-
visit in order to revise; repeat the same difficult passage of existence in order to plunge further into it, make the necessary
changes, get it right; and this meant only too often that he had
to drink himself back into madness again, to resee what was
to be rewritten: to fall down in a ditch, to find vultures perched
on the washbasin, fold fearfully up in a corner like a pair of discarded trousers, or bruise his head between toilet and sink in
some dirty anonymous john.

> But he now became conscious of something more frighten-
> ing yet taking place in his mind. It was a feeling that per-
> meated the high ill-lit yellow walls of the hotel beer par-
> lour, the long dim corridor between the two beer parlours,
> on which the door now seemed to be opened by an invisi-
> ble hand . . . , a feeling which seemed a very part of the
> ugly, sad, red-and-brown tables and chairs, something
> that was in the very beer-smelling air, as if—the feeling
> perhaps someway arising, translated to this surrounding
> scene, from the words themselves—there were some hid-
> den correspondence between these words and this scene,
> or between some ultimate unreality and meaninglessness
> he seemed to perceive adumbrated by them . . . , and his
> inner perception of this place: no, it was as if this place
> were suddenly the exact outward representation of his in-
> ner state of mind: so that shutting his eyes for a long mo-
> ment of stillness . . . he seemed to feel himself merging
> into it, while equally there was a fading of it into himself:

it was as though, having visualized all this with his eyes shut now he *were* it—these walls, these tables, that corridor. . . .[7]

Words, walls, percepts, feelings, this or that cantina, this small victory, that great defeat: all were one behind the colon, a line drawn through his writing to indicate a sum. As he merged with his environment the way numbers enter one another, disappearing entirely without losing themselves, he heard, as if in his own voice yet in a voice now no longer his, prophecies in labels, omens in emblems, spying eyes like whispers looking out of objects, threats in signs.

> La persona que destruya
> este jardín sera
> consignada a la
> autoridad . . .

And as his guilt grew and his terrors multiplied, as his hands refused to write and his fuddled head fell farther toward his knees, he became more and more dependent on Margerie, not only for mothering and other small corrections, but for experience itself, since they went everywhere together, suffered everything together, resolved to begin a new pier, new cabin, new journey, new book, new life together, the glass which poisoned all these plans, although he often drank from it alone, held jointly; so it was Margerie's fault he was such a sot, he felt, and he saw how the powers he possessed were slowly passing to her: he needed her to punctuate his prose; he needed her to smooth out the creases in his style; he needed

---

[7] From the astonishing "Wandering Jew" chapter of *October Ferry to Gabriola* (New York: World, 1970), a work which, while now enclosed by covers, is no more than a pile of rusted and beautiful wreckage.

her guidance and her notes; he would need her to publish his posthumous works. He lived, furthermore, in the presence—literally beneath the gaze—of the person he had most injured, before whom it was no longer possible to put on a new soul like a suit for Sunday—who knew his fears, his incapacities, so many of his secrets, who knew that so many of his lies were lies. He was intolerably uncovered, and there was nowhere finally to go . . . both petal and anvil had arrived.

In the little English town of Ripe (place names follow him snickering even to the grave) . . . Lowry chases his wife away with the shattered neck of a gin bottle.

It was a sort of suicide, a swallow larger and more reckless than usual, this death by misadventure, as the coroner kindly decides to call it, and dying in a scatter of food and glass was no doubt dingy enough to satisfy the Consul, though it had entelechy, like a habit which has finally completed itself. After this death, which Day describes so well, the weekly Brighton *Argus* headstoned and then columned him:

Wisconsin Death Trip

History passes over them like the angel of death; not only these people of Jackson County, Wisconsin, the occupants of this book,[1] alive and dying in Black River Falls and environs during the two decades around which the century turned, but also the enormous anonymous mass of men who have perished that we might be here, in our turn, to perish too.

And although there'll be photographs which embalmers (for a fee) will guarantee to take of our rouged and cottoned cheeks, photographs of the coffin banked by glads and guarded by wire-rigged wreaths; and even though there'll be brief notices of comfort and commemoration (paid for by the grieved) placed in columns beside the Want-Ads and resembling the For Rents, like the one here from *The Badger State Banner*; and though we shall no doubt leave behind us albums of images, snaps of us in all our ages, with weddings, births, and vacations by the Lake or at the Dells predominating; still, history will ignore these traces just as it always has before—because historians want their documents to state sums or be signed by ministers and kings; because we belong to the poor and nonpolitical and cannot pay them; because we are among

[1] Michael Lesy, *Wisconsin Death Trip* (New York: Pantheon, 1973).

those whom George Eliot described as living faithfully a hidden life and resting in unvisited tombs.

Wisconsin Death Trip represents an effort to recapture the consciousness of a neglected people and in this way contribute to the understanding of an old contrast—city vs. country—a polarity so traditionally important to the interpretation of American history. Michael Lesy has collected and arranged a number of remarkable old photographs; he has culled accounts, principally of death, depression, and disease, from local papers; recorded a little local gossip; snipped pertinent paragraphs from the region's novelists; then to accompany these composed a brief though eloquent and perceptive text, and put all this handsomely and artfully before us.

The result is an impressive example of the poetry of history, linear in form as history naturally tends to be, yet curiously still and fixed like a piece of statuary or one of those stiffly posed photographs he's both reproduced and doctored here. As we read, we do not so much pass from death to death as we more deeply enter one life on its painful way there, and we enter it the way water enters stone, through the steadily repeated smack of similar little facts spattering on its face to dissipate into the air.

Photographs represented occasions once upon a time. You dressed for them as you might for church; they cost money; they recorded important moments; you faced front; you seldom smiled, since levity was not the mark you wanted put across your face forever; yet the result of this resolute Egyptian solemnity was to separate people as they sat or stood together, man and wife or members of a band, to emphasize the withdrawn, inward look they all had, because there was nothing in front of them but a lens as cold and darkly caped as God's eye. Even the dogs were docile, cow-jawed, stiff as porcelain. There were, of course, no cats.

The people were often strangely posed: if not before a painted drop, then in the middle of a chicken scratch or vast infertile field, chair and occupant put down there as if by a terrible wind; now and then a storefront or a string of fish was taken, people and fish alike overlapping, and an entire family snapped stoically sitting in a yard of weeds; or the film was exposed at that hour of the day when even a city's wooden sidewalks and dirt streets seem as empty and endless as a wilderness; or a woman in her best black would be stood against a white clapboard wall, the lines behind her already folding into one another at infinity, to make so negative a space you'd think she was the entrance of a cave; and though the younger men's faces seem beautifully stupid and naïve sometimes, the sunken mouths and eyes of the older women wear their suffering the way clothes and furniture show theirs, the skull behind the skin burning like a dim bulb.

The loneliness trapped in these figures is overwhelming, and one thinks of the country, and how in the country, space counts for something, and how the individual is thrown upon his own resources, how he consequently comes to sense his essential self; and then you notice with a guilty twinge three generations posed in front of a small unpainted shack, and you realize that these families are as closely thrown together as potatoes in a sack; that, like men on a raft, space is what confines them; and that the tyranny of the group can here be claustrophobic, crushing, total.

Times were tough, the earth was not easy, businesses failed, banks went bust. Tramps roamed the countryside—stealing, burning. The men drank. The women relied on patent medicines and madness. Diphtheria and other epidemic diseases, as Lesy says, "inverted a natural order—that is, they killed the youngest before the oldest; they killed the ones who were to be protected before their rightful protectors; they killed the progeny before the forebears; they killed the children before their parents."

There were open fires, faulty chimneys, careless cooks, lamps, candles, kerosene, log and board buildings, brush, scrub, barns full of grain, hay in stables, wood in sheds, each easy to set afire and difficult, once burning, to put out, for it was often a long way to water, and then it lay in wells; there were few brigades; and there were hungry men roaming the woods so callused their bodies were clubs, women and even children who had nothing more in their hearts but malice and nothing to live for but revenge, so that although fires were set for profit, by accident, or to cauterize a house infected with disease, arsonists were always feared, invariably suspected, inevitably blamed.

The weather didn't help, but Lesy has no clippings about high winds, heavy snows, deep freezes: the long oppressive winters in which cold filled the space you were supposed to be so free in and drove you, as the dark did, under the blankets early. In his best paragraph, he writes: "In winter, the only men left in town were either so young they were in school or so old they were in bed, or so spineless they sold things to ladies. Everyone else was off in the pineries." Surely there were tales of thaw and freeze, but Lesy says: "I concentrated only on the stories and accounts that concerned the psychology or personality of events."

Perhaps for that reason we learn nothing of how the animals died, except for the man who gave "a colored boy $1.00 to shear a big Newfoundland dog and anoint him with kerosene oil," a fuel they later set alight (although there are photos of a shy-cocked horse with a mane like Goldilocks); there is nothing a politician said; while perhaps for other reasons there are no reports of weddings, christenings, sewing bees and circles, the length of the year's longest pike, or what might be called amusing anecdotes of human interest: what the band played in the park on the 4th of July, or how many fell sick eating chicken salad at the Norwegians' picnic.

Still, there is the tantalizing history of Mary Sweeny, the compulsive window-breaker, another, equally compulsive, who was a woman hugger, some misers, a few charges of rape and incest, a little lesbian by-play, an ossified man, a charming bit about a woman who expelled a frog from her stomach, the Negro barber who had given himself over to startling opinions, and several stories of misfortune falling so thickly on a single sad head you had to affront Job by laughing. Things reach us in this work which normally never do, yet, in general, the world which can't be quoted in the weeklies can't reach history. The rest we must infer.

People became "shack-wacky." No wonder. At any rate, they went insane with a frequency which would be significant if we knew what was meant by it. There were hearings: a judge determined the matter; and you were sentenced to asylums as people were to prison. The inhabitants believed in madness as they believed in arson. As we once believed in Communist conspiracies. They were crazed. They knew it certainly, the way doctors knew diphtheria, and what Lesy gives us is a record of their convenient, resolute, excited, fearful diagnoses. The photographs encourage us to see it . . . to pass through those enlarged eyes into the desolate outdoors.

The lovely countryside was filled with suicides. They hung themselves from trees, of course, and exploded their brains from their heads with guns. They threw themselves in front of trains, cut their own throats, used morphine. They ate the heads off matches, swallowed cigar stubs, carbolic acid, arsenic, Paris green. They drowned themselves in rain barrels, rivers, ponds, wells (as, in pique, a child did). They hammered in their own heads, set fire to themselves as they had torched that dog, and with dynamite blew apart their painful being. Occasionally they murdered others first. Or ran away into the woods. They became hermits. They froze to death, rime on their limbs like blond hairs. But the plague of man was as relentless as that of nature.

They died, in addition, by accident. We all do. Through inadvertence. By mistake.

Unfortunately Lesy's snippet method encourages the

sense, combined with a dose of nostalgia and a dash of quaint, that you are reading an anthology of weird tales culled from the Readers' D, the kind of lives you find in small print at the bottom of pages; but eventually this feeling disappears, awe overcomes every scruple, and you really try to penetrate these pictures to the pianos pictured, the dresser scarves, the curtains, doilies, and the lamps . . . the large eyes like dials . . . the funeral wreaths, the hats . . .

But it is poetry all the same—a construction—for couldn't we put together our own death trip out of any batch of local papers? There would be a different ratio of deaths due to X rather than to Y, to be sure (a difference which is vital), but the total picture might be equally grim or, with the right shears, made to seem so, anywhere. Perhaps human misery can neither be created nor destroyed, merely transformed, distributed, endured. In any case, there can be no question that this original work makes us deeply feel one form that misery has taken; and in causing us to feel as well as consider, *Wisconsin Death Trip* has enlarged on the uses of history.

Mr. Blotner,
Mr. Feaster,
and Mr. Faulkner

Be attentive: Mr. Feaster is emerging from his bath. There he has spent some fifteen minutes soaking, the warm gray water high as his collar. He has been considering what the heat of his tub has done to his sperm, for he has read that such heat kills, penetrating even the soft protective sacking of the scrotum; and he has been pondering, consequently, the possibilities lost, the thousand or moreso lives unrealized, the risks untaken, sparks unstruck, the deaths for which he cannot be held accountable—not by the state, or even by the papacy.

We must be attentive because everything we now observe will pass: the water of his bath will disappear as easily as Mr. Feaster's breath. It will untub with a sound too common to comment on. The ring which remains is silent. Planes at O'Hare aren't heard either. The multitude is always moaning. They would bloat our bellies like soaked beans if we'd let them —crowd our thoughts—though unlike food and water, consciousness, itself, fills nothing up.

We must be attentive because Mr. Feaster's not on camera; his moves have not been registered; the angles his elbows have assumed do not remain like played cards; and his thoughts . . . as for them, they do not fluster the air so much as an arm wave. Feaster cannot complain. Presently he will forget all this. What is most of his life, even to himself, but background noise?

Many millions of men exist for no purpose now, and to no effect whatever. Their presence shall not be missed; their passing neither mourned nor noted. We have more than we need even to support our economies. Perhaps snaps of their bodies—victims of flood, murder, earthquake, war, famine, suicide, disease—will occasionally appear on our screens, in our papers and magazines, where we shall see them clogging roads or rivers; and certainly centuries of nameless mortals have gone before us; the whole earth is simply a grave; yet we do not have to put them behind us as we each must our parents; they have never been a part of us, noticeably loved or harmed us; they have never been human; they have merely been foreigners, poor men, madmen, Persians, Protestants, Huns—faceless hordes, census numbers—and it is only their corpses which still cause us any concern, since consciousness, as I've already observed, is nothing . . . *no thing*; because one gunny sack full of Polish teeth takes up more room in the world than all the agony of their extraction.

History, as it has been generally composed by our historians, has regarded the multitude, as Mr. Feaster does his freckles or his unspent sperm, with an occasional odd curiosity. The closing lines of *Middlemarch*:

> . . . for the growing good of the world is partly dependent on unhistoric acts; and that things are not so ill with you and me as they might have been, is half owing to the number who lived faithfully a hidden life, and rest in unvisited tombs.

. . . they are a novelist's curtain speech, and are rather more optimistic than might be, for the increasing illness of the world, indeed the history of the world for good or ill in a measure heretofore unrecognized, may depend on unhistoric acts;

though if, in any way, it does so, we may properly wonder why they are so unhistoric. Is it because, and only because, the lives of which these acts comprise the greater part are hidden? and why do they pass so unremarked?

Ah, but Feaster, if a sudden frost were to fix you as firmly as it's all been described in *Orlando*, or the ash of a burning mountain poison yet preserve you for a thousand years, then the future would marvel at these tiles and taps, these vials and soaps, rough rags and soft papers. It would mount in a museum your high school ring, wonder at your watch, your St. Christopher medal; and then your body, from dental crown and crew cut to appendix scar and circumcision, would become, as all enduring human matter does, abstract and general; you would not be a member any longer, but a species, a measure like the meter bar in Paris.

Yet what a price the rest of us would have to pay to get Feaster and his bathing house into history. We should have to hope for, then suffer, a cataclysm. As it is, the steamed mirror only faintly reflects him; his plump feet track the mat; he dampens a body-long rough Italian towel with his furry red chest, and, inconveniently, unaccountably, he sneezes. Exit the soul. God bless.

Joseph Blotner's massive Egyptian work[1] is not so much a monument to a supremely gifted writer as it is the great man's grave itself, down which the biographer's piously gathered data drops like sheltering dirt, and if there is a resurrection of any kind it consists of the reemergence of William Faulkner in the featureless form of Henry Feaster.

Faulkner and Feaster—well, they're both private men, men who prefer that no notice be taken of them . . .

About the biography. Dont tell the bastards anything. It cant matter to them. Tell them I was born of an alligator

---

[1] Joseph Blotner, *Faulkner: A Biography* (New York: Random House, 1974).

and a nigger slave at the Geneva Conference two years ago. Or whatever you want to tell them.

. . . who live between the cracks of great events and cultivate their solitude as others do glads or redolent begonias, yet they differ in one rather critical respect: Feaster's life is like Feaster, unhistoric, the rest of the world would have to recede and leave him before we should pay any heed to his comically waterworn presence, while the singular events which Faulkner lived through so quietly, the way a palm stings between claps, were of his own devising, and we cannot consequently say that he did not wish the world to know him. He insisted it was to know him, however, on his own terms, in *his* myths: as the pilot with the limp, the reserved and mysterious poet who drank to discourage the pain he said came from a silver plate in his head, the bedraggled and barefoot bohemian, the courtly gent, or eventually and more honestly as the distinguished author of his books, thus never in the weakness and secrecy of bed or binge, or anywhere he did not seem as solid and imposing as his grandfather's cemetery statue, its stone head

> . . . lifted a little in that gesture of haughty pride which repeated itself generation after generation with a fateful fidelity, his back to the world and his carven eyes gazing out across the valley where his railroad ran, and the blue changeless hills beyond, and beyond that, the ramparts of infinity itself.

Still, Feaster remains in motion. His arms meet on his belly as indifferently as tweezers. Is this a hug, this ambiguous gesture, or does Feaster feel a chill as the bathroom fan sucks the moisture from his freckles? Those freckles—alas—he's scarcely seen them. They live beneath the hairy leafage of his breast unnoticed as aborigines. We can't be too attentive. Feaster is saying bye-bye to his bath. Shall we allow his head to have a sad wag? Down the drain, so to speak, he muses.

Glug-a-lug. Yes. Inconceivable—the prodigality of Nature. Incalculable—the costs of History.

And anyone who ever saw Faulkner in the street, sat beside him in the classroom, sometimes had a conversation or a drink, is dutifully reported here, is cited, is described: little Myrtle Ramey, for example, who had a delicate throat, and who remembers how well Billy Faulkner folded paper into cubes—she couldn't—or Ralph S. Muckenfuss

> . . . a stocky, bright-looking, blue-eyed boy, whose hair was parted precisely in the middle . . .

with whom Billy jumped to victory in a three-legged race, and who observed that Faulkner drew a lot of pictures during class: "one of a cowboy being bucked over a corral fence by his horse." Thus Faulkner becomes a figure in the autobiographies of a thousand Feasters. Their histories overlap, darken, finally obliterate his. To find Faulkner a Feaster among Feasters is a bitter irony because his fiction constitutes, in part, as Proust's does, a vast rescue operation:

> All that I really desired was . . . [to] try by main strength to recreate between the covers of a book the world as I was already preparing to lose and regret, feeling, with the morbidity of the young, that I was not only on the verge of decrepitude, but that growing old was to be an experience peculiar to myself alone out of all the teeming world, and desiring, if not the capture of that world and the feeling of it as you'd preserve a kernel or a leaf to indicate the lost forest, at least to keep the evocative skeleton of the desiccated leaf.

Nothing was too mean for his imagination because he did not believe there was any insignificance on earth. A dirt road was worthy of the most elevated consciousness. An old woman or an old mule: he found in them the forms and forces of History itself. To build a house, found a family, lay rails across a state: these were acts an Alexander might have been engaged in. The Civil War was War, high water along the river was The Flood, the death of a dog was Sorrow. He managed to give even the mute heart speech, and invest a humble, private, oftimes red-necked life with those epic rhythms and rich sounds which were formerly the hired pomp and commissioned music of emperors and kings.

A terrible turn-around. Nevertheless passages of his prose bubble up in Blotner to frighten and amaze us, as if there were a still-breathing figure beneath this wash of uncircumstantiality and tireless cliché . . . the sonorous opening chords of *Absalom, Absalom!*, for instance, with their impressive adjectival orchestration, the careful fastening of consciousness to its object, and Faulkner's characteristically increasing rhetorical beat, a precise local observation blown through a metaphor like a herald announcing . . . what? always . . . the palpable appearance of Time.

> From a little after two oclock until almost sundown of the long still hot weary dead September afternoon they sat in what Miss Coldfield still called the office because her father had called it that—a dim hot airless room with the blinds all closed and fastened for forty-three summers because when she was a girl someone had believed that light and moving air carried heat and that dark was always cooler, and which (as the sun shone fuller and fuller on that side of the house) became latticed with yellow slashes full of dust motes which Quentin thought of as being flecks of the dead old dried paint itself blown inward from the scaling blinds as wind might have blown them.

It is as if remembered things themselves had memories, as if matter *were* memory. The muscles that hoed the garden remember the moves they made. To *see into*—for Faulkner—is to *think back*.

If the question were put to him, I imagine Mr. Feaster would suppose he had a history, and that he even remembered parts of it; but if Feaster were, like Thucydides, to say: "I shall merely set down what my life's been like, for I have suffered it myself, and have seen others suffering similarly through theirs," or if he were interviewed by our modern journalist's mesh-faced mike as though he were the scarred survivor of some terrible bathboom, not everything he might report would be remembered in the same way because remembering is not a single, straightforwardly simple, thing: recalling how to swim, speak French, or tie a knot; suddenly realizing you have left the water running, or that it is your wedding anniversary; knowing that twice seven is fourteen or that Washington was our first president; recollecting rather generally that the house of your birth had but three rooms, and then bringing fully and vividly back to mind the way your mother moistened the hankie she tidied your face with when you were a child, a bubble of spit on the tip of her tongue like a white berry—these are not all acts or objects of the same sort, and the reliability, or even the relative importance, the actual reality, of such different "memories" cannot be determined by a single method.

The autobiographer, even if he stays unusually close to home, records a good deal more than events he has "seen with his own eyes." People remember the date of their birth the way they remember the date of the Declaration of Independence; that is, they remember what they have been told. It's unlikely they remember *when* they were told, or *how it was* to learn it. Moreover, we can only remember what it's possible to forget; for example, it is possible for a man to overlook his birthday, or even to forget his birth date, but it isn't possible for him to forget he was born. This is not an idle distinction. It crosses Being like a crack in a plate.

Similarly, we can "lose track of time," but we can scarcely forget it; we can forget how far it is to Phoenix, but we cannot forget blue, sour, speed, space. "Ah," we can say,

"I'd forgotten what it feels like to ride a roller coaster," but what does it mean if I claim, reriding now, that I am "remembering" the good old days? There is also rhetorical remembering: how can you forget what happened to Napoleon? or, who does not remember Rudolf Valentino? and exhortational remembering: the Maine! Pearl Harbor! the Alamo! me! A good deal of history and biography, I'm afraid, consists of "memories" of these latter kinds.

And Mr. Blotner has those artful literary memoirs to manage, with *their* forms and falsehoods, the fiction itself, with *its* disguised, partial, and elusive truths, newspaper interviews and stories, by nature narrow and publicly pointed, telegrams self-conscious of their cost, letters full of the pleading self, business accounts and contracts with their standardized phrasing and ruled lines, magazine articles enlivened by inaccuracy, opportune criticisms, reviews (reviews! my god, by every Clifton Fadiman who ever lifted a book), as well as all the material Blotner has created himself, the tapes he's taken, the letters he's solicited, "facts" which would never have reached the world, which would have passed to oblivion like the sperm which Mr. Feaster fears he's overheated, if Mr. Blotner had not been discreet, polite, obliged, and so on, quietly persistent, dogged where necessary, etcetera, eager to cite, to give credit where credit, and to due its due, and so forth, careful never to ask the wrong kinds of question or appear otherwise than reverent, or whatever was necessary and seemed right; yet one will rarely find a narrative so extensive, so obviously bent on totality, which is, at the same time, so unaware of the mechanics of its kind, the physics of its own unfolding.

Each piece of information—check stub, clipping, tape length, letter—brings its symbol system with it, and some of these systems are so ontologically incompatible that their presence in the same paragraph or sentence is as sensible as those other incongruities, disproportions, and imbalances of time, importance, and causal connection, which biographers, like

blocks and babies, create in happy innocence of any fall or failure . . . the narrative leap, jig, and stumble of which this is a
minutely exaggerated example:

> Feaster put on his old-school tie to go to jail. There he lan-
> guished for nearly thirty years, memorizing snowballs and
> conversing with Ted. The Warden was named Feaster too.
> He had white hair and a Harvard degree. His dog was un-
> kind to cats and his wife broke plates. On Feaster's re-
> lease, Feaster, assuming the new name of Encyclopedia
> Smith, went to his mother's room to finish polishing his
> shoes, although his mother had already died.

Every biographer must measure out three quantities—
space in the text, data in the dossier, and time in the life—and
these should not continuously and outrageously contradict one
another, as is so often the case. Blotner fills pages with the
founding of New Orleans, but when, shortly after their wedding, Estelle Faulkner gets drunk and, in a gorgeous silk dress,
tries to drown herself in the Gulf of Mexico, he sails peacefully
past in a paragraph and won't even throw her a ring.

It is perhaps one of the more characteristic marks of consciousness that it can without difficulty contain radically heterogeneous contents. It seems to be that long-sought universal
solvent. Here, and here only, can things past and present meet
and mingle; here alone can thought, emotion, pleasure and
perception, ideas of every order, dreams and square roots, actually interact. Whether biography ought to imitate, at least so
heedlessly, the rich incongruities of human consciousness, or
pretend to be a kind of memory without first finding out which
kind, or remain innocent of the perplexities of point of view
and every other technique of rendering, are questions so rarely
put we almost all deserve the easy rhetorical answer I've just
suggested for them.

Blotner has tried to write a biography of Faulkner's books,
too. He has literally tried to supply us with the knowledge

Faulkner drew on when he imagined them, and that is surely a laudable enterprise; but this is not Lowes's *The Road to Xanadu*, because Blotner is not in the least interested in the creative result, and his long descriptions of the plots of every Faulkner novel, story, project, poem (and we are spared none of the poems), each in terms of the most degenerate theory of fiction conceivable, are models of the "missed point."

Faulkner's life was nothing until it found its way into Faulkner's language. Faulkner's language was largely unintrigued by Faulkner's life.

Feaster's thoughts are lengths of language, too, of course, but rarely does he put his experience into words like a sports announcer or reporter at a wedding; consequently they pass to oblivion comparatively unformed, since he has not decided, for instance, whether to call the water "tepid," "luke," or "safe," when he tests it with his hand . . . he has not had to. He thinks, in effect: the water is now the right temperature so it's okay to slope under. *In effect*, but not in so many words. When Faulkner is Feaster, he's in no different case.

We know that Feaster's experience has been formed, too, because the relation, nature, and value of its objects have been culturally defined. It is a commonplace to observe that the contents of his medicine chest will comprise a kind of psychological inventory, and we can be certain that he never imagines that the water watches him turning its tap in order, then, to gush forth obediently. The mouthwash which is sitting on the floor in the corner, we can also be confident, is "out of place." A crumpled Kleenex is "waste." He feels no life in his toothbrush despite its hum, while the vibrator with which he tickles his testicles has not even the humanness of his own hand.

Principally, the things around him will be seen as in or out of chests, drawers, or closets. Doors and windows will be either open or closed. Feaster himself will be either going or coming. Switches and machines will be either on or off, containers full or empty, people occupied or idle, and these simple alternations will no doubt dominate his day. Yet what conceivable importance are such matters to Mr. Feaster?—he serenely overlooks them—or to biography?—which will not observe them either.

They are dreary, insignificant details—yes—but repetitive like rites, and that is the key, for a steady drip can drive men mad; the feet of the faithful, the repeated steps of the common people, can slope a granite stair, and a cancer can begin in the corner of the mouth where for thirty years a pipe's been gripped. Indeed, it's the daily diet—angers, fears, humiliations—Dr. Johnson's tea, Balzac's coffee, Freud's cigars—which lead the liver to overlabor, stomach to puncture, heart to fail, the quiet worker to go berserk and ghetto to erupt, though it's only the seizure, stroke, or strike which reaches the papers.

Our present biographers love to accumulate details until their books are longer than the lives their subjects led (look at the booklines of our literary aces which have been drawn out lately: Lewis, Dreiser, Hemingway, Strachey, Hart Crane, Woolf, Cocteau, Proust, Flaubert, Fitzgerald, Ford, Frost, Faulkner now, Browning, Joyce, and James), and in most cases these details are held together with the biographer's sweat like wet sand.

They are extraordinary details, the details which fill these books. They are not unicorns, for unicorns are quite particular departures from reality. Neither private sensation nor public fact, an event of the moment nor a general law, neither Hume's impressions nor Plato's Ideas, they fall into that soggy never-never land of biographical summary; yet the philosophical difference between "I just saw a cow," and "I lived in Hollywood for three weeks," seems never to be felt. Though, of course, Faulkner himself felt it. And he used abstractions to achieve immediacy.

A book like Blotner's teeters between the historical past and the habitual future—between "he had" and the familiar from now on "he would"—like a walker on a wire. Letters sometimes flash Faulkner before us epiphanously, and in the curtain-like context of Blotner's text make us feel like Peeping Toms. When the woman with whom he is having an affair tells him how much his letters mean to her, he responds:

> Of course you like mine. Who wouldn't like to read the letters Faulkner wrote to the woman he loves and desires? I think some of them are pretty good literature, myself; I know what I would do if I were a woman and someone wrote them to me.   *(Blotner, p. 1445)*

The clips we get from these letters are like short lengths of hair.

Otherwise, here are records of visits paid, dinners attended, grades reached, bottles drunk, birds shot, letters written, remarks made, when what we want to know is whether the Great Man ground his teeth; we need the feel of the normal and everyday; we don't desire merely a list of Our Hero's laundry, but we covet the pattern there may be concealed in the way he dirtied it; that Feaster, for instance, likes to plug the drain with his big toe is only of passing interest, but that he holds his hand over his nose, bites his breath, lets coins sift slowly through his fist, and would stop time with talk if he could— each is, together, a clue to the shapes his consciousness assumes.

For look at the kind of consciousness Faulkner constructed:

> There was snow on Thanksgiving and though it did not remain two days, it was followed early in December by an iron cold which locked the earth in a frozen rigidity, so that after a week or so actual dust blew from it. Smoke turned white before it left the chimney, unable to rise, becoming the same color as the misty sky itself in which all day long the sun stood pale as an uncooked biscuit and as heatless.

White before it left the chimney. In passage after passage (I am quoting from "The Long Summer") cold, heat, wind, light, shadows, stenches, are rendered with an accuracy of imagination which is unique. No American has written down the weather as Faulkner has. No one asks how. No one wonders why.

What we want to know, then, is the difference between the structure of Feaster's consciousness, a consciousness of no account like all the rest of everyday awareness and soon to go gooooog as a fast drain does . . . (thank god, can you imagine consciousness piling itself up in basins, tubs, and pots, and needing to be garbaged off, or consciousness simply emptied like a lung into the available air the way peasants pee against walls?) . . . no, what we need to know is the distance and the difference between the life of Feaster and a sentence of Faulkner, because Feasters, alas (and by assumption here), are a dime a dozen, while Faulkner wrote sentences—who cares?—which had never been seen before, felt before, sentences with feverish impatient bodies, sentences which enclosed whole paragraphs, rising through their clauses like stairs, and which sometimes folded back upon themselves, came suddenly open and were suddenly shut in the same way the book they were a part of opened in the reader's hands, anywhere the reader was, and shut like the amusing mouth of a paper dragon or eyelids in an illness, as Clytie folds the following sentence over, neat as a note you prefer remain private:

> She passed the rest of that week in the one remaining room in the house whose bed had linen sheets, passed it in bed, in the new lace and silk and satin negligees subdued to the mauve and lilac of mourning—that room airless and shuttered, impregnated behind the sagging closed blinds with the heavy fainting odor of her flesh, her days, her hours, her garments, of eau-de-cologne from the cloth upon her temples, of the crystal phial which the negress alternated with the fan as she sat beside the bed be-

tween trips to the door to receive the trays which Clytie carried up the stairs—Clytie, who did that fetching and carrying as Judith made her, who must have perceived whether Judith told her or not that it was another negro whom she served, yet who served the negress just as she would quit the kitchen from time to time and search the rooms downstairs until she found that little strange lonely boy sitting quietly on a straight hard chair in the dim and shadowy library or parlor, with his four names and his six-teenth-part black blood and his expensive esoteric Faun-tleroy clothing who regarded with an aghast fatalistic ter-ror the grim coffee-colored woman who would come on bare feet to the door and look in at him, who gave him not teacakes but the coarsest cornbread spread with as coarse molasses (this surreptitiously, not that the mother or the duenna might object, but because the household did not have food for eating between meals), gave it to him, thrust it at him with restrained savageness, and who found him one afternoon playing with a negro boy about his own size in the road outside the gates and cursed the negro child out of sight with level and deadly violence and sent him, the other, back to the house in a voice from which the very absence of vituperation or rage made it seem just that much more deadly and cold.

He might have been called Maestro Crescendo, like Rossini, and it is assuredly true that he overwrote with a regularity rivaling the seasons. Hoping like Conrad to increase the mystery and majesty of his prose, Faulkner crammed it with abstractions beginning with *im-*, *in-*, and *un-*, prefixes of lordly largeness and menacing absence; he tightened and rhythmed his rhetorical forms, trebled his modifiers, and doubled his *o*s and his *m*s and his *p*s. He fancied fine words in the fashion of the self-taught and used them to render their opposites, the vulgar, illiterate, and innocent, with sometimes thrilling, often laughable, results, although his intuition that it would take repeated spins of the most pointed intelligence to ignite the dullest life seems now sound enough. The grotesque made him lyrical, and as he lowered the mental threshold of his characters, the sensual flood rose, so that when, for instance, the idiot Isaac waits in the wet dawn to greet his beloved cow, Faulkner embraces his reader with words the way Ike, who has wordless desires and otherwise only sensations, is embraced by sensation itself:

> He would smell her; the whole mist reeked with her; the same malleate hands of mist which drew along his prone drenched flanks played her pearled barrel too and shaped them both somewhere in immediate time, already married. He would not move. He would lie amid the waking instant of earth's teeming minute life, the motionless fronds of water-heavy grasses stooping into the mist before his face in black, fixed curves, along each parabola of which the marching drops held in minute magnification the dawn's rosy miniatures, smelling and even tasting the rich, slow, warm barn-reek milk-reek, the flowing immemorial female, hearing the slow planting and the plopping suck of each deliberate cloven mud-spreading hoof, invisible still in the mist loud with its hymeneal choristers.

. . . malleate hands . . . minute magnification . . . rosy miniatures . . . hymeneal choristers . . . what a disaster, the critic is inclined to exclaim, and many did, and many do, and they would have been right in fine had they not been wrong in large.

> Then he would see her; the bright thin horns of morning, of sun, would blow the mist away and reveal her, planted, blond, dew-pearled, standing in the parted water of the ford, blowing into the water the thick, warm, heavy, milk-laden breath; and lying in the drenched grasses, his eyes now blind with sun, he would wallow faintly from

thigh to thigh, making a faint, thick, hoarse moaning sound.

"I am taken to task for my long sentences, and my style is called *pompous* and *ponderous*. But good Lord, it is graceful toe-dancing compared with the overcrowded, overburdened, dragging, and thoroughly opaque periods that Faulkner for some reason thought appropriate for this book," Mann wrote about *A Fable*, and it is not just this book his judgment is relevant to. Everywhere full of tent damp, hog wash, shoe dew, cracker-barrel wisdom, spellbinding, storytelling, and bombast . . . yet, as in Carlyle's case, this writing holds a wind which glorifies its bag: so vigorous, so outspoken, so personal, perceived, original, so significant, serious, continuously strong and deeply felt, it blows the whistle back between our teeth— the whistle which was to accompany our wonder at such tastelessness, such boggy sentiments, such thoughts, such nerve, such genius.

While Ike and others like him have an animal's vulnerability to man and live in a kind of drooling harmony with nature, Faulkner's tragic figures have the dignity and force of his grandfather's statue fixed above the earth like a cold granite phallus. They are drunk with dreams, these heroes, alive through pride the way the rest of us resort to air; they won't bend in the face of adversity; they refuse to recognize change (with enemy and cannon in front of them, after unfolding their flags like flowers, wonderfully, ridiculously, nobly, on wooden nags, they charge); yet Faulkner, persistent moralist, does not ask that we survive, he asks that we endure, and the damage his inflexible dreamers do to themselves and others (to Faulkner's father and Faulkner, for instance), is nothing compared to the evil of the opportunists, the adaptable, the unscrupulous realists, the scramblers, the starlings, the Snopes.

Because . . . And Faulkner offers us an explanation for whatever actions he's imagined which, surrounded by nots and

other negations—not this, not that—like wisely untaken yet informative blind alleys, is invariably vast, detailed, obscure, indeed inexplicable, and the fruit of a family past. His narrative
loops from present punishment to ancestral crime with a mil-
liner's absent mind, and in the same matter-of-fact way, he
chews apart destiny's threads with his teeth. The seam is complete. The knot is tied. It's time.

   Yet he had to write for the *Post*, to pile up pages as you
might heap potatoes, to dicker with editors and agents, write
drivelly and usually useless scripts for Howard Hawkes mov-
ies, cut his gift with sugar for the street. He drank continuously, intermittently, moderately, heavily, in bursts and bouts,
in long languid arcs, not at all, or murderously. He could be
terribly silent. He would tell wonderful stories about the
Snopes family. He was polite, even courtly, rude. He would
spiff up, lose his shoes, collapse in the street.

   Faulkner always needed money, but he and his wife both
drank, he supported two households, servants, had two cars,
flew a plane, and Fox paid him nearly $20,000 in 1936. In the
same year an ad in the *Memphis Commercial Appeal* announced that William Faulkner would not be responsible for
his wife's debts. Later he bought a farm, a boat, at considerable sacrifice to himself lent money to his friend, Phil Stone,
and in letter after letter bitched beautifully about the whole
business of writing for a living and being hemmed in by henfolk
as well as other kinds, kiths, and kin.

   He was rarely among people who understood his achievement, not that this might have lifted his loneliness very much
(solitude was the space of more than his imagination), and the
needs, sensations, and feelings—the pity, the pure fury—
which one time had created those incredible lengths of language, those new and powerful forms, became themselves rhetorical habits, last rites, passionless gestures of passion like
the bouncing bottoms and sighing faces in porno films, and of
mainly monetary significance, too: that empty extended hat in

Feaster's hand, for instance, or, for all that, the hat he holds over his heart at the sound and hearing of the band, since we all die Feasters. Thus it is solemnly written. Becoming and remaining one—a Feaster—may be the first step in life, but it is also, and unequally, the last step toward the dust and disappearance and the silence of History.

Gertrude Stein
and the
Geography of the Sentence

When Gertrude Stein was a young girl, the twentieth century was approaching like a distant train whose hoot you could only just hear. A whole age was about to end. Nations would rededicate themselves, an entire generation bite into a fresh loaf, turn over a new leaf . . . tremble, pray. Despite this threat from the realm of number, though, most of the world went on as before, repeating itself over and over in every place, beginning and rebeginning, again and again and again.

Kipling had just written *The Phantom Rickshaw*. Stevenson was about to bring out *The Master of Ballantrae*, Howells to publish *A Hazard of New Fortunes*, while recently young Miss Stein had composed a melodrama called *Snatched from Death, or the Sundered Sisters*.

Henry James had also been busy. *The Bostonians* and *The Princess Casamassima* appeared in the same year, almost moments ago, it must have seemed, and *Scribner's Magazine* was now serializing *A London Life*. Writing machines were prominently advertised in the same periodical, as well as a restorative medicine made of cocainized beef, wine, and iron, said to be invaluable for nervous prostration and brain exhaustion, among other things, cases of the opium, tobacco, alcohol or chloral habit, gastric catarrh, and weak states of the voice or generative systems. Indeed, women were frequently in need of similar elixirs to combat depressions of the spirit: neurasthenia, sick headache, dyspepsia, and loss of appetite, were the most common. Nevertheless, Adelina Patti was recommending Pears Soap. There were several new developments among stoves. Lew Wallace, Dr. Abbott, Motley's *Works*, Walter Besant's novels, Charles Dudley Warner, Rider Haggard, and a series labeled "The English Men of Letters" were being smartly puffed, as well as the stories of Constance Fenimore Woolson (grandniece of the novelist she was middle-named for and friend of Henry James, in Venice dead of self and fever) and an edifying volume by Charles Reade called *Bible Characters* (12mo, cloth, 75 cents).

At Gettysburg, on the twenty-fifth anniversary of the battle, George Parsons Lathrop read a very long commemorative ode.

> *And, with a movement magnificent,*
> *Pickett, the golden-haired leader,*
> *Thousands and thousands flings onward, as if he sent*
> *Merely a meek interceder.*

And at the great Paris Exposition, among the Americans represented, Thomas Hovenden showed his picture, *The Last Moments of John Brown*, of which one critic said: "It is easy to believe that we are looking at a faithful transcript of the actual scene, and that photography itself could not have made a more accurate record." "It is the best American painting yet produced," wrote another. Holloway's reading stand was deemed particularly good for ladies, combining a book rest, dictionary holder, lamp stand, and invalid's table. It was sold where made in Cuyahoga Falls, Ohio.

The profession of letters had been wide open to women for perhaps seventy years. Many of the best-selling novelists had been and were women, just as nearly all of any novel's readers were. If there were genders to genres, fiction would be unquestionably feminine. Swashbuckling historical romances were liked, Gothic scares, and folksy up-with-country sagas too. Irving Bacheller's *Eben Holden*, a pale copy of that great success of two years before, *David Harum*, would still sell 250,000 copies in 1900. But above all by the turn of the century the domestic novel, in which the war on men was waged relentlessly right under their innocent noses, had become as necessary to female life as Lydia Pinkham's Vegetable Compound.

For some time Gertrude Stein had been absorbed, she claimed, in Shakespeare (of course), and in Wordsworth (the long dull late and densely moral poems particularly), Scott's wonderful *Waverley*, which made novel reading acceptable and popular in the United States, in the clean poems of Burns, Bunyan's allegories, Crabbe's country . . .

> *Fled are those times, when, in harmonious strains,*
> *The rustic poet prais'd his native plains . . .*

in Carlyle's *Frederick the Great*, Fielding, Smollett, and even Lecky's formidable *Constitutional History of England:* eminently heavy and respectable works of the sort I'd cite, too, if I were asked.

Prognostications of doom were also common, and increasing. Arks were readied, mountaintops sought out. Number for some was still number: a mark on a tube was magical . . . a circled day . . . a scratch on a tree . . . layer in a rock. The International Date Line runs like a wall through the ocean.

We can only guess whether the calendar had any influence on her, although later no one was to champion the new century more wholeheartedly, or attempt to identify America with modernity. The United States was the oldest country in the world, she said, because it had been in the twentieth century longer. In any case, Gertrude Stein, at age fifteen, thought frequently of death and change and time. Young girls can. She did not think about dying, which is disagreeable, even to young girls, but about death, which is luxurious, like a hot soak. The thought would appear as suddenly as moist grass in the morning, very gently, often after reading, on long reflective walks; and although it distressed her to think that there were civilizations which had perished altogether, she applauded the approaching turn. It was mostly a matter of making room. "I was there to begin to kill what was not dead, the nineteenth century which was so sure of evolution and prayers, and esperanto and their ideas," she said. It would be a closing, as the opening of puberty had been. A lid. Her own ending, even, did not disturb her. Dissolution did—coming apart at the seams—and she had, as many do, early fears of madness, especially after reading *The Cenci* or attending a performance of *Dr. Jekyll and Mr. Hyde*. She held little orgies of eating, liked to think and read of revolutions, imagined cruelties. She consumed anything, everything, as we have seen, and then complained that there was "nothing but myself to feed my own eager self, nothing given to me but musty books."

Scribner's Magazine was serializing *A London Life*. It contained plot, customs, characters, moral issues, insight, endless analysis, a little description, and went over its chosen ground often like an elephant in mittens. There was another of those essays on the decline of the drama in a recent *Harper's*. This one was quite decent really, by Brander Matthews, and in it he argued that one reason for the apparent death of the drama was the life of the novel—the present art form of the public—in particular, the immense early success of Scott's *Waverley* novels. *Scribner's* July issue of 1888 catches up *A London Life* at the beginning of Chapter V:

"And are you telling me the perfect truth when you say that Captain Crispin was not there?"

"The perfect truth?" Mrs. Berrington straightened herself to her height, threw back her head and measured her interlocutress up and down; this was one of the many ways in which it is to be surmised that she knew she looked very handsome indeed. Her interlocutress was her sister, and even in a discussion with a person long since under the charm she was not incapable of feeling that her beauty was a new advantage.

In "Composition as Explanation" Gertrude Stein would argue that between generations and over time, the "only thing different . . . is what is seen and what is seen depends upon how everybody is doing everything." "Everything is the same except composition."

She became, as she grew, increasingly unsure of who she was, a situation now so normal among the younger members of the middle class as to seem an inevitable part of middle-human development, like awkwardness and acne. Gertrude was a bit of a gawk already, aloof, cool, heavy, more and more alone. Her mother was an ineffectual invalid, gradually draining in her bed until, even before she died, she was emptied out of the world. Her father was a nuisance: stocky, determined, uneducated, domineering, quarrelsome, ambitious, notional, stern. When she was seventeen her father died, and "then our life without father began a very pleasant one."

Chapter V. In the old books there were chapters and verses, sections, volumes, scenes, parts, lines, divisions which had originated with the Scriptures ("chapter," for instance, a word for the head like *tête* and "title"); there were sentences, paragraphs, and numbered pages to measure the beat of each heart, the course of a life, every inference of reason, and the march, as they say, of time.

In *Four in America* she exposed the arbitrary conventionality of these often awkward cuts of meat.

> I begin to see how I can quiver and not quiver at like and alike.
>
> A great deal can be felt so.

Volume XII

HENRY JAMES one.

Volume XIII

The young James a young James was a young James a James. He might be and he might be even might be Henry James.

Volume XIV

Once upon a time there was no dog if there had been a dog nobody wept.

Once upon a time there was no name and if any one had a name nobody could cover a name with a name. But nobody except somebody who had not that name wept.

Naturally the young James did not know, with William around, that he was or would be the Henry James, and Gertrude Stein had not yet covered her name with a name. In this same book, she imagines what kind of novelist George Washington would have made. She does not fail to observe that he was born in February.

Any autumn day is different from any summer day or any winter day.

George Washington is pleased to come that is all who are ready are ready to rule.

Page 7

PLEASE do not let me wander.

Page 8

SHE is very sleepy. George Washington.

She is very sleepy. The autumn scenery when seen at a distance need not necessarily be tempted by wind. They may clear skies. But not a new moon. In autumn a new moon is well advanced. And a cloud can never cover it partly or be gracious rather to like red and blue all out but you. George Washington is famous as a nation.

Books contained tenses like closets full of clothes, but the present was the only place we were alive, and the present was like a painting, without before or after, spread to be sure, but not in time; and although, as William James had proved, the present was not absolutely flat, it was nevertheless not much thicker than pigment. Geography would be the study appropriate to it: mapping body space. The earth might be round but experience, in effect, was flat. Life might be long but living was as brief as each breath in breathing. Without a past, in the prolonged narrowness of any "now," wasn't everything in a constant condition of commencement? Then, too, breathing is repeating—it is beginning and rebeginning, over and over, again and again and again.

After all, what is the breath-before-last worth?

The youngest, she had been pampered as a baby, and she took care to be pampered all her life. "Little Gertie," her father once wrote, "is a little schnatterer. She talks all day long and so plainly. *She outdoes them all.* She's such a round little pudding, toddles around the whole day and repeats everything that's said or done." Yet she became, as she grew, increasingly unsure of who she was. Her eldest brother, soon off to college and career, seemed distant in his age, while the next, named Simon, she thought simple—as, indeed, he was. "My sister four years older simply existed for me because I had to sleep in the same room with her. It is natural not to care about a sister, certainly not when she is four years older and grinds her teeth at night."

She loved her brother, Leo, but she had no trust of men. It becomes a central theme. "Menace" was the word they went around in. Still, she and Leo were invariably "two together two," although Leo always led, and when Leo went to Harvard, Gertrude later came to Radcliffe, and when Leo began to study biology at Johns Hopkins, a regular tag-along, Gertrude enrolled in medicine there, and when her brother went to Italy finally, she soon abandoned her studies to join him. They were to-

gether for a while in London, shared a flat in Paris, gathered
paintings almost by not moving, like dust.

She shared something else with this brother, something
deeply significant, something fundamental: an accidental life.
When they thought about it, Gertrude said, it made them feel
funny. The Steins had planned on having five children, and
then, efficiently, had had them. However, two of these children died early enough they never "counted," and this made
room for Leo, first, and then for Gertrude, so that when, at the
beginning of *The Geographical History of America*, she writes:
"If nobody had to die how would there be room enough for any
of us who now live to have lived," she is not merely paraphras-
ing Hume's famous reply to Boswell, who, as the philosopher
lay becalmed on his deathbed, injudiciously asked if it was not
possible that there might be a future state: "It is also possible
that a piece of coal put on the fire will not burn," Hume answered, meanly remaining in the realm of matter. "That men
should exist forever is a most unreasonable fancy. . . . The
trash of every age must then be preserved and new Universes
must be created to contain such infinite numbers."

I do not believe she had any knowledge of Frederick Jackson Turner's frontier hypothesis, but her understanding of
American history was based on something very like it: "In the
United States there is more space where nobody is than where
anybody is." There is no question that she, like Turner,
thought human behavior was in great part a function of the
amount of free land available. On the frontier, Turner believed, civilization was regularly being reborn. When westward
the course of empire no longer took its way, Americans moved
"in" and went east to Paris in order to go west within the mind
—a land like their own without time. And Gertrude Stein believed Americans were readier than Europeans, consequently,
to be the new cultural pioneers. The mind . . . The human
mind went on like the prairie, on and on without limit.

It is characteristic of her method by and large that every

general thought find exact expression in the language of her own life; that every general thought in fact be the outcome of a repeated consideration of solidly concrete cases—both wholly particular and thoroughly personal—and further, that these occasions be examined, always, in the precise form of their original occurrence, in which, then, they continue to be contained as if they were parts of a sacred text that cannot be tampered with substantially, only slightly rearranged, as a musician might lengthen the vowels slightly or repeat the words of a lyric to compose a song, skip a little now and then, or call for an extensive reprise. "I was there to begin to kill what was not dead. . . ."

And what is Mrs. Berrington doing as we come to the end of this month's episode?

> "Where are you going—where are you going—where are you going?" Laura broke out.
>
> The carriages moved on, to set them down, and while the footman was getting off the box Selina said: "I don't pretend to be better than other women, but you do!" And being on the side of the house, she quickly stepped out and carried her crowned brilliancy through the long-lingering daylight and into the open portals.
>
> *(To be continued.)*

Much must go, however good, for Gertrude Stein to be. A place must be made. But much of Gertrude Stein would have to be subtracted once she discovered who she was.

Born in Allegheny, Pennsylvania. It does seem unlikely, but in American letters the unlikely is not unusual: Hart Crane came from Garretsville, Ohio; Pound was born in Idaho; neither Michigan nor Mississippi has any prima facie promise; Wallace Stevens saw exquisite light in Reading; Katherine Anne Porter in Indian Creek, Texas; Edward Arlington Robinson in Tide Head, Maine; and for T. S. Eliot even St. Louis is odd. They mostly moved anyway. Who thinks of Robert Frost

as a tyke in San Francisco? And the Steins left almost immediately for Vienna, where her father hoped that family connections there might help him in his wool business. He really did
write back that little Gertie "toddles around the whole day and
repeats everything that's said or done." After a period in
Paris, the Steins returned to Baltimore, but soon they swapped
houses, climates, coasts again, and crossed the country to live in
Oakland, California, where Gertrude's father became successfully connected with, for god's sake, a cable railway company.

To be hoist up a hill. And with certain exceptions modern
American writing has been overwhelmed by space: rootless-
ness, we often say, that's our illness, and we are right; we're
sick of changing house, of moving, of cutting loose, of living
in vans and riding cycles, of using up and getting on (that's how
we age), until sometimes one feels there's nothing but geography in this country, and certainly a geographical history is the
only kind it can significantly have; so that the strange thing is
that generally those years which both Freud and the Roman
Catholic Church find crucial to our character are seldom connected to the trunk, except perhaps as decals: memorials of
Mammoth Cave, ads for Herold's Club. Well, what's the point
of being born in Oak Park if you're going to kill yourself in
Ketchum? Our history simply became "the West" where time
and life went. So what's the point in St. Paul if you are going
to die in Hollywood of an alcoholic heart? Like Henry James
we developed an enlarged sense of locale, but we were tourists. And Gertrude Stein lived in hotels, shops, trains, rented
rooms, at aunts', with friends, in flats, with chums, and grew
up with her books, her body, and her brother—nothing more,
and no one else.

Of course, you could say that democracies have never
had a history; that they cannot run in place; they must expand;
they must have space. In New England, in the South, life went
sometimes in another direction, and it was, naturally enough,
one of the lures of Europe: to be in the presence of people who

had lived for a long time alongside things and other people who had been allowed to live for a long time alongside them; consequently to observe objects and relations come into being, alter, age, fade, disappear, and to see that process rather constantly; to feel in things one's own use of them—like old clothes, maybe, streets, shops, castles, churches, mills—as one's own person felt one's self—in hills, paths, lakes, fields, creeks— since we seldom gawk at our own changes as though passing by on a bus, but learn to live them with the unconscious ease which daily life and custom gradually confer, like the wear of water and the growth of grass; still Gertrude Stein blew "the American trumpet as though it were the whole of Sousa's band" and always spoke European brokenly; she was perhaps the last of our serious writers to, in the square sense, love her country, and she moved her writing even through her own enthusiasms (Henry James and Richardson and Eliot), as painfully as through a thicket, straight into the present where it became, in every sense of this she understood, "American" and "measureless."

But not in a moment was this accomplished. In a life. The resolution required would be heroic. Shortly after she began living in Paris with her brother, she completed a manuscript which was not published for nearly fifty years: a curiously wooden work of relentless and mostly tiresome psychological analysis which she called, with crushing candor, *Quod Erat Demonstrandum*. However, in this brief novel about the personal relationships between three depersonalized paper women, plotted as a triangle on which the lines are traveled like a tramway, the points incessantly intersected—in which, though much is shown, nothing's proved, and everyone is exhausted—Gertrude Stein's sexual problem surfaces. Clearly, she has had a kind of love affair with another woman. Clearly, too, the circumstances of her life were now combining against her, compelling her to rely more and more upon a self she did not have. She lacked a locale which might help to define her and a family she could in general accept; she had grown into a hulksome female and become a bluestocking, yet she remained professionless and idle; in fact, she was a follower at present, fruit fly, gnat, silent in front of Leo while he lectured to their friends on his latest fads and finds: she was a faithless Jew, a coupon clipper, exile anyhow, and in addition, she was desperately uncertain of her own sexuality. The problem of personal identity, which is triumphantly overcome in *The Geographical History*, would occupy her henceforth, particularly in the most ambitious work of her career, *The Making of Americans*.

Furthermore her brother was beginning to ridicule her writing.

Still she listened to Leo; she looked at Cézanne; she translated Flaubert; and this subordination of ear, eye, and mind eventually released her, because Flaubert and Cézanne taught the same lesson; and as she examined the master's portrait of his wife, she realized that the reality of the model had been superseded by the reality of the composition. Everything in the painting was related to everything else in the painting, and to everything else equally (there were no lesser marks or moments), while the relation of any line or area of color in the painting to anything outside the painting (to a person in this case) was accidental, superfluous, illusory. The picture was of Mme. Cézanne. It had been painted by her husband. It was owned by the Steins. Thus the picture had an *identity*. But the painting was an *entity*. So a breast was no more important than a button, gray patch, or green line. Breasts might be more important than buttons to a vulgar observer, but in biology, where a mouse and a man were equal, in art, in our experience of how things are presented to us in any present moment, in mathematics—indeed, in any real whole or well-ordered system—there was a wonderful and democratic equality of value and function. There was, she said, no "up" in American religion either, no hierarchy, no ranking of dominions and powers.

Identities were what you needed to cash a check or pass a border guard. Identities had neighbors, relatives, husbands, and wives. Pictures were similarly authenticated. Poems were signed. Identities were the persons hired, the books and buildings bought and sold, the famous "things," the stars. She drew the distinction very early. In *The Geographical History* she would describe it as the difference between human nature and the human mind.

Gertrude Stein liked to begin things in February. Henry James has written *The Golden Bowl* and it will take a war to end the century, not the mere appearance of a pair of zeros on the mileage indicator. Never mind. Although the novel as it had been known was now complete, and Gertrude has meanwhile doubled her fifteen years without appreciable effect, still there was in what was being written (*Nostromo*, last year; *The House of Mirth*, just out; and *The Man of Property*, forthcoming), for instance, that socially elevated tone, the orotund authorial voice, the elegant drawing-room diction, that multitude of unfunctional details like flour to thicken gravy; there were those gratuitous posturings, nonsensical descriptions, empty conversations, hollow plots, both romance and Grub Street realism; and there so often remained the necessity, as Howells complained, to write with the printer at one's heels, therefore the need to employ suspense like a drunken chauffeur, Chapter Vs and other temporal divisions as though the author commanded an army, and all of the rest of the paraphernalia required by serialization and the monthly purchase of magazines.

She saw how the life of the model had been conferred upon the portrait. And in the central story of *Three Lives* (they were still stories), she captured the feeling she wanted in words.

All that long day, with the warm moist young spring stirring in him, Jeff Campbell worked, and thought, and beat his breast, and wandered, and spoke aloud, and was silent, and was certain, and then in doubt and then keen to surely feel, and then all sodden in him; and he walked, and he sometimes ran fast to lose himself in his rushing, and he bit his nails to pain and bleeding, and he tore his hair so that he could be sure he was really feeling, and he never could know what it was right, he now should be doing.

The rhythms, the rhymes, the heavy monosyllabic beat, the skillful rearrangements of normal order, the carefully controlled pace, the running on, the simplicity, exactness, the passion . . . in the history of language no one had written like this before, and the result was as striking in its way, and as successful, as *Ulysses* was to be.

Neither *Three Lives* nor *The Making of Americans* eliminated the traditional novel's endless, morally motivated, psychological analyses, though she would manage that eventually. *A Long Gay Book* was begun as another investigation of the relationships between people, in this case mainly pairs, but it gradually wandered from that path into pure song. "I sing," she said, "and I sing and the tunes I sing are what are tunes if they come and I sing. I sing I sing." For instance:

Wet weather, wet pen, a black old tiger skin, a shut in shout and a negro coin and the best behind and the sun to shine.

She was readying herself for *Tender Buttons*. But what would never disappear from her work, despite her revolutionary zeal, was her natural American bent toward self-proclamation and her restless quest for truth—especially that, because it would cause her to render some aspects of reality with a ruthlessness rare in any writer, and at a greater risk to her art than most.

The household balance slowly tipped. Leo became enmeshed in an oddly passionless love affair, unsuccessfully

underwent analysis, and looked more and more, in Mabel
Dodge's judgment, like a suspicious old ram, while Gertrude,
discovering the pleasures of "lifting belly," developed a "laugh
like a beefsteak." Although the twentieth century had begun
with Grant's massed attacks on Lee around Cold Harbor, the
nineteenth had hung on despite Gertrude's efforts, only to ex-
pire somewhere along the Marne and in the mud of the
Somme; but centuries don't end in an instant or easily, sometimes only in a lifetime. The Romantic Century took a lot of
killing.

Alice Toklas came to live, to type, to correct the proof of
Three Lives, which Gertrude was printing at her own expense,
to manage, companion, cook, protect, while Leo at last left to
fulfill his promise as a failure, taking the Matisses and the Re-
noirs with him, and allowing his sister finally her leeway, her
chance to define herself, which she firmly, over decades, did:
as an eccentric, dilettante, and gossip, madwoman, patron, genius, tutor, fraud, and queer—the Mother Goose of Mont-
parnasse.

2

Buttons fasten, and because tender buttons are the buttons we
unbutton and press, touch and caress to make love, we can
readily see why they fasten. These extraordinary pieces of
prose, which Gertrude perversely called poems, do much more
than simply resemble the buttons she liked to collect and sort,
though they are indeed verbal objects, and their theoretical af-
finity with the paintings of advanced cubism is profound. Like
many of the canvases of Cézanne, Matisse, and Braque, each
piece is a domestic still. They employ many of the methods of
collage, too, as well as those of Dada disassociation.

Thematically, they are composed of the implements, activities, colors and pleasures of home life, its quiet dangers,
its unassertive thrills: cooking, cleaning, eating, loving, visit-

ing, entertaining, and it is upon this base that the embossing of these buttons takes place. Plates are broken, pots and tables polished, meat sliced, food chopped, objects are repaired, arranged, contained. The highest metaphysical categories of sameness and difference, permanence and change, are invoked, as are the concerns of epistemology, of clarity and obscurity, certainty and doubt.[1]

Like a cafeteria tray, *Tender Buttons* has three sorting sections (Objects, Food, Rooms), but it is also built with three floors, so that its true shape is a cube. Objects are things external to us, which we perceive, manipulate, and confront. Next are the things which nourish us, which we take into ourselves: information, feeling, food. Finally, there are things which enclose us as our body does our consciousness, like a lover's arms, or as people are embraced by rooms. If the X-axis is divided as I've described, the Y-axis is marked off into Work, or household chores, Love, or the complicated emotional exchanges between those who spend their daily life together, and Art, or in this case, the composition of odd, brilliant, foolish, accidental, self-conscious, beautiful, confused, or whimsical sentences.

For example, clinging to objects and dulling their glitter is *dirt:*

WRITING	obscurity	—change—	clarity	ARTISTS
LOVING	concealment	(cleaning)	candor	SAINTS
WORKING	dirty		shining	"WIVES"
	OBJECTS	Process	OBJECTS	

Negative ------------------------ Positive

---

[1] Opinions about the methods, meaning, style, purpose, nature, sources, influence, or value of *Tender Buttons* vary wildly, though a consensus may be slowly emerging as time passes and tempers cool. To sample the range, for both bewilderment and profit, I suggest the reader consult: Richard Bridgman, *Gertrude Stein in Pieces* (New York: Oxford, 1970); John Malcolm Brinnin, *The Third Rose* (Boston: Atlantic Monthly

That is, objects are either clean, so that they shine and glitter, gleam and dazzle, or like the tarnish on copper pots, the grayness of dusty glass, the dinginess of soiled pillows, they are dull and dirty, as our lives become when we are left unloved and unemployed.

Throughout, the crucial word is *change*. Some processes, like cleaning and mending, are basically restorative. They remove the present in order to return to and conserve the past. Others, like sewing, decorating, and cooking, principally through operations which alter *quantity* (by shaping, enlarging, reducing, juxtaposing, mingling, and so on), create *qualities* which have not previously existed. Many times these qualities are positive, but naturally not always. In the human sphere, to which these activities are precisely proportional, similar consequences occur. Finally, both these areas are metaphorically measured against the art of writing and found to be structurally the same. Words can be moved about like furniture in their sentences; they can be diced like carrots (Stein cuts up a good number); they can be used in several different ways simultaneously, like wine; they can be brushed off, cleaned and polished; they can be ingeniously joined, like groom and bed, anxiety and bride. Every sentence is a syntactical space (a room) in which words (things, people) act (cook, clean, eat, or excrete) in order to produce quite special and very valuable qualities of feeling. Cleaning a room can be a loving or a vengeful act, a spontaneous tidying, mere routine, or a carefully planned Spring Scrub, and one's engagement to the task can be largely mindless or intensely meant. Similarly, not a few of these buttons are as accidental as kicked stones (my

Press, 1959); B. L. Reid, *Art by Subtraction* (Norman, Oklahoma: University of Oklahoma Press, 1958); Allegra Stewart, *Gertrude Stein and the Present*, (Cambridge, Mass.: Harvard University Press, 1967); Donald Sutherland, *Gertrude Stein: A Biography of Her Work* (New Haven: Yale University Press, 1951); and Edmund Wilson, *Axel's Castle* (New York: Scribner's, 1931). Gertrude Stein talks about her intentions in *Lectures in America* (New York: Random House, 1935).

typewriter writes "spoiled cushions" instead of "soiled" and I wonder whether I shouldn't leave the phrase that way), others are painfully self-conscious and referential, as planned as a political coup, while a few seem wholly momentary whims whose consequences have been self-indulgently allowed to stand.

Although the "poems" do not avoid nouns, as their author suggests she was trying to do, and have nice tasty titles ("SINGLE FISH," "SAUSAGE," "CELERY," "VEAL"), they avoid naming. Picasso's hermetic *The Clarinet Player*, for instance, painted during the same period *Tender Buttons* was being composed, offers no comment, visual or otherwise, on clarinet playing, players, or the skill of playing. After the motif has been analyzed into its plastic elements, these are modified and recombined according to entirely abstract schemes in which colors and forms predominate and respond solely to one another. The world is a source of suggestions, nothing more, and every successful work supersedes its model and renders the world superfluous to it.

Yet we are already in a tangle of terminology, because Gertrude Stein was always doing "descriptions," and she furthermore felt that naming was the special function of the poet. *Tender Buttons* is, she insists, a book of poems; poems are based, she claims, on the noun; and tender buttons are portraits, as she puts it, not of living people like Mabel Dodge and Sherwood Anderson, but of ordinary objects and common processes and simple spaces. Naming and not naming, describing and not describing, subject or sign: can we straighten this out?

In the first place, nouns are full of remembrance since they represent collections of past experience, and although it may seem reasonable to encounter the present well-padded by the past, this tends to give to every meeting of bell and clapper the same dull clonk: ah, there you are again, Socrates. We cease to listen, cease to see. So we must rid ourselves of the old titles and properties, recover a tutored innocence, and then, fresh as a new-scrubbed Adam, reword the world.

I began to wonder at at about this time just what one saw when one looked at anything really looked at anything. Did one see sound, and what was the relation between color and sound, did it make itself by description by a word that meant it or did it make itself by a word in itself . . .

I became more and more excited about how words which were the words that made whatever I looked at look like itself were not the words that had in them any quality of description. This excited me very much at that time.

("Portraits and Repetition")

When she did her portraits, Gertrude Stein spent a great deal of her time listening, because each of her subjects was, as we all are, a talking machine, and of course what she listened to was in part a response to herself, to her talking. Now she wanted to stress seeing, because, of course, though frying pans speak and one might mutter to one's knitting, objects mainly spangled space with color and reflection.

We have bought a poodle. What shall we name it? We can, of course, confer upon it a name we idly like, and force it to conform, or we can study the beast until it says "Basket."[2] Yet the poet seeks the names of things because she loves the names. Al-ci-bi-a-des, we call out. Ai-e. Ai-e. Alcibiades.

. . . you can love a name and if you love a name then saying that name any number of times only makes you love it more, more violently more persistently more tormentedly.

("Poetry and Grammar")

To denoun and undenote, then to rename, and finally to

---

[2] Anyone interested in Gertrude Stein's attitude toward names and their relationship to the thing named should consult the Wilbur Wright and Henry James sections of *Four in America* (New Haven: Yale, 1947).

praise the old world's raising of the new word out of the moni-
toring mind:

> Poetry is concerned with using with abusing, with los-
> ing with wanting, with denying with avoiding with adoring
> with replacing the noun. It is doing that always doing that,
> doing that and doing nothing but that. Poetry is doing
> nothing but using losing refusing and pleasing and betray-
> ing and caressing nouns.   *("Poetry and Grammar")*

Suppose then that I have a carafe of wine in front of me.
My aim is to peel language from it like a label, and I shall then
allow these words, put in attractive proximity, to draw other
senses, sounds, and sentiments, from one another. A CARAFE,
THAT IS A BLIND GLASS is the name of the first Object (if these
titles indeed are names),[3] and we observe at once (1) that, although the Object is an occasion for these words, it is the author who accounts for their singular character; and (2) that the
heading possesses a maliciously ambiguous structure. The single comma is a kind of curiosity, and only one will appear in
the first sentence of text which lies beneath it. Shall we read:
"A carafe, that is to say, a blind glass," as if we were being
given a definition; or shall we think of it as a carafe which happens to be a blind glass, in which case its blindness is not defining; or is it an exclamation, and should we come down hard
as a hammer on 'that': "A carafe, wow, is *that* a blind
glass!"? Obviously the order runs from exclamation back
through accident to necessity like a wound which leaves a scar.

The rest of the button is finished off as follows:

> A kind in glass and a cousin, a spectacle and nothing
> strange a single hurt color and an arrangement in a system

---

[3] I have chosen this one not only because it is first, but because it has been heavily
commented upon. Compare the treatment in Bridgman and Stewart.

to pointing. All this and not ordinary, not unordered in not resembling. The difference is spreading.

Not every decanter is made of glass, but this is one of the glass kind. (The word 'kind' will reappear.) Its opaqueness makes it a cousin to the clear. Blind people wear dark glasses because they do not desire us to see they cannot see and be disconcerted by rolling pupils or the glaze of a sightless eye. Thus this glass is not made for seeing but for being seen: it is not a pair of spectacles but a spectacle. A spectacle is normally something grand and extraordinary, however here there is nothing unusual, nothing strange.

A bruise varies in color from purple through pale green and yellow, and as it ages, fades. I cannot say directly which of these colors the glass is, but each hue is one which wine has: apple clear or straw or ruddy. The blind person's tinted glasses signify a hurt too, and it is of course an irony when glasses are used to say that someone cannot see. Everything in a carafe flows up the neck like a pointing finger or a fountain. As we shall see. Words, as well, appear to point or fountain. Though these poems do not point, they have one. As asparagus.

Now I (the poet, the perceiver, the namer, the praiser) reflect: not upon the Object but upon the pattern I've made of my words and how they space themselves, for their space is inside them, not openly disposed upon the page as poetry normally is. I notice that my verbal combinations are, on that account, unusual (I shall brag about it), and that, although they resemble nothing else which passes for poetry, they are nevertheless not without their own system and order . . . these sentences which form triangles, crowds, or squares, go verbless as one goes naked, or which wind around Being like a fateful spindle.[4]

---

[4] "I really do not know that anything has ever been more exciting than diagraming sentences . . . I like the feeling the everlasting feeling of sentences as they diagram themselves. In that way one is completely possessing something and incidentally one's

A kind	in glass	and a cousin,
a spectacle		and nothing strange
a single hurt color		and an arrangement
	in a system	

to pointing.

Gloss 1: These poems are like a wine-colored glass carafe. Their most common shape is that of a truncated hour-glass (an anticipatory interpretation).

Gloss 2: The carafe is like a blind person's glasses.

So these poems are opaque containers. They have been made to fasten us through pleasure together, as indeed wine does . . . and most household objects and the acts which center on them: pots, pans, pillows, cooking, cleaning, love. The difference between these buttons and other swatches of language is going to deepen, she says, and there are going to be more and more of them, not only because the book will pour them out on us, but because the principles of their composition will be widely imitated.[5]

The next button, GLAZED GLITTER, continues the theme of change with a first line which is immediately followed by a commentary:

Nickel, what is nickel, it is originally rid of a cover.

The change in that is that red weakens an hour. The change has come. There is no search. But there is, there is that hope and that interpretation and sometime, surely any is unwelcome, sometime there is breath and there will be a sinecure and charming very charming is that clean and cleansing. Certainly glittering is handsome and convincing.

---

self." ("Poetry and Grammar") These simple spatial pictures (hardly diagrams) are designed to reveal the functional rhetorical forms of her sentences.

[5] If this is what she meant, she was of course mistaken, because the principles by which *Tender Buttons* was composed are only narrowly understood.

Let us attempt to answer that initial question. Responses rise like hungry fish. Many household utensils are nickel-plated because the metal they're made of may wear, rust, redden, or otherwise become unwholesome to use. Nickel is naturally shiny and easy to maintain (i.e., is a benefit without labor, a sinecure). Nickel has, in short, an impermeable surface, a glaze, which has a glitter.

But had the question been: nickels, what are nickels? we might have replied: small change.

However, if we listen intently, we shall hear inside the word two others of woeful association: 'Nick,' the name of the Devil himself, and 'Hell,' his hot location. Our license for following this procedure is, first, that Gertrude Stein regularly requests us to find other words within her words in exactly this way[6]; second, that a little research into the history of the term tells us that the original nickel was a German coin called *Kupfernickel* because, although it was a copper color, it yielded none of the metal, and for this deceit, like fool's gold, was accused of being the devil's ore; and third, that the lines which immediately follow, as well as all of the remaining poems, require it.

Snuffling at roots gives us another method for finding words in words, as well as another fundamental sense of what a tender button is: a swollen, underground stem or bud, a truffle.[7] That is, these poems are buds based on hidden roots. The fourth poem, A BOX, is explicit about this.

---

[6] In LUNCH she splits an acorn: "a corn a corn yellow and green mass is a gem." The title of the last Object, THIS IS THIS DRESS, AIDER must be read "this is distress, aid her," among other things, as we shall see. That poem contains the phrase, "make a to let," in which the rent sign is missing its toy. Allegra Stewart has nice notes on these. There are innumerable others.

[7] Allegra Stewart's essay on *Tender Buttons* (in *Gertrude Stein and the Present*), perhaps the most complete we have, not only sees the importance of the light imagery, and correctly names the central subject: purification, it also stresses the search for roots. Unfortunately she frequently pushes past the operable derivations into Sanskrit. You cannot usefully explain tomorrow's murder by citing yesterday's creation of the world. The encoding, the disguising, the circular imagery, which she again locates

She often permits 'this,' 'there,' 'they,' and 'it' to float free of any single reference because she wants so many. These terms are like holes in buttons through which the threads pass. And in the opening line that bewildering 'it' stands for all original nakedness and exposure. Stainless steel souls, one imagines, need no cleansing, no catharsis, no cover. They are the ultimate solution to the problem of sin.

The spatial organization of this paragraph is revealing, and shows what I meant by sentences turning on the spindle of Being:

```
The change in that              is
              that                      red weakens an hour.
The change                              has come.
                        There is                  no search.
                        But there is,
              that hope        there is
and          that interpretation
and               sometime
        surely    any(time)          is un wel come,
                  sometime there is                breath
and                        there      will  be     a  sine-
        cure
and charming
very charming                        is
              that
        clean
and  cleansing.
        Certainly  glittering       is   handsome
and convincing.
```

beautifully, is soon smothered in Jungian obfuscation. The neglect of surface sense also lames her account, as well as an inexplicable reluctance to spell out the sexual references. *Tender Buttons* is an in-private, *sub-rosa*, discussion of the "marriage" of Gertrude (who, after all, is "dear spear") and Alice Toklas (probably, "child-less").

Having lost our innocence and put on knowledge with our leaf, we had to earn our keep, labor, sleep, and learn to wash. Like Alcibiades to the cloak of Socrates, cleanliness crept next to Godliness and made itself beloved by health and hospitals equally. Coverings grew grand and hid our weaknesses. We covered sculpture's plaster glands, legs of pianos, tables too, and all our thoughts with discretions. These poems are themselves excessively discreet.

To red up is to rid oneself of whatever is extraneous and out of place (a small change, 'e' for 'i'), and the uppermost meaning here is how the work of tidying tires out both time and ourselves. Still we cannot forget that red is the past tense of reading, the color of blood and wine, of Jezebels, the suit of Satan, and the cent it takes five to make a nickel of. And any reader who observes Stein's sly small small-change in this passage (to mention but one of so many), must begin to be of different mind about her alleged subconscious methods of composition.

We hope of course that one day we shall be able to take it easy, draw an idle breath, purify ourselves the way we polish hardware and pots, clear tables, or better yet, cure sin, and cook without dirtying a dish. Cleaning, like confession, is a rite, and the spells it casts are effective, because a tidy house does seem for a time to be invulnerable.

> There is no gratitude in mercy and in medicine. There can be breakages in Japanese. That is no programme. That is no color chosen. It was chosen yesterday, that showed spitting and perhaps washing and polishing. It certainly showed no obligation and perhaps if borrowing is not natural there is some use in giving.

The medical theme (one thread: hurt-spreading-rid-red-weakens - hope - interpretation (diagnosis) - breath - cure - clean and cleansing) is joined by the sacramental (another thread:

"wine"-"Satan"-"the Fall"-hope-interpretation(hermeneutics)-
breath-sinecure-cleansing) to become momentarily dominant. We do not receive mercy from God because He is grateful to us, nor does the physician feel he is discharging a debt.

"The change has come." If the change has come (unlike
the coming of the Kingdom, to be sure, but love has been made
with Alice for some time, and Leo has been replaced), it has
come without our fumbling for it (reds, nickels, dimes, quarters, halves). One may borrow a nickel (after all, what is a
nickel?) without any obligation to repay. Actually one rarely
asks for the loan of such a small sum, and indeed a nickel is
easy to give away. Later one learns how these little daily things
add up, for a dollar contains ten dimes the way loving is made
of lots of light caresses.

			There is		no gratitude	in mercy
and						in medicine.
			There	can be	breakages	in Japanese.
	That			is	no programme.	
	That			is	no color chosen.	
				It was		chosen	yesterday,
	that showed spitting					
and		perhaps washing				
and		polishing.				
				It		
	certainly showed				no obligation	
and perhaps				if		
		borrowing		is	not natural	
			there is		some use	in giving.

GLAZED GLITTER is a "poem" with a subject: roughly, the
price of change and restoration, repairs and healing, the charm
of coming clean.

A SUBSTANCE IN A CUSHION

The change of color is likely and a difference a very little difference is prepared. Sugar is not a vegetable.

Callous is something that hardening leaves behind what will be soft if there is a genuine interest in there being present as many girls as men. Does this change. It shows that dirt is clean when there is a volume.

I have quoted only two of this important section's ten paragraphs, yet these, and the two poems already so cursorily examined, make the fundamental moral and metaphysical issues apparent: the contrast between surface and depth, for example, the relation between quantity and quality, permanence and change, innocence and knowledge, giving and receiving, art and life, in and out.

Sugar cane, of course, is a vegetable, a grass, but the process of refining it transforms the juice of the stalk. Sugar is often a surface addition, as on cereal; it sweetens our coffee, for which we may be grateful; it enhances, but it does not nourish.

Again: if we multiply dust until it becomes earth, it is no longer dirt, and so long as Gertrude lived with her brother there was no suspicion, but when Alice moved in to form, in effect, a *ménage à trois*, or after Leo left, the whispering began. One must become hardened.

So sometimes work, sometimes writing, sometimes love, are uppermost; sometimes one metaphorical carrier (cooking, cleaning) rises above another; key words are obsessively repeated, not only in particular paragraphs, but throughout; sometimes the sentences look over their shoulders at where they've been, and we are not always prepared for the shifts.

Although the text is, I think, overclued, the language plain, and the syntax so Spartan as to be peculiar, naked as a Dukhobor whose cause we cannot yet comprehend; nevertheless, the "total altogether of it" remains cryptic, and we are likely to feel that our interpretations are forced unless they are confirmed by readings from another direction. Some knowledge of Gertrude Stein's daily life and obsessive concerns is essential, as well as familiarity with the usual associations she makes among words, and the in-common subjects of her works. Then, not only must we fasten ourselves to Webster, as Empson chained himself to the OED, and avail ourselves of slang dictionaries too, we must go to Skeat or Partridge as eagerly as a cat for cover on a cool day.

Thus this is certainly not an airtight text. It leaks. But where? and why should we care? It will not tell us what day the bridge is to be bombed, the safe rifled, or buck passed. We must set to work without reward or hope of any, and submit ourselves to the boredom of an etymological narrative.[8]

A BOX

Out of kindness comes redness and out of rudeness comes rapid same question, out of an eye comes research, out of selection comes painful cattle. So then the order is that a white way of being round is something suggesting a pin and is it disappointing, it is not, it is so rudimentary to be analysed and see a fine substance strangely, it is so earnest to have a green point not to red but to point again.

A box protects and conceals. It is frequently wrapped and tied. It is usually of wood or paper. Ribbons are found on it. A box contains surprises. Gifts. Pandora had one. Although a box is something one can get caught in, it is also something one can get out of. A jack is often in a box. A word is a box out of which we can draw other words. A woman has a box into

---

[8] To see what happens when you don't resort to etymology, compare the reading to follow with Harry Garvin's in "The Human Mind and Tender Buttons," *The Widening Circle*, Fall, 1973, p. 13.

which penises are put and from which babies are taken. To
have such a box in our world, certainly in Stein's, is to be in
a box (*hemmed* in). And so the passage assumes the structure
of a series of Biblical begettings. Or are we listening to a recital
of the pedigrees of prize stock? Etymology affirms everything
at once, for the root of 'box' is tree (the boxwood). A FAMILY
TREE. THE TREE OF KNOWLEDGE.

The *manifest* text invokes two *covert*, or, in Stein's terms,
covered, colored, or red, texts: a main one, the Old Testament
tale of Adam and Eve, which establishes the linear order of
ideas in advance of any other expression which may be placed
on top of it, and whose verbal character is relatively *fixed*; and
a second, subordinate one—the story of Pandora and the box
of Prometheus—which is not fastened to any single formulation, and so *floats*. The *alignment* of the two covert texts is
parallel, and the *relationship* between them is one of struc-
tural identity, thus the *function* of the secondary tale is to interpret and heighten and universalize the first. God makes
Adam out of clay, for instance. Zeus shapes Pandora out of the
same substance. Both are seen as vessels into which the breath
of life is blown, and thereafter they hold that life like a liquid:
wine or water. Clearly the two texts are accompanied by sets
of traditional *interpretations*. For example, it is often supposed
that Adam took a carnal interest in Eve only after the Fall.
Both tales are anti-feminist tracts. Both involve disobedience
to the chief. Both are about revenge. Both explain why mankind must live in sorrow and die in delusion. And both invoke
male saviors.

The principal covert text manifests itself immediately in
two ways: through a *key* word or phrase—in this case, 'box'—
and by means of a *mirrored* rhetorical *form*, the Biblical be-
gats. The key in the latter case, of course, is the phrase 'out
of.' Even more darkly mirrored, with a parallel alignment and
the same key, is the form of the livestock pedigree. Eventually
the proportion: as men are to the Lord, so are women to men,

and cattle to their owners, will control our understanding of the argument. Both forms, because of their associations, contribute substantially to the meaning of the passage. They are, that is, *significant forms*.

The manifest text contains a *coded commentary* on the covert texts. Each word must be regarded as standing for many others, the title A BOX referring to a blow as well as a container. Not only is *Tender Buttons* a *polytype* text, it is frequently *polytokenal* too (see the formation of 'kindred' in the first line). There is evidently a *metatextual metaphor* operating here. The paragraph before us is a box containing words which are also regarded as boxes. In short, the passage does not describe some object which the title designates as much as the title describes the passage. *Tender Buttons*, itself, is a metatextual metaphor.

The meanings we discover when we open these boxes are, like the covert texts, both floating and fixed; that is, certain associations are general: with the 'red' which comes out of 'kindness' we may connect a blush of pleasure, but we are not confined to exactly these words, as we shall not be to 'shame' and 'embarrassment' later. However, when we extract roots, such as 'recircle' from 'research,' we are. These meanings have no serial order. They are *clustered* like grapes, and the way they are eventually fitted together depends not upon the order of words in the manifest text, but upon the way each illuminates various aspects of the covert text. At first we may want to think of 'kindness' as kindness, but it is difficult to continue in that vein. Digging down we find a few roots. We might favor 'inborn' first, but 'kind' seen as 'nature' snaps into '-ness' understood as 'state,' with a satisfying certitude. We must not abandon 'kindness' as kindness, though, because it is in fact the complaisance of the woman which leads to sin and kinning; but the incorporation of this surface sense into the total interpretation of the passage has to come later, after most of the ground floor has been built. Thus there is no preestablished order. We must wait until a place to fasten the meaning to the emerging sense can be found.

Except for the fact that the manifest text hides Adam and Eve like a leaf, the text is not *layered*. Certain themes or threads can be continuously followed, but sometimes one will be more obvious or dominant than another, so it is more accurate to describe the text as *woven*. Since the text often looks at itself, it is *reflexive*, and since meanings which emerge rather late in the manifest text must often be sent back to the beginning like unlucky players, the *presentation of meaning is spatial*, not temporal the way, for example, 'John hit Jack' is temporal. It is temporal, that is, until we decide that 'John' is Jack and 'Jack' John. Then the sentence spatializes, swinging back and forth.

John hit Jack	Jack hit John	John hit Jack . . .
is	is is	is
John was hit by John	Jack was hit by John	

This swing can be corralled, as Gertrude does in the case of her overly famous tag:

Civilization begins with a rose.

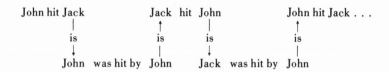

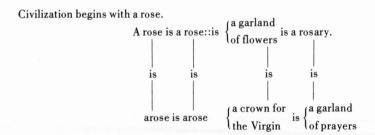

These chaplets retain the plainest syntax, but beneath the simple grammar of these Buttons lie meanings which have nearly

lost their syntactical value, becoming astonishingly *plastic*.
Let's take a look at some of the etymological clusters.

```
            -ness=state   -ness              -ness
Out of   kindness  comes redness and out of   rudeness comes
         kind ────────→ red=kindred          rude=rubble, rubbish
         kind=nature      (dread of kin)      rud  =red
             =in-born     =blood                  =c·rude
         kin  =genus   rudd=(fish)spawn       LL. eruderare: to clear of
             =gender                          rubbish, to purify, hence
                GENESIS                           =impurity
         (kine)
```

```
                              -ion=state
rapid           same        question,                    out of an
rapt                  =image,  quest=judicial interrogation
rap=to snatch         likeness    =inquisition
rape
```

```
                          se=separation
                        ╱              ╲
            re=back to original      -ion=state
eye comes   research, out of    selection comes
            search=circle        lect=gather, pick (fruit)
            seek                 legere oculis: assemble letters with the eye
eye ────────── see ──────────────→ se(e)  =read
```

```
painful         cattle.         So then the order is that a
pain=punishment chattel=property, esp.      ord=rank of threads in weaving
                     domesticated bovines.
```

```
                              some=same       sug=under
white                 way of being round   is something    suggesting
        =gleaming   wag=move         =roll  =assembly       gerere=bear
                    via=route        =role  =court          geste  =tale
                                    rota=public way          jest
                                    rote=repetition          gestate
```

```
              dis=separate
              appoint
a pin and is it   disappointing, it is not, it is so     rudimentary
   point             pungent=prick                   rud, etc.
   pen               punctuate
   penis             pugil=boxer
                     pug  =fist


         ana=on, up, un-                    sub=under
to be   analyzed and see a fine             substance      strangely,
         lose          final                stance         externally,
         loose=free    finis =boundary=     stand=resist  from the outside
                          mark on tree
                          =end (good)
                       fine=monetary  settlement


it is so earnest  to have a      green                    point not to red
                 =pledge      =to grow green as grass is    q.v.
                 =observe closely        vide:graze
                 =contest (duel)


but to point again.
    q.v.  =gain-say: contradict
```

The entire passage is held together by underlying meanings which are greatly akin and often simply repeat one another—a familiar characteristic of Stein's manifest texts—and the passage is pushed forward as much by the progressive disclosure of these deep meanings as by ordinary linear onset. There is a cluster around what might be called the idea of an early state; there's one around gestation, blood, and pain, as well as punishment and judgment; there's still another around resistance, repetition, and property. There is finally a solution expressed in the dimmest imagery of all: the target with its black bull's-eye.

I recall particularly that Zeus, desiring to punish Prometheus for stealing fire from the gods and giving it to man, fashioned a beautiful woman out of clay, clothing her like a queen and, with the help of the Four Winds, breathing life into her according to the customary recipe. This done, he sent his glittering clay creature to the brother of Prometheus as a gift, but Epimetheus, warned not to accept any favors from Zeus (as though to "beware of gods bearing gifts"), politely refused her until Zeus frightened him by chaining his disobedient brother to a pillar high in the mountains where a vulture ate by day the liver which grew heedlessly back by night (just as waking life was to be ruinous for us ever afterward). Pandora, of course, capricious and willful and curious, opened the box in which Prometheus had bottled all the evils which might beset man, among them delusive hope whose sting keeps us from suicide and still alive to suffer the bites of the others.

Similarly, Satan ('red'), speaking through a serpent and by tradition from a tree ('box'), tempts Eve in Paradise ('kindness') to pick ('selection') and eat the apple ('box,' 'red'). A whole set of derivations indicates that we should interpret this act as a case of praiseworthy resistance. (No time is wasted on Adam.) *Kindness is thus reduced to rudeness*. God soon ('rapid') seeks out ('research') the impure pair ('rudeness') and holds an official investigation ('question'). He finds that their eyes ('eye') are now open; they see ('research') that they are naked, and are consequently full of shame ('red'). His judgment ('question') is that Eve shall belong to her husband like a chattel and bear her children ('kindred') henceforward in pain and labor ('painful cattle'). At the point of the first full stop, there is a definite break in the text. In order to go on, we must go back.

And who are "we" at this point? Not even Gertrude would have read this far.

Without the myths of Eve and Pandora I should have no sounding board, no principle of selection, nothing to paste my conjectures to, however remarkably I imagined them. So far what have I been made to do? I have been required to put roots and shoots and little stems and tendrils together much as their author did, to wander discouraged and confused as Hansel and Gretel through a dark wood of witches, to strike the hot right way suddenly, but just as suddenly to mire, to drag, to speed, to shout Urreek! to fall asleep, to submit to revelations, certainly to curl a lip, to doubt, unnose a disdainful snort, snick a superior snicker, curse, and then at some point not very pleasantly to realize that the game I'm playing is the game of creation itself, because *Tender Buttons* is above all a book of kits like those from which harpsicords or paper planes or model bottle boats are fashioned, with intricacy no objection, patience a demand, unreadable plans a pleasure. So I am pulling a poem out of this BOX. The words on the page do not contain it, but their conundrum does.

Adam and Eve now beget children who, though innocent infants for a time ('rudeness') have the same in-born impulses ('kindness'), so that shortly ('rapid') they manifest the same lusts and suffer the same punishment as their parents ('rapid same question'). The cycle ('research') of generation ('kindness') is viciously continuous ('redness'), and soon ('rapid') women are being picked ('selection') as Eve once was ('eye'), and bred ('rapid') like cattle.

So God's command ('order') is that the common way ('round,' 'way') is a repetition ('round') of that first fornication and painful multiplication ('something suggesting a pin'). There is, in effect, a second break in the argument here, so with a little help from the final lines I shall loop back over these still unclear combinations. The Virgin Mother was spared both sin and pain, shame and copulation. Her child was engendered by the prick of light from a star (see the section, A WAIST). While gloomily researching 'point' (whose 'disappoint' deprives the 'pin' of its pain), I come upon the phrase '*de pointe en blanc*' (from a point in the white of a target), and everything rattles into place like iron gates. But will it rattle for you unless you labor? Something fired point blank is fired from the outer white toward the bull's-eye; that is, from a point so close that an arrow needs no compensatory arc in its travel to the target. Its path ('way') is straight (as a pin). So the chaste way of becoming pregnant is through that gleaming straight arrow of light from a star, while the common way requires mating with a bull.

The consequences of our investigation of this basic and traditional myth, reducing it to small rubblelike bits ('rudimentary'), the paragraph goes on to say, is not disappointing because it shows how the penis may be removed ('disappointing'), and how the woman's struggle ('substance,' 'earnest,' and so on) to escape male domination ('analysis') can be won ('fine'). She ('a green') must turn not to her complementary, the male ('red'), but to his opposite, her own sex ('to the point again').

In sum, A BOX is an ironic argument (the jest in 'suggesting') for lesbianism on the ground that such sexual practices preserve virginity, avoid God's punishment, and do not perpetuate original sin.

Now that A BOX has been broken down, we can look back at that CARAFE, THAT IS A BLIND GLASS, with eyes from which the scales have fallen. Fitzgerald's Omar, among others, testifies to the commonness of the metaphor which, on Old Testament authority, pictures man as a clay vessel containing a gaseous spirit or liquidy soul.

XLIV

Why, if the Soul can fling the Dust aside,
And naked on the Air of Heaven ride,
*   Wer't not a Shame—wer't not a Shame for him*
In this clay carcase crippled to abide?

Mankind, before eating from the tree, was a blind glass, a carafe (an object and a word of Spanish and Arabic origin). Women were also a "kind," in-born, cousin to man, taken out of his side by caesarean; thus neither sex was a stranger to the other, and both were designed from the first for copulation. Nevertheless, as time passes and people disperse and multiply, the differences between men and women aggravate and widen.

The techniques at work here do more than allow Gertrude Stein to disguise her drift. They permit a simply astonishing condensation. The word 'difference' alone contains *to carry apart, delay, disperse, to bear (as fruit)*. And this inner economy facilitates the interweaving of contradictory strands of meaning within a single sentence.

When we try to grasp the significance of these truly peculiar pieces, it helps to remember that their composition was stimulated by a trip Gertrude and Alice made to Spain in 1912; that Robert W. Service brought out *Rhymes of a Rolling Stone* the same year; that Gertrude's household was breaking up and her affections had been rearranged; that not a line of Joyce or Eliot had appeared, though there'd been some Pound and a little of the greater Yeats; that Havelock Ellis had been arguing for the equality of women with great reasonableness and little effect, though the suffragettes were out in strength; that Rilke's thing-poems, in print, quite miraculous, quite beautiful, quite other, were in effect as invisible as the spirit of the vagina'd Spanish saints, although everywhere both writers saw sanctity's black battledress and the southern region's austere landscape redolent with renunciation like a vine; that in fifteen years *The Well of Loneliness*, genteel, inept, and as unlibidinous as beets, will still cause a scandal; that the Dadaists haven't uttered their first da yet, let alone their second; that a play can be driven from the boards because it shows one woman giving another a bunch of violets, and that when Colette kissed Missy on the mouth in one such there was a howl of rage; that in those Andalusian towns where Jewish, Muslim, and Catholic cultures came together with a crash, their ignorant collision created buildings—rather than rubble—whose elastic functions, dubious faith, and confusing beauty, were nearly proofs, even to a Jew, of a triune god; that people in the United States are really reading Rex Beach or James Oliver Curwood; and that only Apollinaire might have preceded her in her aims, a few methods, and some effects.

Words, of course, were tender buttons, to be sorted and played with, admired and arranged, and she felt that language in English literature had become increasingly stiff and resistant, and that words had to be pried out of their formulas, freed, and allowed to regain their former Elizabethan fluidity,[9] but it is now evident, I think, that she had other motives, indeed the same ones which had driven her into writing in the first place: the search for and discovery of Gertrude Stein, and the recording of her daily life, her thoughts, her passions.[10]

One does not need to speak in code of Adam and Eve, though if you are going to take Eve's side against the serpent, God, and Adam—all—you had better begin to dip your tongue in honey; but what about the pleasures of cunnilingus or the dildo, of what she was later, as she grew more frank, to call "lifting belly"? Even Natalie Barney was less bold in print than in the dalliance and dance and undress of her notorious salons. And Gertrude had Alice to contend with, a reader who was not as eager as she was to see their intimacies in print, and who could coldly withhold her favors if she chose.

> *This must not be put in a book.*
> *Why not.*
> *Because it mustn't.*
> *Yes sir.*　　　("Bonne Annee,"
> 　　　　in *Geography and Plays*)

---

[9] See Brinnin, pp. 164–65.

[10] Bridgman's discussion of all these points is very useful. See especially Chapter 7 of *Gertrude Stein in Pieces*. He says, however, that "Physical passion had been virtually absent from Gertrude Stein's work since *The Making of Americans*, or at least sufficiently disguised to be invisible." I think the latter is the case.

She might have to disguise it, but she was damn well going to write about it: "Suppose a collapse in rubbed purr, in rubbed purr get," for instance, a line which explodes, upon the gentlest inspection, into a dozen sexual pieces. There is 'suppose,' which means *to place under*, followed by the neck and lap of 'collapse,' which contains the French 'col,' of course (the next line begins, "Little sales ladies . . ." a phrase I construe as "little dirty girls"). 'Collapse' also yields the root, *to fall* (sin) *together*, immediately after which we must deal with 'rub,' 'purr,' 'get in bed,' 'rub her,' 'rubber,' and Gertrude's pet name for Alice, which was Pussy.

Here is the third to last button in the box labeled Objects:

PEELED PENCIL, CHOKE

Rub her coke.

Remember those paper pencils you sharpened by peeling? Don't Jews do the same to the penis? Oral sex with such will make you choke. Certainly the writing instrument is one of Stein's household gods, as Penates are, gods of our most interior and secret parts. It's what we reach when we peel off the leaves of an artichoke: the hairy center. But isn't this a joke? The pencil has an eraser and a graphite core. A woman's core is her clitoris, which one rubs to please her. With what? a rubber cock. It *is* a joke.[11]

Let's push the culminating button and see what buzzes.

THIS IS THIS DRESS, AIDER

Aider, why aider why whow, whow stop touch, aider whow, aider stop the muncher, muncher munchers.

A jack in kill her, a jack in, makes a meadowed king, makes a to let.

---

[11] William Wasserstrom has the right gloss on this in his fine essay, "Gertrude Stein: Sursymamericubealism," in *Twentieth Century Literature*, XXI, No. 1 (1975), p. 103.

This poem contrasts male and female love-making. There is disgust for the former, joy in the latter. The word 'aider' is not only a sound shadow for *aid her* and a muffled form of 'Ada,' one of Gertrude's code names for Alice, it is also the original Old French root, meaning *to give pleasure to*. I have already claimed that we must read the title as THIS IS DISTRESS, AID HER, but the distress is partly explained by the twice-hidden 'his,' by the fact that 'distress,' itself, gives us 'strain,' which immediately yields 'stretch,' as in the various expansions consequent to begetting. 'Dress,' in turn, has its roots in the Latin *directus* and the French *drecier*, and these extend toward 'make straight,' or 'put in proper position,' 'prick up.' Hence, we have (1) Ada, help me take off this dress (dis · dress), and give me pleasure, for I am in sexual need, and (2) it is his doing, this stress and strain of begetting, save her from him. In short, Gertrude is to save Alice from men, while Alice is to save Gertrude from sexual want. In this passage, the square-off of male vs. female, and the balance of pleasure and pain with rescue and reward, is perfect.

Stein now imitates, perhaps too predictably, the stop/ don't stop alternation of sexual excitement, but this allows her, at the same time, to render the resistance of the female and the painfulness of male penetration.

(1) Ada, why what are you doing? wow, how, wow, stop, oh touch, Ada, wow, Ada stop . . . and Ada, of course, is graz-ing, a cunnilingual metaphor.

(2) Help, help, ow, ow stop ouch, help, ow, stop the muncher . . .

(3) Aid her. Why aid her? how to stop the touching and help her, how?

The relation of 'how' and 'cow' (hence 'munch' and 'mead-owed king') is not infrequent in Gertrude Stein. "A Sonatina" (written in 1921) is only one poem which makes the connection explicit:

> A fig an apple and some grapes makes a cow. How.
> The Caesars know how. Now.[12]

A similar ambivalence governs the construction of the final sentence. Shadowing 'A jack in kill her' are at least three
other Jacks: Jack the Giant Killer, Jack and Jill, and Jack in
the Box.[13] Jack is normally any male, a knave, a jakes or john,
and a penis, both real and artificial, while 'a jack in' imitates
the pump and rock of sexual stimulation. The dildo imagery,
which some readers may wish to resist, becomes increasingly
explicit. For instance, in "A Sonatina" again:

> Do you remember that a pump can pump other things than
> water . . . Yes tenderness grows and it grows where it
> grows. And do you like it. Yes you do. And does it fill a
> cow full of filling. Yes. And where does it come out of. It
> comes out of the way of the Caesars.

So: (1) if a man gets hold of her, he can kill her as a consequence of rape or pregnancy, to say nothing of the pain, the
shame and humiliation. When Jack and Jill go up the hill together, Jack falls down and breaks his crown, but Jill comes
tumbling after. Men merely rent the body anyway, and make
the woman a toilet for their secretions; (2) when there is a dildo
in her, however, she will know pleasure (die), and this jack will
kill the giant one, and let in instead the meadowed king (the
bull). 'Let,' which means both *permit* and *hinder*, perfectly
represents the alternating currents here. The same toy and
toying sound which seduces Ada pleasantly when she is mas-

---

[12] From *Bee Time Vine*. Gertrude is one of the Caesars. "Cows are very nice," she
says. "They are between legs." See Bridgman, pp. 149–54. The connection is in any
case nearly inevitable, as, for example, in Cummings's famous "anyone lived in a
pretty how town."

[13] Allegra Stewart flails away at this passage, mentioning every Jack she can think
of but missing Jill, and because she does not play her jacks on the page, misses the
scatological and sexual connotations. The poem, consequently, does not come apart
for her.

tered by the meadowed king, would turn her into a toilet bowl
if she were jacked by a man.

Strong stuff. *Not* a joke.

In 1951 Edmund Wilson conjectured

> . . . that the vagueness that began to blur [Gertrude
> Stein's writing] from about 1910 on and the masking by
> unexplained metaphors that later made it seem opaque,
> though partly the result of an effort to emulate modern
> painting, were partly also due to a need imposed by the
> problem of writing about relationships between women of
> a kind that the standards of the era would not have al-
> lowed her to describe more explicitly. It seemed obvious
> that her queer little portraits and her mischievously baf-
> fling prose-poems did often deal with subjects of this
> sort . . .[14]

but he later felt he might have overestimated the motive of sexual concealment.[15] If the reading I have given the Object sec-

---

[14] Edmund Wilson, *The Shores of Light* (New York: Farrar, Straus & Young, 1952),
p. 581. I also came to that conclusion in 1958. See "Gertrude Stein: Her Escape from
Protective Language," in *Fiction and the Figures of Life* (New York: Knopf, 1970).

[15] Wilson couldn't find much evidence of it when he read *Two: Gertrude Stein and
Her Brother*, after it had been posthumously published by Yale, so he ascribed the extremely abstract quality of that work to "an increasing remoteness in her personal relationships." The subject naturally led her already dry style into mathematical meditations ("If one is one and one is not one of the two then one is one . . .") which were
transparently about the position of the self in a family of two. James Mellow points
out that Wilson must have missed the portrait in that volume called "Men," which
is very obviously about homosexual behavior. *The Charmed Circle: Gertrude Stein &
Company* (New York: Praeger, 1974), p. 134. *Two* was written at about the same time
as *Tender Buttons* (which hid its luridity under a bushel but was nevertheless lurid
enough to require the basket), and was concerned about the cementing of her relationship with Miss Toklas as well as the breakup of the one with her brother. The subject
was full of potentially dangerous material. Leo, who had served as a father replace-
ment, was replaced in turn by Gertrude herself, who, as husband to Alice, became
her own father figure. If the appropriate joke about the women's movement is that it
needs a good man to direct it, the attitude of Gertrude Stein was that although the
male role was the one worth playing, the only good man was a woman.

tion of *Tender Buttons* is even somewhat sound, however, Wilson will have been right the first time.

Evasiveness, of course, becomes a habit, a style, a method which overreaches its original excuse and must seek another justification, just as the quadriplegic, who must paint with his teeth, will eventually find reasons why the bite is superior to the squeeze. Although, in a few works—the popular public ones like Alice's and Everybody's autobiographies, *Brewsie and Willie*, and *Wars I Have Seen*—Stein's style is as simple and open and even giddy as we might imagine the letters of a young girl to be, much of her work is written, like *Tender Buttons*, in a kind of code, even when, as in *How to Write*, the subject does not appear to require it; and there is no question whatever that the coding dangerously confounds the surface; for even if a passage effects a concealment, as when a body is covered by clothing, from the artistic point of view, those clothes had better dazzle us as much as the truth would, unless the concealment is only gestural and temporary, and we are expected to penetrate it at once, because the object of art is to make more beautiful that which is, and since that which is is rarely beautiful, often awkward and ugly and ill-arranged, it must be sometimes sheeted like a corpse, or dissolved into its elements and put together afresh, aright, and originally. Stein is painfully aware of the problem. Coming clean is best. "Certainly glittering is handsome and convincing."

The manifest text of *Tender Buttons* is only one segment of its total textual surface. That CHOKE is 'joke' is a surface phenomenon, as is AIDER's 'aid her.' In a swirl of lines a horse's head may be hidden, some clouds do in fact look dragonish, and a drawing may turn itself inside out before our very eyes; thus 'get in bed' lies disguised in 'rubbed purr get,' and an unseen 'i' will fit between the words 'to let.' The problem is that in *Tender Buttons* the unconcealed surface usually makes no sense. AIDER, for instance, is not an active English verb, and might as well be a word in the *Wake* or in "Jabberwocky." Occasionally, instead of the word being wounded, the syntax will be: "Please a round it is ticket." Most often, however, the confusion in the surface is semantic. "This is no authority for the abuse of cheese," she will suddenly say severely, and we think we are listening to the Red Queen. "Suspect a single buttered flower," we are warned, but what is the warning?[16] In contrast, the other segments of the surface are usually fairly clear. "Aid her" is plainly what we are being asked to do.

Some covert texts are hidden like the purloined letter, others are concealed the way the family portrait hides the safe, still others the way the safe contains its money. That 'color' is a cover, or that 'cow' is cunt or that 'a white way of being round' refers to immaculate conception, is nothing that can be read directly off the page. Since many of the meanings of *Tender Buttons* are etymological, the covert text can be said to be sometimes *inside* the surface text. We have only to enter the word on these occasions. However, the idea that the innocent dust which makes up Adam and Eve is a 'blind glass' can be safely said to lie *beneath* its covering phrase.

We are familiar with the before and after of words and sentences because that is the way they are read and written, but now we must learn to diagram them differently.

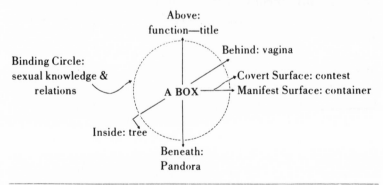

The manifest surface of A BOX is represented by the idea, container. There is a covert surface, too, that of contest or blow. Each such covert text adds to the *width* of the surface, just as its *length* is determined by the basic unity of the verbal series chosen for examination (A BOX, in this case, rather than merely BOX). In this example, we have a surface two words long and two texts wide. *Inside* A BOX is its root, 'tree.' *Behind* it is the slang meaning, womb or vagina. Pandora is *beneath*, while hovering *above*, though not like an angel, is its characterization as the label of a button. Because A BOX is set up as a title, it has no *immediate* before or after; there is to be imagined, before the opening of each book, an endless preceding silence, just as an equally endless one follows its close; but these are the silences of one text alone, not the quiet of all texts, for the whole of literature surrounds every work like water.

Here, then, is a notable explosion of language out of time into space. Although the button which follows A BOX makes sense, and is even funny (if the labor of reaching the punch line does not itself supply the reel which should result), it is, by and large, without the swift sensuous intake which is essential, since our response, as readers, must always run even with, if not ahead of, understanding. Basically, our knowledge of a poem serves simply to explain why we were shaken. It will never, alone, do the shaking.

In *Tender Buttons* the conflict between concealment and expression is especially intense. This kind of contest can sometimes lead to the most beautiful and powerful of consequences, so long as the victory of concealment remains incomplete, so long as the drapery leads us to dream and desire and demand the body we know it covers, so long as passion speaks through rectitude, so long as impulse laughs with the lips of duty. We can, of course, rip the clothing off anyway, as I have; but it is the promise of the nipple through the slip, the tender button, which matters to us here, and is the actual action of art; it is the hint of the hollow which holds us, and the way a stone arm encircles nothing but atmosphere so lovingly we want to believe in our being there, also surrounded, and only then as alive in our life as that stone.

"Celery tastes tastes where" (she asks) "in curled lashes and little bits and mostly in remains." It is a careful observation. "A cup is neglected in being full of size." It is a rich saying. Many of these buttons are as tender as tusks, but Gertrude Stein also wrote densely and brilliantly and beautifully and perversely and with intense contrivance and deep care and a skill which no one could recognize. In the Food section, for instance, there are passages like this one which escapes through honkytonk and even Blake into true feeling:

> Lovely snipe and tender turn, excellent vapor and slender butter, all the splinter and the trunk, all the poisonous darkening drunk, all the joy in weak success, all the joyful tenderness, all the section and the tea, all the stouter symmetry.

Or consider this extraordinary conclusion to ROASTBEEF, a passage which only she could have written, at first glance on a commonplace theme (the cycle of the seasons), yet as dense and transformational as fog, and like a chant in Latin, lovely before, during, and long after, comprehension.

> There is coagulation in cold and there is none in prudence. Something is preserved and the evening is long and the colder spring has sudden shadows in a sun. All the stain is tender and lilacs really lilacs are disturbed. Why is the perfect reëstablishment practiced and prized, why is it composed. The result the pure result is juice and size and baking and exhibition and nonchalance and sacrifice and volume and a section in division and the surrounding recognition and horticulture and no murmur. This is a result. There is no superposition and circumstance, there is hardness and a reason and the rest and remainder. There is no delight and no mathematics.

3

I write for myself and strangers. The strangers would go—eventually, even the self.

It took many years; she had to bring out most of her books herself; usually they appeared long after they'd been written, in silence, to indifference, incomprehension, jeers; but in time there were too many strangers: curiosity seekers, sycophants, opportunists, disciples. She hugely enjoyed her growing celebrity, but she noticed what she thought was a change in herself, and she began, vaguely, to be alarmed. In 1933 *The Autobiography of Alice B. Toklas* was published in the U.S.A. with great success, portions of it appearing in *The Atlantic Monthly*. Suddenly there was money she had earned. *Three Lives* went into the Modern Library. She was nearing sixty, $4 \times$ her 15 yrs. It seemed like a good time to go back.

Gertrude Stein would return to the United States like a lion, she said, and word of her arrival did run in lights around the *Times* Building, reporters met her boat and filled twelve columns of the city papers with news and mostly friendly comment about her.

> . . . we saw an electric sign moving around a building and it said Gertrude Stein has come and that was upsetting . . . I like it to happen . . . but always it does give me a little shock of recognition and non-recognition. It is one of the things most worrying in the subject of identity.

She had come home but, although she was recognized in the streets of New York by strangers, she could not find again the San Francisco of her childhood.

> . . . it was frightening quite frightening driving there and on top of Nob Hill where we were to stay, of course it had not been like that and yet it was like that, Alice Toklas found it natural but for me it was a trouble yes it was . . .

Along with the face of Gracie Allen, she was caricatured by Covarrubias in *Vogue*; in Chicago she had a chance to see her own *Four Saints in Three Acts*; at Princeton police were used to hold back the crowd which came to hear her lecture. "Americans really want to make you happy." And she would plunge into traffic with a child's trusting unconcern. "All these people, including the nice taxi drivers, recognize and are careful of me."

Queerly companioned and oddly dressed, deep-voiced, direct, she loved being a celebrity and was consequently charming, her autograph was sought, and she and Alice met old friends, publishers, passers-by and tradesmen, students, journalists, teachers, many who were rich and famous from all parts of a country they were both seeing from the air for the first time, the mountains subsiding like a fountain, the desert like a waterless floor of the sea, the whole land lying in lines which Masson, Braque, or Picasso might have drawn. She saw the same flatness, after so much European brick and tile, in the wooden buildings of America, but it was the map in the air which delighted her most because it taught her what the human mind was capable of: flying without wings, seeing without eyes, knowing without evident data. Yet in East Oakland, on the shabby streets where she had played as a child, experience proved empty. What is the point of being born a little girl if you are going to grow up to be a man?

Back in France she tried to digest the lessons of her fame. A woman and artist who had been for much of her life without self or audience, she now had both; but what, after all, did it come to—this self she was famous for? In *Vogue*'s "Impossible Interview," Gracie Allen is made to say: "Now Gertie, don't you start to make sense, or people will begin to understand you, and then you won't mean anything at all." These reporters, followers, and friends—they were merely hearts that spaniel'd her at heels . . . She'd looked back, snuffled at her roots, found, seen, felt—nothing.

The Geographical History of America is a culminating work, though not the outcome of her meditations. Those she summed up in an essay, "What Are Masterpieces?" written a year later. This book is the stylized presentation of the process of meditation itself, with many critical asides. In the manner of her earliest piece, *Q.E.D.*, it demonstrates far more than it proves, and although it is in no sense a volume of philosophy (Gertrude Stein never "argues" anything), it is, philosophically, the most important of her texts. If we follow her thought as Theseus did the thread of Ariadne, I think we find at the end the justice, if not the total truth, of her boast that the most serious thinking about the nature of literature in the twentieth century has been done by a woman.

Life is repetition, and in a dozen different ways Gertrude Stein set out to render it. We have only to think how we pass our days: the doorbell rings, the telephone, sirens in the street, steps on the stairs, the recurrent sounds of buzzers, birds, and vacuum cleaners; then as we listen we suck our teeth; those are our feet approaching, so characteristic the tread can be identified, and that's our little mew of annoyance at the interruption, too, as well as the nervous look which penetrates the glass, the fumble with the latch, the thought: I must remember to oil this lock; whereupon we are confronted by a strange man who is nevertheless saying something totally familiar about brooms. Suppose he is truly a stranger. Still, we have seen salesmen before, men before, brooms; the accent is familiar, the tone, the tie, the crooked smile, the pity we are asked for, the submissive shoulders, yet the vague threat in the forward foot, the extended palm like the paw of a begging bear. Everything, to the last detail, is composed of elements we have already experienced a thousand and a thousand thousand times. Even those once-in-a-lifetime things—overturning a canoe in white water or being shot at, pursuing a squirrel through the attic, sexual excess—are merely unusual combinations of what has been repeatedly around. Our personal habits express it, laws of nature predict it, genes direct it, the edicts of the state encourage or require it, universals sum it up.

The range of our sensations, our thoughts, our feelings, is generally fixed, and so is our experience of relations. Make an analysis, draw up a list. Life is rearrangement, and in a dozen different ways Gertrude Stein set out to render it. We are not clocks, designed to repeat without remainder, to mean nothing by a tick, not even the coming tock, and so we must distinguish between merely mechanical repetition, in which there is no progress of idea, no advance or piling up of wealth, and that which seriously defines our nature, describes the central rhythms of our lives.

Almost at once she realized that language itself is a complete analogue of experience because it, too, is made of a large but finite number of relatively fixed terms which are then allowed to occur in a limited number of clearly specified relations, so that it is not the appearance of a word that matters but *the manner of its reappearance*, and that an unspecifiable number of absolutely unique sentences can in this way be composed, as, of course, life is also continuously refreshing itself in a similar fashion.

There are novel sentences which are novel in the same old ways, and there are novel sentences in which the novelty itself is new. In *How to Write* she discusses the reason why sentences are not emotional and paragraphs are, and offers us some sentences which she believes have the emotional balance of the paragraph.

a. It looks like a garden but he had hurt himself by accident.
b. A dog which you have never had before has sighed.
c. A bay and hills hills are surrounded by their having their distance very near.

Compare these with Sterne's:

d. A cow broke in tomorrow morning to my Uncle Toby's fortifications.

Or Hawkes's:

> e. It was a heavy rain, the sort of rain that falls in prison yards and beats a little firewood smoke back down garret chimneys, that leaks across floors, into forgotten prams, into the slaughterhouse and pots on the stove.

Or with this by Beckett:

> f. Picturesque detail a woman with white hair still young to judge by her thighs leaning against the wall with eyes closed in abandonment and mechanically clasping to her breast a mite who strains away in an effort to turn its head and look behind.

All right, we have answered the bell. Suppose we broke that action into parts: opening the door, coming down the stairs, mewing with annoyance, and so forth—how easily we might combine them in other ways, in new sentences of behavior, new paragraphs of life.

Mewing with annoyance reflects a state more subjective than the others. Mewing with annoyance is an event of lesser size, though it, too, is divisible. All are audible acts, unlike the secretion of saliva. Our sentence must manage them—their motion, weight, size, order, state of being—must be themselves events, must pass through the space the way we pass when we skip down the stairs to the door.

Let's begin with a sentence without any special significance, selected the same way you might curiously pick up a piece of paper in the street.

In the middle of the market there's a bin of pumpkins. Dividing this sentence as it seems natural to do, we can commence its conquest:

> a. There's a bin of pumpkins in the middle of the market.
> b. There, in the middle of the market, is a bin of pumpkins.

     c. A bin of pumpkins? There, in the middle of the market.
     d. A bin of . . . pumpkins? There? In the middle ᴏf the
       market?

We can make our arrangements more musical:

     e. In the middle. In the middle of the market. In the mid-
       dle there's a bin. There's a bin. In the middle of the
       market there's a bin.
     f. In the middle. In the middle of the market. In the mid-
       dle of the market there's a bin. A bin. In the middle of
       the market there's a bin. In. A bin. In. In the market
       there's a bin. In the middle of the market—pumpkin.
     g. Middle of market. Middle of. Middle of. Middle of mar-
       ket. Middle of bin. In the middle of market a middle of
       market, in the middle of market there's a middle of bin.
       In the middle of market, in the middle of bin, there's
       a middle of bin, there's a middle of pumpkin, there's
       a middle of in.
     h. Pumpkin. In in in. Pumpkin. In middle. In market. In
       bin.

Much of this is dreadful singsong, of course, but the play has
only begun. Besides, this is just a demonstration record. The
words themselves can be knocked apart, rhymes introduced,
or conceptual possibilities pursued.

     i. Middle of market. Riddle of. Middle of. Riddle of mar-
       ket. Middle of bin. Not thin when in. When hollow in
       huddle then kindle pumpkin.
     j. Pump. Pump ump. In the middle. P p. Um, there's a
       bin. Pumpkin.

And so on. And on so.

    Such games soon give us an idea of the centers of concep-
tual energies in any sentence, its flexibility, a feel for the feelings possible for it, all its aural consequences; and to a child

who is eagerly looking for a skull to carve some Halloween horror on, our celebration of the sentence will seem perfectly sensible.

The procedure is thoroughly analytical, however. It treats the elements of the sentence as if they were people at a party, and begins a mental play with all their possible relationships. Gertrude Stein's work rarely deals very happily with indivisible wholes.

Sometimes she treats a sentence as if it were a shopping list, and rearranges every item in happier orders, much as we might place knicknacks on a shelf, considering whether the spotted china dog might be seen to better advantage in front of the jade lizard and nearer the window, or beside the tin cup borrowed from a beggar in Beirut.

Sometimes she lets us see and follow every step, but often she neglects to give us the sentences she began with, and we find ourselves puzzled by distant results.

Think next what might happen if we considered the sentence to be composed of various voices: in short, a play. For what else is a play? It simply cites the separate sources of its sentences.

h.	1.	Martha.	Pumpkin.
		Mary.	In in in.
		Martha.	Pumpkin.
		Joseph.	In middle.
		John.	In market.
		M. & M.	In bin.

A musician would have no trouble in seeing how a single sentence might be treated as the consequence of a chorus, nor would a modern painter find it hard to imagine the dissolution of his plate, bread, vase, and fish, into plastic elements he then rearranged in a new, more pleasing way.

Gertrude Stein did more with sentences, and understood

them better, than any writer ever has. Not all her manipulations are successful, but even at their worst, most boring, most mechanical, they are wonderfully informative. And constantly she thought of them as things in space, as long and wiggling and physical as worms. Here is a description of some of them from "Poetry and Grammar":

> . . . my sentences . . . had no longer the balance of sentences because they were not the parts of a paragraph nor were they a paragraph but they had made in so far as they had come to be so long and with the balance of their own that they had they had become something that was a whole thing and in so being they had a balance which was the balance of a space completely not filled but created by something moving as moving is not as moving should be.

She understood reading, for instance. She sometimes read straight on, touching the page as lightly as a fly, but even as her mind moved there would be a halt, a turning, the eyes rising and falling in a wave, and she realized that the page, itself, was artificial, arbitrary with respect to the text, so she included it in the work as well, not as a thing or an action, but as an idea.

j. 1.	Page one.	Pump. Pump ump.
	Page two.	In the middle.
	Page three.	P p.
	Page four.	Um, there's a bin.
	Page five.	Pumpkin.

The understanding was, as she read, not only tormented by the physical makeup of the book, it was often troubled, too, by the content, which it had difficulty in making out. The poem does not repeat itself, but I do. I read the first four lines, and then I reread the first two. Now I am ready to go on, and I jump without a qualm to the second quatrain. Soon, however, I am back at the beginning again. There are interruptions, too. Alice asks me what I would like for dinner. Company comes. Time passes. Other texts may even intervene, many strange words from all directions. Why not, she thought, formalize all this, create something new, not only from the stops and starts and quarrels of normal thought, but from the act of attention itself, and all its snarls and tangles, leaps and stumbles.

She is not always satisfied merely to render the phenomenon. Sometimes she chooses to involve us in it. By removing punctuation, for instance. I am reading her sentence about her sentences, which I quoted above, and sliding over words as though through mud:

> . . . not filled but created by something moving as moving is not as moving . . .

I must pick myself up. Reread until I get the hang:

> . . . not filled, but created by something moving, as moving *is*, not as moving should be.

By the time I understand what she means, *I* have been composed. Thus the repetitions which mimic my own when I read make me repeat even more when I read them written down.

Listen. We converse as we live—by repeating, by combining and recombining a few elements over and over again just as nature does when of elementary particles it builds a world. Gertrude Stein had a wonderful ear and she listened as she listened to Leo—for years—not so she could simply reproduce the talk, that sort of thing was never her intention, but so she could discover the patterns in speech, the *forms* of repetition, and exploit them. At first she saw these shapes as signs of the character of the speaker, but later her aim was to confer upon the words themselves the quality she once traced to the owner of the tongue. That was Cézanne's method—the method of the human mind.

We not only repeat when we see, stand, communicate; we repeat when we think. There's no other way to hold a thought long enough to examine it except to say its words over and over, and the advance of our mind from one notion to another is similarly filled with backs and forths, erasures and crossings-out. The style of *The Geographical History of America* is often a reflection of this mental condition.

Repeating is also naming. Pumpkins have names. They are called pumpkins. But what is the word 'pumpkin' called? Not Fred, not William, not Wallaby, but 'pumpkin' again. And so we seem to be repeating when we are speaking in the metalanguage, or the overtongue. A division of 'pumpkin' into 'pump' and 'kin' is not a carving of pumpkin. Nor is the finding and baking and eating of one any damage to the word. An actor's gestures name the real ones. Suppose, behind your back, I am making fun of you by imitating your hurried, impatient, heavy-shoed walk, or like an annoying child I echo your talk as you talk; then a round is being formed, a ring made of reality and its shadow, words and their referents, and of course I can dance with my image or with yours very well, mock my own methods, and suddenly discover, in the midst of my game, a meaning that's more than a vegetable's candle-lit face.

The ice cream eaten is desired again, the song sung is resung, and so we often say things over simply because we love to say them over—there is no better reason.

Furthermore, Gertrude Stein knew that masterpieces were, like life itself is everywhere, perfect engines of repetition. Just as leaves multiply along a limb, and limbs alike thicket a trunk, a work of art suffers simultaneous existence in many places, and eventually is read again and again, sometimes loved by the same lips. As Borges has demonstrated so well, when that inspired madman, Pierre Menard, succeeded in writing a chapter or two of *Don Quixote*, word for word the same, his version was both richer and more complex than that of Cervantes. The reverse can also be the case: *Three Lives*, written by any of us now, would not be nearly so remarkable as it was then.

4

How pleasantly a doll can change its age. I do not even have
to dress it differently. My eye alters and a few rags bundled
about a stick assume a life, a life at any point or period I like,
with any sex and any history I choose—pets, presumptions,
peeves—mortal or immortal ills. Whether I imagine it's a swat-
chel or a queen, the stick with its scrappy sleeves remains and
is like another Homer to me, focus for my fancies; yet when
I open an old album and find my photo, what tells me what the
image is, since I've no faithful wad of fabric or enduring spinal
tree to fix on? . . . a lingering resemblance? am I that solemn
little moon-faced boy in the ribboned hat whose photographic
stare is as dumbly inked upon its paper as these words are?
am I that weak-eyed, pork-cheeked creature? . . . possibly;
but is it a likeness which leaps out at me, one I feel, or do I
have to hunt for it, piously believing that a resemblance must
be there, and easily fooled by a substitute, a switch, because
a dozen other boys that age may look more like me now than
I do then. A sentence with such moods and tenses shows in
what strange ways our lifeline's twisted, how precariously it
passes from one pole of recognition to another, because, as
Hume reported:

> For my part, when I enter most intimately into what I call
> myself, I always stumble on some particular perception or
> other, of heat or cold, light or shade, love or hatred, pain
> or pleasure. I never can catch *myself* at any time without
> a perception, and never can observe any thing but the per-
> ception. When my perceptions are remov'd for any time,
> as by sound sleep; so long am I insensible of myself, and
> may truly be said not to exist.

I may dress Shakespeare, like my dolly, in the costumes
of other centuries, interpret him according to the latest scientific myths or social magics, nevertheless there is something—

some pale text—some basin, bowl, or bottle I am peeing my opinions in; but as I turn the album pages—black not without a reason—I only dimly remember the bow and arrow in one snapshot, the knickers in another, or the man who was my father holding me wearily in his arms at the entrance to Mammoth Cave. The little boy I was is no longer living with me. Of course, we say that some people never grow up, but the little boy I am at forty is actually the little man I am at forty, no one else.

Rilke's celebrated remark about Rodin sums up what Gertrude Stein's American trip taught her:

> Rodin was solitary before he became famous. And Fame, when it came, made him if anything still more solitary. For Fame, after all, is but the sum of all the misunderstandings which gather about a new name.

Or work of art. It is the same.

When Gertrude Stein wrote that there was little use in being born a little boy if you were going to grow up to be a man, she did not intend to deny causality or the influence of the past. She did mean to say that when we look at our own life, we are looking at the history of another; we are like a little dog licking our own hand, because our sense of ourselves at any time does not depend upon such data, only our "idea" of ourselves does, and this "idea," whether it's our own or that of another, is our identity. Identities depend upon appearances and papers. Appearances can be imitated, papers forged.

She also said: I am not I any longer when I see. Normally, as Schopenhauer first and Bergson later argued so eloquently, we see like an animal. We see prey, danger, comfort, security. Our words are tags which signify our interest: chairs, bears, sunshine, sex; each is seen in relation to our impulses, instincts, aims, in the light of our passions, and our thought about these things is governed entirely by what we consider their utility to be. Words are therefore weapons like the jaws of the crocodile or the claws of the cat. We use them to hold our thought as we hold a bone; we use them to communicate with the pack, dupe our enemies, manipulate our friends; we use them to club the living into food.

When, for instance, we give ourselves to a piece of music —not to drink, daydream, or make love, but to listen—we literally lose ourselves, and as our consciousness is captured by the music, we are in dreamless sleep, as Hume says, and are no more. We become, in becoming music, that will-less subject of knowing of which Schopenhauer spoke so convincingly.

Human nature is incapable of objectivity. It is viciously anthropocentric, whereas the human mind leaves all personal interest behind. It sees things as entities, not as identities. It is concerned, in the Kantian sense, with things-in-themselves. The human mind knows that men must die that others may live; one epoch go that another may take its place; that ideas, fashions, feelings, pass. The human mind neither forgets nor remembers; it neither sorrows nor longs; it never experiences fear or disappointment. In the table headed Human Nature there is, therefore, time and memory, with all their beginnings, their middles, and their ends; there is habit and identity, storms and hilly country, acting, audience, speaking and adventure, dogs and other animals, politics, propaganda, war, place, practice and its guiding truths, its directing sciences, while in the table of the Human Mind there's contact rather than connection, plains, space, landscape, math and money, not nervousness but excitement, not saying but showing, romance rather than mystery, masterpieces moreover, and above all, Being.

Gertrude Stein was no longer merely explaining herself. She had begun to wonder what it was inside her which had written *Three Lives* rather than the novels of Lew Wallace; what it was that made masterpieces. Besant's books had sold very well and he had been admired. But he had sold to people of principally the same sort and had been read during a finger-snap of time. Masterpieces escaped both country and climate, every condition of daily life; they hurdled history; and it was not because daily life, climate, country, and history were not contents, as if in those sweetly beautiful Angelicos there were no angels. What accounted for it? in reader? writer? work? Her conclusions were not original, although their largely Kantian character is a little surprising for a student of William James and Santayana.

It was not because she was a woman or was butch—her poodles or her Fords, her vests, her friends, her sober life, her so-called curious ways, her Jewishness, none counted. Allegheny, Pennsylvania, had nothing to do with it. Her "scientific" aim in writing *The Making of Americans*, her desire to define "the bottom nature" of everyone who had or could or would be living, was mistaken and had to do with human nature, not the human mind. She had gone on repeating because she thought the world did. The world did, but what the world did, did not matter. *Tender Buttons* was pure composition, like Cézanne, or at least one could pretend it was, but the *Autobiographies* and *A Long Gay Book*, *Three Lives*, *The Making of Americans*, many of the portraits and the plays, although they were about human nature, were fortunately written by the human mind. And it took another human mind to understand them.

There were people who were no more than their poodles. If their little dog didn't know them, who would they be? Like mirrors they reflected what fell into them, and when the room was empty, when the walls were removed and the stars pinched back in the sky, they were nothing, not even glass.

Naïvely, she thought free people formed themselves in terms of an Emersonian self-reliance; she believed in the frontier, and in the ethic of the pioneer. After all she was one. Naïvely she thought that the average man, here in America, understood the spiritual significance of space, and was less a slave to human nature. Consequently here the human mind should flourish, the masterpiece emerge, the animal sleep. However, *Finnegans Wake* would demonstrate best the endless roundness she had in mind, and the perfect description of her ideal had long ago appeared, in 1894: Paul Valéry's *Monsieur Teste*.

Just as the order of numbers in a sum makes no difference, just as there is no special sequence to towns on a map, the mind and the masterpiece may pass back and forth between thoughts as often and as easily as trains between Detroit, Duluth, and Denver, and chapter headings are, in fact, only the names of places. Oral literature had to be sequential (like music before tape), but type made possible a reading which began at the rear, which repeated preferred passages, which skipped. As in an atlas, the order was one of convenience, and everything was flat. A geographical history rolls time out like that. Of course, there are stories still; an evening's entertainment, that's all human nature asks for; but masterpieces have to bear repeating and repeating. There are no surprises, no suspense, no tears, no worries in them. We know what will happen to Ahab. Duncan's dead, and Anna's under her train. I can tell you the page. *The Wings of the Dove* lies spread before us now as openly as Iowa. Literature in the eyes of the human mind is like land seen from a plane. And so is Gertrude Stein when we find her. Macbeth shall murder sleep again, Tom Jones receive a beating, Heathcliff . . . ah, well . . . "Oblige me," she says, "by not beginning." Netherfield Park is let at last. Mr. Gradgrind is still proceeding on the principle that two and two are four, and nothing over. Bloom is carrying a piece of soap about. The next century is approaching like a distant train. John Barth has just written *Chimera*, Beckett has brought out *The Lost Ones*, Nabokov a book called *Transparent Things*. And they are reissuing *The Geographical History of America* almost a hundred years from the author's birthday. Oblige me, she says, "Also by not ending."

Three Photos
of Colette

First
Photo There is a much-folded photograph reproduced in Yvonne Mitchell's charming and richly illustrated biography of Colette which shows Monsieur Willy and his wife at lonely table.[1] A white rail of the sort you might find in a baroque church divides the dining room from the rest of the apartment. This rail passes in front of us, opening only to provide an entrance to the space, and we can easily imagine taking a rising or descending step toward the chalk-white cloth, which, in the photograph, advances to occupy the railing's compositional place; but whether the step should be up or down, it is difficult, and even undesirable, to say.

Colette was always able to project an expressive image upon the photographer's plate, just as her own style gave the objects it described a lively face: the grass snake coiled like a snail shell by her hand or the heath spiders she says are pink and round as pearls; indeed, the quality of every quality, the rhythm of every contour, is rendered as by a composer, so that, with the immediacy of music and thus as suddenly as Marguerite is brought before Faust by the magic of Mephistopheles, we are seated in a country schoolroom in company with Clau-

[1] Yvonne Mitchell, *Colette: A Taste for Life* (New York: Harcourt Brace Jovanovich, 1975), pp. 68–69.

dine or on the big embarrassed bed of her girlfriend, Luce, who has fallen from the provinces to Paris like the fruit she chews, and now serves her fat "uncle" in return for silks. The camera, too, has brought us to a flat on the rue de Courcelles, and put us in front of this frozen tableau, the gray domestic world of women: full of cosmetics and clutter, yet ordered and empty, expensively utensiled, but patently futile, noisy and corseted and fussy, deathly still.

To the right on that white rail squats a cut-glass decanter which appears nevertheless to contain a candle, and on the left rests a large, probably brass, bell. Two half-full Burgundy bottles, well-corked, clearly white and red, flank Willy's plate. He is eating fruit, and a basket of apples draped with grapes sits on the table in front of him. A Persian rug embarrasses the edges of the luncheon linen like a poorly fitting petticoat. When the meal is removed (. . . the bell does not look rung, though perhaps once it rang . . .), the rug remains to enliven the tabletop and disguise its scars.

It is a long way from the much-loved landscape of Colette's childhood, the woods which she described in perhaps the first pages she ever wrote:

> No small creatures in those great woods; no tall grasses; but beaten earth, now dry, and sonorous, now soft on account of the springs. Rabbits with white scuts range through them and timid deer who run so fast that you can only guess their passage. Great heavy pheasants too, red and golden, and wild boars (I've never seen one) and wolves. I heard a wolf once, at the beginning of winter, while I was picking up beech-nuts— those nice, oily little beech-nuts that tickle your throat and make you cough. Sometimes storm-showers surprise you in those woods; you huddle under an oak that is thicker than the others and listen to the rain pattering up there as if on a roof. You're so well-sheltered that when you come out of those

depths you are quite lost and dazzled and feel ill at ease
in the broad daylight.   *(Claudine at School)*

In a mirror beyond the married pair, who sit in profile to
us, the room behind our backs floats like a world on water.
There is a lamp, a corner cupboard like a standing corpse, and
in the distance, deeply submerged, a dark frame shorelining
something that looks like a boarded-up lake. I don't see
Willy's image, though over the low mantel the mirror seems
well placed to perceive him. His attention is fixed on some
book we cannot see, or on perhaps a bit of biscuit, crumb of
cheese, or sheaf of notes. A white collar obliterates his throat.
He is absorbed, composed. He wears a dark suit and a second
beard behind his ears. He is distinguished and sits well forward on the caned seat of his chair.

Across from him, Colette is held firmly inside her clothes
the way her napkin lies rolled and ringed beside her. A silk
blouse, gray in the photograph as stone, grasps each wrist; a
beaded collar closes about her neck; and a satin belt is cinched
about her waist. To make room for her elbows and remove her
life, she has pushed away a plate on which there remains the
indistinct skin of a grape, and she is leaning forward now to
rest her breasts on the table and her right cheek heavily on the
peak of her clasped hands.

Her stare is nowhere, and her unnaturally pale face seems
fastened to her head like a mask. Above the black velvet bow
in her flattened hair there is a ghostly photo of Willy, top-
hatted, hanging on the wall, while on the oriental rug at her
skirt-covered feet is a white blob like a darning egg—a toy, one
supposes, a ball for Toby-Chien. The creases in the photograph appear as cracks in the plaster, as broken glass, as lines
of worry on the walls, ill fortune in the furniture, as judgments,
omens, anger.

Who but Willy, who adored his image and desired its presence everywhere; who had a thousand depictions of himself—

including caricatures and paintings—made and printed and posted about in Paris like the herald of a social cure; who even persuaded Colette to dress herself like Polaire, the Algerian actress then playing Claudine to full loud houses, in order to enhance certain lesbian allusions, and who dared to have himself photographed standing behind his "twins" as though he were their evil Svengali, not merely their benevolent Papa; who but Willy would have posed for such a domestic picture, or permitted Colette's unhappiness or his own indifference—their total estrangement—to be so nakedly stated? Perhaps it was his own fist which folded their images together in a kiss—a curse—when he saw more than boredom in her emptied gaze, but in addition how his young wife's eyes had fallen like early apples onto a hard and distant interior earth.

It is not difficult to see ourselves what the Parisian public saw and enjoyed in these novels about Claudine which Colette had written almost accidentally, first at the suggestion and then the insistence of her greedy usurious Monsieur; but what can we find in them now but Colette? for we have read Violette Leduc since then, among others, and have played all the schoolgirl games; we have had quite enough of lewd and giggling innocence, of unaimed spite and wide-open ego, of coltish spirits, silly presumption, ignorant courage, or naïve trust. Natural wit's old hat; sweet fears, fresh hope, we've had instance after instance of; and the contrast between mistress and maid, cynicism and faith, the unripe and the spoiled, cannot strike us any more with tragic weight or moral force. What worms we are, like Willy, to have forsaken the fruit to cannibalize its grubs!

In any case, there are no silly schoolgirls anymore, and if the public nowadays wants to know what young girls think, they are served a stronger brew than *Daisy Miller* or *What Maisie Knew*. Wedding nights are still disappointments, but scarcely surprises; the war between the sexes has never been noisier, meaner, or emptier of sense, adultery more snoozily middle-class, or homosexuality more sordid—no, and trivial commonplace lives, for Colette a specialty, have never been more blandly Cream-o'-Wheat, more catsup leaked on steak, reaching stale middling heights; nor has the production of vapid conversation or cretinous creature comforts, shimmering baubles and other visual distractions—football, films—fallen off, on the contrary, or the use of the carnal drug; and loneliness is as large as it ever was: paper napkins snuffed in plastic glasses testify to it, the floor of every closet cries out "love me!," wadded towels too, windows on which the images of waiting faces have been fixed, long halls like highways, and on kitchen counters, where waxy cartons speak of it to knives smeared with crumbs and purple jelly; so that the fascination we now find in these novels about Claudine, and it is certainly there, is due solely to the ever-fresh charm—the instinctive grace—the greatness of Colette, which is certainly immense.

Colette was not the sort of natural genius whose eventual vocation appears spelled out on baby's Beethovian brow. Her intelligence, her curiosity, would not allow her to remain safely at home where she really wanted to be, but let her be taken in by Willy's worldliness and sophistication, as so many were— perhaps by his masterful gaze, his sexy voice—and carried out of her little Burgundian town, where indeed hard times were another incentive, to the great city, no doubt the way captives were once brought to Rome for amusing display. She must almost immediately have felt as Rilke's hero, Malte, did: surprise that people came there to live when the place seemed best fitted to sustain physical distress, loneliness, and fear, and supplied only the facilities for dying. In any event, it was this paunchy old publicist, who picked brains better than crows clean carrion, who introduced Colette to the smoky world of men, and he did it with a thoroughness to inspire praise and discourage imitation.

The recognitions began immediately, if the wedding night is immediate enough, but only gradually did the full measure of her mistake stretch the dressmaker's tape to its tip. By and by (fine words for what it emotionally meant), her toes growing cold in the too-big bed, she was twisted by jealousy like a wet towel until she wept, and was compelled to admit that her husband did a good bit more than neglect her like a friendless pet. She was in fact left alone all day in a small cold flat with a poisonous stove where she dined on nuts and fruit like a monkey and nibbled candy like someone kept. Then fell evening when she was led through salons like a fox terrier on a chain, as Cocteau said, and thence to musicales which Willy might review but at which, in any case, he must be seen, and finally to cafés full of smirk and innuendo and late hours—what was there to say? to these polished and brittle homosexuals? to these softly jowled fat Don Juans? by a girl from the country? with a thick Burgundian burr? especially since they were none of them red and golden pheasants or even geese come down on a smooth deep lake.

Willy's jaded sexual interests were limited to her innocence, which stimulated him the way new snow invites small boys to trample it, and he had at once begun to cheat, as Colette discovered one day when, by unforgivably demeaning herself, she followed and discovered him with a foul-tongued, back-bumped dwarf, little Lotte Kinceler, whom Colette could only pity, and who later blew her mouth apart like glass, committing suicide with a symbolic substitute for what had murdered her already. Willy eventually brought his other cocottes to Colette's apartment where they would finger her things and speak smut. He also carted his collection of pornography with them when they traveled to the country, either to visit and vacation or to escape creditors. And he clung to the skirts of bankruptcy like a bewildered boy.

This wit and bon vivant and raconteur, moreover, this powerful journalist and man-about-town, signed his name to books he hadn't written, claimed ideas he hadn't had, professed tastes he'd never formed. Willy consumed talent like a pimp, and Colette slowly realized that she'd become his latest literary whore in addition to her other duties; that the true sensitivity, intelligence, and taste, furthermore, were on her side; that grace was hers, and honest animal sensuality, the clear uncluttered eye, even good character, industry, and decent ambition, were hers rather than his; that nevertheless she had no vocation, no real role, no independence, a rudimentary education, no polish, no funds; and so she must do her stint and wait at the window and furnish his life, when he chose to share it, with slippers and prattle and pie; that she must be obedient and willing and patient and pretty, cheerful and faithful on top of it, like dung decorated with whipped cream and a cherry, though now she was braidless and ill and bruised, unfresh and scrambled as crawled-over snow; still she was supposed to be grateful, and eager to unbutton his vest and remove his tie, to clasp his fat back in amorous arms, and closely regard, even admire, that thick neck swollen with blood and exertion which rose from his trunk on those occasions like a peeled raw root, while her own body went through the sorrowful motions of love to a conclusion which had from the first time to the last to be a burning and shameful, embittering lie.

Colette could not write to her mother of her misery—not just yet—and later the *Claudines*, those ostensible fictions, gave her a chance at the truth, while her warm and optimistic letters home to Sido, by virtue of what they left out, were in effect made up. Memoirs mixed with fiction, fictions compounded of fact: these were to remain the poles of her work, and the journalism she eventually produced—made of impressionistic, on-the-spot responses—was like a switch engine shunted between these principal stops. Colette was clearly not a novelist by nature as her beloved Balzac was. She wrote her early novels on demand; the key was turned in the lock. Her plays were also a response to pressing necessities, and she toured in them eventually, and bared her bosom too, and struck eloquent attitudes like one of those seductive figures who advertise perfumes: in order to live, to escape being cast forever in the role of a little girl or superfluous femme; although there can be scarcely any doubt that a large part of her yearned to be fed sweets—comforted, cosseted, ruled.

Writing was furthermore a means of shading her mother's eyes. It earned Willy's parsimonious praise and shifted slowly the direction of dependency between them. As time and her success reduced these complex causes to simple considerations, Colette turned more and more openly to autobiography, to that sort of reposeful meditation which was to make her great: the evocation of nature and the celebration of the senses, the beautiful rewording and recovery of her life.

But in Paris Colette found herself strangely imprisoned in an open ruin—a marriage destroyed because of jealousy, mistrust, infidelity, a series of explosive truths—with physique and spirit weakened by her sense of the futility of everything, aching loneliness, the worn-out view out her window, her empty odd hours and odder diet. So she fell ill—what else was there to do? sickened by fumes from a salamander stove, by the little cruelties of daily life, the slick wig of evil tongues and stupid wag of amorous pastimes, but especially by lies both large and immensely petty. She was burning—that was it—consumed by a nostalgia which became a happy characteristic of her consciousness, when she was well, the way her breasts continued to gladden her body. Yet among all those innumerable disappointments which close over a soul grown small and tender as a snail to be swallowed, there was the persistent reappearance of reality like a hard shell or bitter pit. Always that. And every dream dead of the truth. The future, too—dead of it.

Sido had to be summoned at last. That resilient will which was to be the core of Claudine's charm and the center of Colette's strength during a difficult life had become as loose and limp in her body as the bedclothes on her bed, and slid away whenever she rose. Recovery was slow, but her illness won her a few more trips into the country, a little respite from the gentleman in the black hat.

Second   The second photo shows us Willy, pen in hand, force-
Photo   fully facing the photographer. He is seated at another
        table, also berugged, another mantel behind him,
other paintings, further glass glint, smears of image and reflection, amply figured in an ample darkness.[2] He could well be wearing the same suit. There is a spread of papers signifying industry, a penholder, silver tray, a book or two, perhaps a magnifying glass. To his left Colette sits with her fingers holding down a passage on its page as if it could wiggle away. No doubt Willy wants this important section marked, held for him like a seat at a play. The hands are patient. They serve his needs. While Willy and the camera are tête-à-tête, Colette's gaze, as if she'd carried it between the two pictures like a brimming bowl, slips weakly over the edge of the table and disappears into the void. Her expression is one of quiet but profound sadness. The far side of her face is as white as her blouse, though barely there, and a tie covered with bursts of light falls from a high tight collar like a crack of dark sky between clouds.

To write about school in a copybook—to continue the little themes indefinitely into life—what could be more natural? but fate had to conspire almost constantly to bring it about. She and Willy stayed at her old school for a few days while on vacation one July (she writes about this "return" in *Claudine en ménage*), and back in Paris that fall Willy suggests that she write down and spice up the best of what she remembers of those carefree girlish times. This idea, coming from Willy, was not so surprising, since Willy was used to hiring out such work, and he doubtless expected her scribblings to come to nothing. It was a therapeutic occupation like needlepoint and tatting; perhaps it would provide some private titillation, little more,

---

[2] Mitchell, p. 62.

and direct her chatter from his ear to the no-longer-listening and indifferent page. Indeed, Willy found only dull trivia when he later examined the six exercise books Colette had filled. There was nothing he could use. Too bad, but no matter.

Having nibbled on the pen, Colette did not suddenly become insatiable. When Willy tossed her work deep into his black desk, she was content, as regards that, to return to her candy and her cat; yet she continued to write long letters as she had always done, not understanding how they reflected her true and early love of language, her real vocation. Chance again put these notebooks back in Willy's hands. Two years later he happens on them while cleaning out the rear of a drawer.[3] He finds them interesting—useful—this time, though publishers are not easily convinced, and refuse more than once to issue Willy's saucy little novel about a pack of odd, though ordinary, kids, a pair of overly fast friends, some childish high jinks, and one long worrisome exam; and they continue to refuse even after Willy has had its actual author bend a few relationships toward the piquant and perverse. *Claudine à l'école* was not published until 1900, some six years after its very circumstantial composition. Then twenty-seven, Colette had been married from her twentieth year to the Monsieur Willy who signed the volume and composed its preface, one which put much of the truth inside a joke: that the book had been written by a schoolgirl—Claudine herself.

Sales began slowly, but with favorable reviews and word of mouth, the novel became a sensation. Willy redoubled his visits to the photographer, and set Colette to work on a second

---

[3] Maria le Hardouin says it was a few months (*Colette: A Biographical Study*, London: Staples, 1958), but most biographers fix the time at two years: Mitchell, previously cited; Margaret Crosland in her two books (*Madame Colette: A Provincial in Paris*, London: Peter Owen, 1953, and *Colette: The Difficulty of Loving*, Bobbs-Merrill, 1973); and Elaine Marks in hers (*Colette*, Rutgers Univ. Press, 1960). Margaret Davies (*Colette*, Grove Press, 1961) suggests that it was two to three. Maurice Goudeket's memoir (*Close to Colette*, London: Secker and Warburg, 1957) does not cover this period.

confection—a briefer, poorer book, but an even greater success. Soon hats and collars, ice creams, lotions, perfumes carried Claudine's name. Then there was the play, and more Claudines, each shorter, more ambiguous, less resolutely cheerful. Meanwhile Colette kept herself trim in her little private gym, and began to choose her future—a future open to a woman of her present class and condition—the stage.[4]

Nearly unnoticed amidst the schoolgirl gush of the Claudine books, the amorous titivations, the mounting references to immediate Parisian social life—all calculated to entice—was Colette's angry exposure of the condition of young women in rural France. What was a Burgundian girl to do? In *Claudine at School*, for instance, appears this sudden paragraph of social commentary. The girls are readying themselves for a spelling test:

> There was a great hush of concentration. No wonder! Five-sixths of these little girls had their whole future at stake. And to think that all of those would become schoolmistresses, that they would toil from seven in the morning till five in the afternoon and tremble before a Headmistress who would be unkind most of the time, to earn seventy-five francs a month! Out of those sixty girls, forty-five were the daughters of peasants or manual labourers; in order not to work in the fields or at the loom, they had preferred to make their skins yellow and their chests hollow and deform their right shoulders. They were bravely preparing to spend three years at a Training College, getting up at five a.m. and going to bed at eight-thirty p.m. and having two hours recreation out of the twenty-four and ruining their digestions, since few stomachs survived

---

[4] Nothing went to waste: this music-hall life too, almost accidentally arrived at, would provide the background and some of the form for *Mitsou* (where a playlet is inadequately digested), as well as for *Music Hall Sidelights* (a series of vivid sketches), and *The Vagabond*, perhaps her first fully realized fiction—a novel in which the sexual dilemma of the "working woman" is beautifully defined.

three years of the college refectory. But at least they would wear hats and would not make clothes for other people or look after animals or draw buckets from the well, and they would despise their parents.

Claudine is not in school to come to this. Nor has she been reluctantly badgered there by a mother who wishes her daughter to escape, as one of the girls who fails explains to Claudine:

Mother sent me to boarding-school, father he didn't want it, he said I'd do best looking after the house like my sisters, and doing the washing and digging the garden. Mother, she didn't want it—it was her as they listened to. They made me ill, trying to make me learn—and you see how I come over today.

Although Colette will carry on a lifelong romance with little villages and country gardens, in her less reminiscent moods she will realize that despite her attachment to her mother, her beloved Sido, she could never have stayed put.

Come over here little girl and let me show you something, wheedles the dirty old world, and sweet ignorant Claudine— well—all tiptoes, she does want to be wheedled; she does want to see. Weary of innocence, she does desire to know what the sexual fuss is all about. She is a tight string eager to sound yet fearful of the music; and since she wants to take risks while retaining her safety, she will pass from one school to another, one teacher to another, one parent to another, in every case learning the unforeseen and unexpected, insecure on one leg because, mistrustful of the ground, she cannot chance having both put firmly down together.

So curiosity . . . not your window-shoppers' sort, those strollers whose eyes in muggy weather light like nervous flies on crumbs and sweets yet leave without lessening their prize or fattening themselves; but the curiosity that bites the peach to the pit and allows the mouth to fill with juice like a basin; that licks hard and listens, that fingers and sniffs and above all looks, regards—watches, stares, peers—that observes, receives, as an infant explores its world, all drool and smear, as if the world were a fistful of thumbs . . . such curiosity consumes both Colette and Claudine, and unties them from their homes, and lets them for a time believe that certain dashing older gentlemen will open the earth for them, expose life as they expect to be exposed, and give them the only kind of experience that counts: carnal knowledge of all things.

These Claudines, then . . . they want to know because they believe they already *do* know, the way one who loves fruit knows, when offered a mango from the moon, what to expect; and they expect the loyal tender teasing affection of the schoolgirl crush to continue: the close and confiding companionship, the pleasure of the undemanding caress, the cuddle which consummates only closeness; yet in addition they want motherly putting right, fatherly forgiveness and almost papal indulgence; they expect that the sights and sounds, the glorious affairs of the world which their husbands will now bring before them gleaming like bolts of silk, will belong to the same happy activities as catching toads, peeling back tree bark, or powdering the cheeks with dandelions and oranging the nose; that music will ravish the ear the way the trill of the blackbird does; that literature will hold the mind in sweet suspense the way fairy tales once did; that paintings will crowd the eye with the delights of a colorful garden, and the city streets will be filled with the same cool dew-moist country morning air they fed on as children. But they shall not receive what they expect; the tongue will be about other business; one will hear in masterpieces only pride and bitter contention; buildings will have grandeur but no flowerpots or chickens; and these Claudines will exchange the flushed cheek for the swollen vein, and instead of companionship, they will get sex and absurd games composed of pinch, leer, and giggle—that's what will happen to "let's pretend."

The great male will disappear into the jungle like the back

of an elusive ape, and Claudine shall see little of his strength again, his intelligence or industry, his heroics on the Bourse like Horatio at the bridge (didn't Colette see Henri de Jouvenel, editor and diplomat and duelist and hero of the war, away to work each day, and didn't he often bring his mistress home with him, as Willy had when he was husband number one?); the great affairs of the world will turn into tawdry liaisons, important meetings into assignations, deals into vulgar dealings, and the *en famille* hero will be weary and whining and weak, reminding her of all those dumb boys she knew as a child, selfish, full of fat and vanity like patrons waiting to be served and humored, admired and not observed.

Is the occasional orgasm sufficient compensation? Is it the prize of pure surrender, what's gained from all that giving up? There'll be silk stockings and velvet sofas maybe, the customary caviar, tasting at first of frog water but later of money and the secretions of sex, then divine champagne, the supreme soda, and rubber-tired rides through the Bois de Boulogne; perhaps there'll be rich ugly friends, ritzy at-homes, a few young men with whom one may flirt, a homosexual confidant with long fingers, soft skin, and a beautiful cravat, perfumes and powders of an unimaginable subtlety with which to dust and wet the body, many deep baths, bonbons filled with sweet liqueurs, a procession of mildly salacious and sentimental books by Paul de Kock and company—good heavens, what's the problem?—new uses for the limbs, a tantalizing glimpse of the abyss, the latest sins, envy certainly, a little spite, jealousy like a vaginal itch, and perfect boredom.

And the mirror, like justice, is your aid but never your friend.

Dependent as a young girl is, she has only her body to sustain her. Her body has brought her to Paris. Her body can free her from her husband if she wants to go on the stage or be a whore, but she must possess a pleasant face, a fresh complexion, good limbs, prominent breasts, a narrow waist. She will succeed only so long as she gives pleasure to men. To do that, she must know how to flatter, how to be silent, when to be weak; for women must be weak in public, strong at home, compliant in private.

The prudent woman will not accept gifts from just any body, so frigidity will be the rule. To become dependent there, to allow a male that power over you, to lose the last of your lands without a struggle, the citadel of sensation, is to surrender everything and enjoy even the humiliation of your rape.

The Claudine books do not contain the complete scenario. The independent woman goes to bed with bankers and invests her tips with wisdom on the Bourse, and the time will come when she will keep men as she was kept, requesting their erections, and requiring them to pleasure her as she was once supine and sweetly willing. A woman who has children and who remains married will someday sell her daughters off as she was sold, and by middle age the intelligent, ambitious ones will be so accomplished at managing the world through their husbands —as if soft arms were in those manly sleeves—and so skilled at beating back female competition, so sly with insinuation, clever with wigs and rouge, so unscrupulous about the truth, adept at blackmail and intrigue, hard inside as cinders, that males would fall to their knees in terrified admiration if they believed to their bones what they've hitherto only suspected, and occasionally felt: the scornful condescension which has shivered the small hairs of their skin when they turned away to sleep sometimes in bedrooms shut away from any breeze.

During wars, as it is written in *La Fin de Chéri*, when the men go off to be brave in front of one another, rump to rump and arm in arm and hand to hand (for that's *esprit de corps*), the women, as dangerous as the slaves which the Spartan soldiers left behind, take over. They discover, the way Rosie the Riveter did, that women can shape the real world as well as any man; that manipulating men has made them peculiarly fit for politics and administration; and that they become men then, improving on the species; for it never occurred to Colette (as it never did to Gertrude Stein) to question the roles, only the assignments of the players.

There is one value in this sort of life, one currency which can be cashed like grapes crushed in the mouth, spent in the released limbs, received from one's surroundings as simply as rain, and that is the quiet ease of soul called contentment, the joyful joining of the body to the world which we vaguely spell as pleasure. The realm of animals and nature, quiet open country, unassuming streams and ponds, flowering plants: these yield that pleasure up with greatest certainty and safety, and young Claudine and the mature Colette are sensualists of a greedy straightforwardness and simplicity supreme enough to put Pierre Louÿs's perversities to rout, and J.-K. Huysman's hothouse visions and rococo plans, like out-of-fashion paintings, into the museum basement.

But the body fails us and the mirror knows, and we no longer insist that the gray hush be carried off its surface by the cloth, for we have run to fat, and wrinkles encircle the eyes and notch the neck where the skin wattles, and the flesh of the arms hangs loose like an overlarge sleeve, veins thicken like ropes and empurple the body as though they had been drawn there by a pen, freckles darken, liver spots appear, the hair . . . ah, the hair is exhausted and gray and lusterless, in weary rolls like cornered lint.

Third Photo It is the hair we see in the final photographs, after arthritis has marooned her on that pillowed divan she calls her raft. She wears a futile sweater against the chill which swells from within now like a puff of cold breath, and a fur bedspread is draped over her former body. She is looking at us with Claudine's eyes and Colette's mouth. Her alertness is utterly unlike the hopelessness we earlier saw when she sat beside Willy. It is preternaturally intense. Her jaw juts as it always did; her nose has not lost its longish taper either; the brow has risen, lying beneath her frizzy hair like snow beneath a wintering bush; and her hands, thank god, can still form words. A table crosses her body like a bridge, running toward the window which overlooks the gardens of the Palais-Royal, and bearing, like pedestrians trooping over it, a telephone, pen and little pitcher chocked with spares, her spectacles, some papers (what's that, an address book?), a potted plant overbearingly in bloom, and plenty of bleaching sunshine. One of the immortals, she will soon die, and be given a state funeral and denied consecrated ground on the same day.

Claudine never had enough to do. She had no children, few plants, and her husband's servants. She had her husband, too, who kept her at ends as loose as carpet fringe. She gives way to her impulses and encourages her moods. She recoils from imprisonment but plays at being kept. Yet what can a plaything feel but the handling? Love is the great distraction. Romance can fill you better than pasta, and when it's digested it leaves you thin. Love gives you the sense of having been alive, but the life of love is always in the past tense, in that remembered moment when a curl touched your cheek or an amorous glance felt like a warm palm on the belly—there, where the smallest muscles tremble to the touch like an animal. Chéri, too, a male Claudine in many ways, though without her elasticity, can only hunger and fondle, fuck and sleep; find his intermittent being in his mother-mistress, Léa's arms, as Claudine finds hers in Renaud's, her equally fatherly lover. "Devoting oneself to sensual pleasure is not a career for a respectable man," Colette writes in *L'Etoile Vesper*, or for a woman who would live past fifty either, since by that time . . . time . . .

Love. Always *that* in these silly French novels. Isn't there another subject, Jouvenel had complained, beside incestuous longing, adultery, absence? Well, not really. Look at how this tiny boudoir mirror reflects all the larger relations! Because novels about love are inevitably about its failures, and the failure of love leads directly to the need for an alternative salvation which can lie nowhere else but in one's work, although most work is as impermanent as pleasure, often even hurtful, and pointless to boot; still for a fortunate few (and if they are women they are very few and fortunate indeed), there is the chance for a redeeming relation to some creative medium—in Colette's case, as Fate finally settled it, the written word.

The better word, as she suggested her hunt was—the better word. But the better word did not fall toward her out of space like a star, nor did the untranslatable rhythms of her prose dance like urchins in the street beneath her flat. Words arose, came to her, fell in line, principally as she reflected upon her life, whether it was fiction she was writing or something else. Experience was her dictionary, and what we can observe, as we read through the *Claudine*s, is the compiling of that dictionary, and how, out of that large scrawly book of girlish words, is finally shaped an art of grave maturity, subtlety, perception, grace; one which is at once so filled with Colette's own presence and yet so open to the reader, so resolutely aimed, that it masters a mode: *le style intime*, one would be tempted to dub it, if that didn't suggest it was a naughty perfume.

The memory transcribes loops. It begins here where I am; it departs for the past, then returns to me through possibly fancy slips and spins like a Yo-Yo to the hand. Colette was fond of mimicking such motion, beginning a chapter with Claudine breathless from an outing or a visit, and then returning the narrative through some carriage ride or concert until Claudine is once more at home. In this way the event is bracketed by endings at both ends (and ends as it began). The immediate moment can benefit then from the play of reflection, although there is little benefit from reflection in the Claudine books, which are for the most part shallow indeed. Plunged into iniquity, Claudine emerges as clean as a washed doll.

Events are naturally related in the first person. Even *Chéri*, which is written in the third, has every quality of the quiet "I." The tone is of course girlish in these girlish books, but it is that of the confidential exchange in almost all of them: the personal letter, the intense tête-à-tête, confessions passed between chums like shared toys, or at its most innocent, it has the character of a daughter's report of what happened on her first date (one suspects the presence of Sido, listening almost in the reader's place).

Colette will copy the manner of the diary or journal too, but also include a great deal of designedly empty and idle yet lively chatter. Opportunities will be manufactured for the exchange of confidences, though the effect is nothing like that of Henry James. Equally contrived, the result is merely artificial, and unfortunately often cheap. Verbal voyeurism is the rule. Claudine enjoys hearing how it is to be a kept woman from her former school chum, Luce: "Old thing, you've got to tell me all." "He's old, my uncle, but he has impossible ideas. Sometimes he makes me get down on all-fours and run about the room like that. And he runs after me on all-fours too . . . Then he jumps on me, bellowing: 'I'm a wild beast!' " Claudine's husband Renaud, and Marcel, his homosexual son, are both excited by accounts of amorous encounters. "I implore you, do tell me all about Lucy. I'll be nice . . ." "What next, Claudine, what next?" "I'll tell you everything, Claudine," Annie promises, and Claudine is soon responding: "Go on, go on, just the main facts."[5]

It is not the promise of dirty details which makes the style so personal and beckoning. Confessions can be as public as billboards, and our bookstores are as cluttered by beseech-

---

[5] Robert Cottrell's suggestion that not all this sexual leering can be blamed on Willy is correct, I think: "Titillation resulting from an artful toying with debauchery is one of the veins Colette worked, and it crops up even in the books of her maturity" (*Colette*, Frederick Ungar, 1974, p. 23). This is perhaps the best critical introduction to Colette: brief, clear, balanced, and very perceptive. Marvin Mudrick makes a similar complaint in his *Hudson Review* article, "Colette, Claudine, and Willy" (XVI, No. 4, pp. 559–72), but Mudrick's sometimes eloquent piece is also peevish, and his drearily old-fashioned conception of what counts in fiction leads him to overlook the virtues of these books while somewhat misstating their flaws.

ments and soulful outcries as our highways. It may be useful
to remind ourselves how other masters of so-called female fiction sound, how done up in public prose, not plain brown
paper, most conversations are. Here is an example of pure
melodrama: public to its core. It has no internality. Clarissa
has determined not to run off with Lovelace:

> Fear nothing, dearest creature, said he. Let us hasten
> away—the chariot is at hand . . .
>
> O Mr. Lovelace, said I, I cannot go with you—*indeed*
> I cannot—I wrote you word so—let go my hand and you
> shall see my letter . . .
>
> . . . here we shall be discovered in a moment. Speed
> away my charmer—this is the moment of your deliverance
> —if you neglect this opportunity you *never* can have such
> another.
>
> What is it you mean, sir? Let go my hand: for I tell
> you . . . that I will sooner die than go with you.
>
> Good God! said he . . . what is it I hear!

Good god, what one hears, indeed! Well, Richardson will
not greet us in his dressing gown, you can be certain of that
(though in dots and dashes like something sent in Morse), nor
will Jane Austen go out without her Latinated English buttoned
on; but Colette is always carefully *en déshabillé.* There is the
unguarded expression of emotion (the all-too-frequent exclamation and oo-la-la!); there's the candid opinion dropped as casually as a grape, the gleefully malicious judgments,

> Model pupils! . . . they exasperate me so much with their
> good behavior and their pretty, neat handwriting and their
> silly identical flat, flabby faces and sheep's eyes full of
> maudlin mildness. They swat all the time; they're bursting
> with good marks; they're prim and underhand and their
> breath smells of glue. Ugh!

the broken phrases, sentences darting in different directions
like fish, gentle repetitions, wholly convincing observations,

> That lanky bean-pole stood and made a secret grimace,
> like a cat about to be sick . . .

and above all the flash of fine metaphor, sometimes one of only
local governance like this from *The Last of Chéri:*

> He never went to the hospital again, and thereafter Edmée
> invited him to go only as a perfunctory gesture, such as
> one makes when one offers game to a vegetarian guest.

or sometimes an image which is both accurate summation and
continuing symbol, as this from the same page:

> He grew thoughtful now, prey to an idleness that, before
> the war, had been agreeable, varied, as full of meaning as
> the resonant note of an empty, uncracked cup.

and when we look down the length of her sentences, we see
the energy which rushes up through them like the bubbler in
the park—they are alive—even when otherwise they are callow
and jejune, or even when they move with an almost Jamesian
majesty, as they often do through the stories which make up
The Tender Shoot, or reveal the pruned, precise lyricism, the
romantic simplicity of a finely shaped head beneath a haircut:

> Few memories have remained as dear to me as the mem-
> ory of those meals without plates, cutlery or cloth, of those
> expeditions on two wheels. The cool sky, the rain in drops,
> the snow in flakes, the sparse, rusty grass, the tameness
> of the birds.

Colette did not invent so much as modify her memory,
thus her work required continual return; yet retracing well demands forgetting too, or the early line will soon be overlaid
with other lines and lose all definition. None of us now matches
her skill at rendering the actual contours of experience. How
far can we see out of raised eyebrows? How straight can we
speak with a curled lip? Irony, ambiguity, skepticism—these

aren't attitudes any more which come and go like moods, but parts of our anatomy. However, Colette could recall a young girl's innocent offer of commitment and not dismay it with the disappointments and betrayals which she knew were sure to follow. She did not feel obliged to insist that the confusions of the loving self rise from their depths to trouble every feeling just because she knew they were there and wanted us to know she knew. Our illusions, when they shattered, spilled affection like a cheap perfume which clings to our surroundings, over-scenting, so that the sick smell of ourselves is everywhere, however frantically we move. In English, how many genuine love stories have we had since Ford wrote *Some Do Not?*

Colette is being pushed to pen it; nevertheless, *Claudine in Paris* is often a sadly meretricious book. Despite its causes, and despite the fact that she, herself, has suffered seven years of Willy like the plague, Colette can still remember what her hopes were—how it was—and can render Claudine's feelings for this older man (handsomer than her husband to be sure, but close enough in every other way to guarantee discomfort) with a rare and convincing genuineness. In the best of these books, *Claudine Married*, there are many unreal and merely fabricated things, but the passion is real: at the sight of her beloved's breasts, she aches and fears and trembles, is full of the gentlest and most giving hunger.

Perhaps the impossibility of love should be our only subject (it was certainly one of Colette's), but living was not impossible, only difficult. There was always before her the specter, when love failed, when pleasure went out of the wet grass, and the air hung like further leaves in the quiet trees; there was always the possibility that these scents, these observations, these open mornings when the sky threw itself back out of the way like a concealing sheet; that not only would they pass as all things do, but that they'd leave no trace behind but triviality —snail slime, worm hole, bug bite, mouth with chocolate-covered corners to be buried in.

HE LIKED HIS COCOA THICK
NOT THIN

In one of her beautiful late stories, "The Photographer's Missus," she gives that missus, in explanation of her attempted suicide, the following speech:

> . . . whatever do you think came into my head one morning when I was cutting up some breast of veal? I said to myself: "I did breast of veal with green peas only last Saturday, all very nice, but one mustn't overdo it, a week goes by so fast. It's eleven already, my husband's got a christening group coming to pose at half-past one, I must get my washing-up done before the clients arrive, my husband doesn't like to hear me through the wall rattling crockery or poking the stove when clients are in the studio . . . And after that I must go out, there's that cleaner who still hasn't finished taking the shine off my husband's black suit, I'll have to have a sharp word with her. If I get back to do my ironing before dark, I'll be lucky; never mind, I'll damp my net window-curtains down again and I'll iron them tomorrow, sooner than scorch them today. After that, I've nothing to do but the dinner to get ready and two or three odds and ends to see to and it'll be finished."

It is the beginning of an attempted end.

The late books tell us what the late photos show: in a life of love and even melodrama, a life that was lived within the skin and nerves as few have been, it was her work which won— loved her and won her love; and that finger which once held down sentences for Willy helped write others which need no help and hold themselves. The moral isn't new or arresting. Philosophers have been saying the same thing for centuries.

Proust at 100

Proust's mother, everyone immediately said—(and the echo is with us yet, for it was the kind of conjecture we talebearers love)—was marked before she bore him by that foolish war the inept French were diddled into waging against Bismarck and his Boche, much as the mother of Thomas Hobbes was marked, and infected the future philosopher with the fear she felt at the approach of the Spanish Armada. And certainly the siege of Paris was no picnic: citizens ate the horses and the dogs, then the animals in the zoos; cats cost six francs, rats one; streets were crowded with defeated soldiers, carts of dead and wounded, insurrectionists, and, in the days before the cannonading scattered them, an audience of gossips. The section of the city where Madame Proust was shortly to seek refuge in order to procure for Marcel his welcome from the world received from Edmond de Goncourt, whose prize her son would one day win, a grim *Journal* invocation: "Cursed Auteuil! This suburb will have been deprived of communication with the rest of Paris, sacked by the Mobiles, starved out, shelled, and now is to have the misfortune of being occupied by the Prussians."

Sick, weak from the start, marked, everybody said. There may have been an apprehension in the fetus that not all was well, a feeling for the thinness of the cord with which it was fed, the precariousness of the silence which cushioned it. At his birth, not everyone expected Marcel Proust to live, and, indeed, with what was to be characteristic perverseness, the little fellow grew as sturdily as if weakness were the purpose of the plant.

He became allergic to pollen, dust, damp, smoke, odors of all sorts, especially perfumes and the scents of his favorite flowers; he was easily chilled, easily fatigued, easily offended, thinking often of duels; he frequently gave way to weeping, or had tantrums in which he broke things or crushed his friends' hats; he suffered prolonged spells of melancholy, grew pale, lost weight, and went into mourning the way, ideally, one ought to put on plays; attacks of anxiety made him sweat, gave him cramps; he complained of indigestion, later of dizziness and a paralysis which disturbingly resembled the sort which seized his mother just before her death: it required him to wobble when he walked—to bump most awkwardly into things—and, what was worse, made it difficult to talk, to pronounce well and clearly his sacred French.

He feared for his heart, his sight which was failing, the affections of his friends, those love affairs which could not last, arrangements which could not be consummated—to have a party, pay a visit, take a train, make a move, or love, a purchase, dine—without infinite trouble, endless doubts and consequently paralyzing bouts of indecision, countless pleas for assistance (he wrote many letters so obsequious, so grotesquely ceremonial, they were like spit in the face).

Then there were those floating pains like underwater mines . . . in his back, his wrists, behind the eyes . . . and there was the noise . . . the demanding clamor of the world outside; thus he was, of course, in his condition, prone to flus, rheums, fevers, lung congestions, laryngitis; he wheezed, he coughed, he choked, he sneezed—the continual shuddering of his chest enlarged the cage.

So it became necessary to cork the walls, draw the blinds,

to sleep surrounded by comforters and quilts, warm rubber bottles; he went out in furs, more and more at night, in carriages carefully closed against the weather, to sit in late cafés, to watch, eavesdrop, interrogate, or to attend parties where, very weary, with drug-enlarged eyes, his head supported by his palms as you might prop the heavy bloom of a spindly plant, he talked and talked, his voice going slowly and remotely on as if he were oozing.

Colette remembered, in those last late days, "the sooty telltale traces that an absent-minded malady had smeared haphazardly across his face."

Yet despite his precautions, he often took alarm and turned back, apologizing to his hosts by post and messenger: even the happiest streets can be strange, the most familiar of them foreign, while his health was insecure, all knew—how he regretted it—and besides there were patches of fog, there were menacing rooms, disappointments, chills; and Proust put balls of ivory in his ears, burned Legras powder, took bicarbonate of soda, iodide, drank tisanes, and for his sore throat swallowed, of all things, cascara, a purge with a name like a river.

He lay down for the day to go over the night, placing immense weights on small things, sliding his eyes from tea tray to ribbon, flounce to hairdo, when he remembered the soirées; watching, listening for those nuances of language—word, tone, gesture—which would turn over his feelings as if each were a page, even though he would always discover that the opposing leaf involved a volte-face which confirmed his suspicions; and in this insomniac's way he filled up the blanks and hollows of his graveside life with nervous reflection.

It pleased Proust to have the critic, Paul Souday, remark while writing of *Within a Budding Grove*: "Few novelists have expressed, more forcefully or more bitterly, the feeling of change and incessant instability that makes human life an uninterrupted series of partial deaths." *A series of partial deaths*: that was good. Yes. His body made a drama of its dying. It wrote its own script, although its owner was not above offering some editorial assistance now and then: "*Ma chère petite Maman*, I have come in so exhausted by an incessant cough that I tried it discreetly outside your door to see whether you were asleep. But there was no response to 'that voice of the heart,' which, Lamartine says, 'alone reaches the heart.' "

Well it was true, in a way, that his heart coughed. I cannot breathe, it also said. I am being smothered. Everything is heavy, close, stifling. Just as the first breath of life is an outcry, so I've drawn myself up to scream, to howl, to bellow like a baby for its mother; but somehow the cry is suppressed, and I gasp as one who feels the floor fall beneath him, as a child may at the top of his father's toss, as one about to climax; yet how cold I am in this close, warm room; I need my robe, more blankets; I shiver from a lack of love, from fright; I say I cannot swallow, I cannot stomach things, and my gorge rises, meals empty out.

His body insisted that it could not bear the burdens of its life; see how my bones, my back aches—every aperture—ears, eyes . . . How much did it have to pain him to prove it? And though Proust spent much of his time in bed, like a mountain climber in a nightmare, he could never reach sleep. He swallowed amyl, Trional, Veronal, and then to revive himself received adrenalin in injections, took caffeine. Often unshaven, his linen far from fresh, he allowed his entire apartment to settle into dinginess like dust, and, like his bed, to rumple. His friends could not decide how best to describe him: as a young or aged invalid, a dandy or a maiden aunt, an animal, an addict, a hypocrite or, if sincere, a madman.

The Greeks had ascribed living motion—soul—to breath, and Proust behaved as if they had been right. Hadn't he said that invalids feel closer to their souls? And it was breath which hollowed our primal clay. Although his asthma required him always to be holding his, clinging to the life he both loathed and loved (and of which he was so insecure and jealous) with the same grip he used to hang on to the past, to the world as it was when his mother was alive, nevertheless his vocation as a novelist demanded that all he'd taken in be given its release, so that his writing was really like a repeated sigh—an expiration—and since his book was actually that vital latter half of breathing, he could not finish it while he lived.

He wrote as a river builds a delta—by overlay and accretion. His galleys were as black with corrections as Balzac's. The first section, "Combray," and the last, an afternoon party with music at the house of the Princess de Guermantes, were written first, the rest of the book was middle. To write in interleaf and interline, around the rim as Joyce would do, that was his method. It was our curious good fortune, too, that another war with the Germans interrupted the appearance of the work which Proust himself called, simply, "Swann," allowing it in the meantime to more than double.

This should not surprise us, for it was the untiming of time itself that was Proust's project. He lifted ticks from the clock and froze them as the furniture and lights are frozen in those Vermeers which he favored with some of his best pages. It was not to rescue time itself that he started out, but to redeem himself, to save all that life which he had let so worthlessly flow by—every moment of it—to reclaim it and then invest it with a verbal value it had never had as a human happening; for who knew better than he the genius in him, blooming like the rose which Mallarmé had suggested was absent from every bouquet, the genius who was to display his excellence . . . when? . . . well, every day it was still tomorrow.

Who knew better his baseness, his guilt, the crimes he had contrived? He was, after all, a useless idler, ill half the time and a fake for a fourth of that; he was a jealous whiner and a faithless sycophant, a purchaser of favors and a false friend, a social trifler and a snob. He had a dilettante's interest in music and painting, a brat's love of mama, a fairy's fondness for furbelows, finery, and female life, and a love of gossip that would have left him, had he indulged it fully, without a single back to bite.

How did the great call come? It came, of course, in those celebrated moments when the past rushed back open-armed, contrite, forgiving, like a lover who has quarreled and wishes to make amends; when, in the novel, the narrator tastes the madeleine dipped in tea; when he studies the steeples of Martinville or catches sight of those three trees; when he stumbles on a pair of paving stones or touches a shoe button, feels a napkin on his lips, smells a moldy odor, hears the sound of water in a pipe or a spoon rung by a servant against a plate. Taste, touch, sound, sight, smell: through each of the senses at one point or other the past is recaptured, but noticeably without the anxieties and disappointments of the original occasion, so that even the most shameful times, in these remembrances of them, lack that threatening immersion in immediate emotion they first had; now they can be held like a blossom; they can actually—even the most trivial, the most fearful of them—be transformed, not by the Marcel who experienced them originally, but by another, the Marcel who holds a poet's pen and can contrive a line so beautiful its author can claim a virtue for every vice it limns.

Before and After. Yes, with a little work, they can be saved. It is the present, the immediate moment—the During—that is doomed. Before the narrator watches the actress, Berma, play Phèdre, before he sees the little church in Balbec, both are perfect (inaccessible, he says of the church, intact, ideal, endowed with universal value), such is the art of romantic expectations. But Balbec was a name, he has to confess, that he should have kept hermetically sealed, somewhat like a private letter or perhaps his writing room, because the moment it was broken into, there were loosed—to sully the church and its illustrious Virgin—the images of a branch bank, omnibus office, pastry shop, café.

Experience was in constant danger from these contrasts—

the sublime and the sordidly commercial, for example—the kind of undercutting contradiction which delighted Flaubert (who counted the scratches of the wedding plates) and which could never have dismayed more robust men (our Balzacs and our Zolas, they have their strengths). Nor could the rarer objects—refined tastes, sharp wit, the right people and their real accomplishments, the precious effects he so dearly loved—always be protected by the bibelots of fashionable parlors, where, as likely as not, the wealthy hostess was a bourgeois whore, or the clever baron an affected pederast, while in the glitter of his company the rest were sniveling sycophants and bores. Nor could he come to terms with himself, for what was one to say of an intermittently fastidious though aging and increasingly puffy-faced fop who had a yen, sometimes, at the homo house he helped to suit out with his family's furniture, for strong young men who worked in butcher shops?

In short, then, Proust planned to replace his life with language, to restore it to beauty as you might restore a church, and thus to pull it out of time and seal it like a freezer package, protecting it from every vulgarity as the Balbec church in his book was not. Though he was half a Catholic, it wasn't confession he was after. Confession might suit Gide. Gide had a compulsion in that direction. He thought it allowed him everything. So Gide would complain of Proust's work that it wasn't honest, and that Proust, so close to the edge already, should have cried "I"; that he should have spoken of loving Albert, and not, as he wrote, of loving Albertine (Gide had a point, because these disguises did not work; they merely obstructed, obscured, and lamed).

But it was not in the recovery of any actual past that Proust's genius lay; his was not a novel of remembrance, as I've pointed out, but a novel of analysis and reflection (Proust returned to his childhood the way a modern primitive returns to the woods: with his books, his bankroll, and a stash of pot); and Remy de Gourmont's saying that "one only writes well about things one hasn't experienced" remained importantly true, because what Proust intended to write was not so much an account of his life (he would, of course, condense, amalgamate, rearrange, select), but something that would give it meaning and worth.

Remembrance of Things Past is, like most great examples of the novelist's art, an act of love, of hate and revenge, and finally, of reparation. Proust lives in it as he failed to live in life, and it would be more appropriate to celebrate the hours in which he began it, were there such moments, than the confused and frightened days of his confinement. But before he could embark upon its composition, Proust had to devise a fictional strategy that would radically single his mind, slow the drain of neurasthenia on his spirit, and by indulging his deepest nature find employment for all his vagrant energies; in this way permitting, for example, his morbid suspicion and excessive possessiveness, his inclination to symbolic cruelty and ritual desecration, to have a constructive outlet; and allowing him to exercise exactly the painstaking and painful reappraisal of every occasion which was his constant bedtime occupation.

For then his mind was not one wolf but twenty, it could bring down anything; there his jealous instability was a law of love; and in the scheme he finally settled on, his obsessive concerns (homosexuality, snobbery and the break-up of classes, the pleasures and anxieties of being "in society," the religion of art) became recurrent themes in an enormous Mahleresque composition in which these subjects, themselves, were entered, overcome, and eventually replaced by the style of their own depiction. Remember that description of Madame Swann's gowns which is more laced and bowed and ruffled, more exquisitely daring, more utterly elaborated, than they are, and beneath which she sinks from sight as a thread of grass does in a bouquet of daisies?

Proust was always ready to have his friends defend the organization of *Remembrance of Things Past*, and there can be no doubt his tapestry is intricate and cunningly worked; yet much of the so-called form in Proust is meaningless—an excuse. Like the elaborate Homeric correspondence in *Ulysses*, it is meant only for the mind. It placates critics who chase relations like lawyers trying to settle rich estates. An unfeelable form is a failure. Furthermore, it is hard to imagine what the architecture of this novel would have excluded, since forms, like fences, are meant to keep the cows out as well as the corn in. No, it is largely a wonderful wallow; it can accommodate anything, including little essays on art, love, literature, and life. Nor should we too readily accept the idea that the fuses of those involuntary memories (the madeleine, the shoe button, the paving stone, etc.) really set off the rest of the text; otherwise we should have to believe that, when those little powdered strings are lit, a miracle of physics occurs—one in which the boom blows up the bomb.

Proust despised the esthete with all the hate hog has for hog, and believed that his novel would uncover, in a way no other method could manage, the essential truth of his life; but he was a liar like all the others, a master of dissimulation and subterfuge; there is no special truth in him; he would capture our consciousness if he could and give us a case of his nerves. Still—no danger. When the fuss over Proust's theories about memory and time has faded; when we have taken what we can for psychology from his own reflections on his characters; when we have faithfully observed, as Proust did, the intrusion, like a second row of teeth, of the middle into the upper classes; when we have ceased to be shocked by inversion or amused by period dress and manners (and it's been well past "when" now for many years); then it is only Proust's style that will carry this enormous book: the style of his mind, his sight and hearing, touch and feeling, and above all, the unique character of his language and its extraordinary composition—a style where image and object, like Jack and Jill, go up and down together.

Carry it? The standard French edition is in 15 volumes; the Random House is a pair comprising 2,265 pages; and each page should be sounded, each sentence thought slowly over as a mind on a walk for pleasure. So taken, the pace of every one of them is slow, the path of every one of them is lengthy. When reading, one wonders first if the book will ever end, and then, in despair, if it will ever begin. In comparison, the Russian steppes—were they so vast? Or winters in upper Michigan prolonged? Lawrence said it was like tilling a field with knitting needles, and James, reading *Swann's Way*, confessed to an inconceivable boredom.

Well, we are safe from it, since it is difficult to imagine a work more out of step with modern consciousness, not simply because its sexual revelations are tame, its social preoccupations fairly innocent and out of date, its politics impossibly square, but because the rich and thoughtful musical approach Proust takes, the deep analytical poetry he writes, is both duller and quieter than silence is among the loud impatient honks and heartfelt belches which these days pass for books. "Inconceivable boredom," James said, "associated with the most extreme ecstasy which it is possible to imagine."

Carry it? This style? How? Proust writes a careless self-indulgent prose, doesn't he? Developing trivialities endlessly, as if he were in terror that anything should be thought trivial. Oh, he would sanctify if he could, his every wink, pang, or sniffle. My god, how he fawns over the asparagus, "stippled in mauve and azure." Does he plan to make a mayonnaise with his effusions? And note how he flatters the lilacs. Epithet follows epithet like tea cakes in flutes of paper. You'd suppose every bloom were a baron. Indeed, botanical metaphors are plentiful as plants, and the growth of the action is like theirs—imperceptible, steady, continuous—yes, and it's the same for the revelation of character; it's the same for the course of his thought; thus he slows things to permit the fullest flight of his fancy, the tireless play of his sensibilities, the utmost smother of his love. He slows, then stops; and then his scenes are like those cell cross-sections cut by the microtome and stained till they glow like glass.

It is a style that endangers the identity of the self in its reckless expression of it.

Proust has always had his Proustians, which seems inevitable, though a pity, for they have tended to admire everything in him but his art; they fatten on content; but this work, like all truly great ones, spits life out of time like the pit from a fruit. Out of the architecture of the word, the great work rises, but its reading requires a similar commitment, a similar elevation of the soul above mere living, mere mortal concerns. One hundred years—and we remember him. And perhaps one day soon we shall find ourselves pleasantly immobilized, comfortably hammocked or mildly ill (whatever it takes to make us one of the happy few); one day when the guns are gone and the looters are out of the suburbs; when all the threats have been withdrawn, and time lies as empty in our hands as an office present, then perhaps—I won't say we shall read Proust again (cowards and nincompoops abound and many may not wish to run the risk of the same transformation which made a saint from a sinner)—but then, perhaps, like a shoeless pilgrim, we may make a start.

Paul Valéry

The August evening in Geneva in 1892 which Paul Valéry chose to mislead us by calling his night of crisis, his "turning point," was shot like a scene from a stupid movie. In the spiritual background there was a distantly worshipful and wholly one-sided love affair with an unapproachable married woman, an affair of barely smothered sighs and secret languishments whose very disappointments were romantically necessary. There was, in addition, Valéry's deepening discouragement with his own work as a poet—after all, Mallarmé had already surpassed the possible—and in consequence, as a protection to pride, there had appeared in him an increasing tendency to disparage both poetry and the language from which it was made, just as someone who's cleaned a collar by cutting it off entirely is required to imagine that in this fashion he's better dressed. Nearly a year before, he had written this desperate la-de-da to Gide: "Please don't call me Poet anymore . . . I am not a poet, but the gentleman who is bored."

Inevitably there was, as well, a willingness to find insufficient superiority even in the supreme. "The most original of our great men—Wagner, Mallarmé—stoop," he announced to the same correspondent in the smug tones of the youthfully aggrieved. They *imitate*, he reported, feeling the triumph and the shock of one who, for the first time, has seen the great chef sneeze into the soup. He had "analyzed, alas!" their expressive means and encountered everywhere, even among the most wonderful writers (he mentions specifically Poe, Rimbaud, and again, Mallarmé), the loveliest illusions concerning the genesis and production of their poetry. Pledged to a profession that obliged them constantly to surpass themselves, they failed to remember who they were; they (it was such a snob's word) . . . they *stooped*; yet Valéry did not feel himself ready to fall in just that way just yet.

We know none of the details, and can only darkly guess the cause, but if the background of the scene of crisis contained the characteristic *Sturm und Drang* of an ambitious, gifted, randy youth of twenty-one, the foreground was filled with simple, bolt-upright sleeplessness and fright: in his head he heard the badly bowed music of his nerves, the familiar theme of *sic et non*, while, outside, this interior cacophony was accompanied the night through by a vulgarly obvious but appropriately violent thunderstorm.

Absurdly set and conventionally shot ("his whole fate played out in his head"), Valéry had his trial and his illumination in the desert, nonetheless, and came back a brave. Deciding, as Descartes did, to put his trust solely in himself (or rather in one part of himself—that part which was prepared to flee to pure awareness where it could be, he said, "an unmoved observer"), he became a stubborn student of his own mind, of his mental acts and processes, and of the structures and subtle modulations of consciousness.

For Valéry poetry had been, on principle and from inclination, an escape from the world ("By 'world' I mean the whole complex of incidents, demands, compulsions, solicitations, of every kind and degree of urgency," he wrote, "which overtake the mind without offering it any inner illumination . . ."). But now the world blew through him like a wind—poetry was no shutter to it. He felt insecure in its care. Somehow the inde-

pendence of the self was threatened, and despite his "intellec-
tualized" view of poetry, the poetry he wrote was predomi-
nately erotic.

In addition to the predictable appearance of Venus, Orpheus, Helen and their friends, the use of films and gauze, the
dreary azures, lilies, fountains, fruit, hair, swans and roses of
conventional symbolist poetry, the moon and the murmurous
wood, the ritual expostulations (hollow ohs and fatuous ahs),
the early poems are stuffed, as though for Christmas, with
images of images: tree, leaf and sun shadows, dream and fire
flicker, countless kinds of reflection. Here the footprint has
more substance than the foot; the face finds its resemblance
in another medium, floats in fountain water like a flower, trembles independently of its owner as if it had its own sorrows,
looks back from the language of its own description like a lover
or an accusation. The Narcissus theme has already been introduced: "I can love nothing now but the bewitching water."

He also writes a poem called "Caesar," and admires in the
figure he portrays there ("all things beneath his foot") the same
quality he finds the young Napoleon showing in his critical
hour.[1] It is a characteristic he discusses with some shrewdness
and more detachment in his essays on dictatorship: the burning concentration of will, mastery, the instant disposal of
means. It is not Descartes's system, but Descartes's self he
makes us a present of, and although his interpretation is so
oddly perverse that only a psychological need can account for
it, there is no question that Valéry thinks of the philosopher's
famous moment of illumination, the moment in which analytic
geometry is conceived, and the poet's own sheet-chewing night
of crisis, as importantly alike, for in such moments, Valéry

---

[1] In his translation of Rilke's "Orpheus, Eurydice and Hermes," Lowell adds the line,
"The dark was heavier than Caesar's foot." That is how, as Valéry might have said,
the undisciplined mind *moves*: in a lurch through Valéry and Caesar to Lowell and
Rilke, and, considering the curious accumulation of references, remains to touch
Borges as if he were home base.

writes: ". . . a whole life is suddenly clarified, and every act will henceforth be subordinated to the task which is its goal. A straight line has been staked out." Napoleon had to conquer his dominions, but "Descartes created *his* Revolution and Empire at a single stroke." Valéry chose a world where he could be, as he repeatedly said, master in his own house: his head. It was a world of wait and watch.

Order, clarity, precision, shape: these properties seem so often an enemy of powerful feelings that, although they may usefully employ them the way steam is put to work by the piston, to invoke them is the same as calling the police. Anything—the starry heavens which so terrified Pascal (the one author for whom Valéry exhibits contempt)—can be scientifically observed, but the man of science, Valéry believed, "*switches off* the whole emotive system of his personality. He tries to turn himself into a kind of machine which, after recording observations, sets about formulating definitions and laws, finally replacing phenomena by their expression in terms of conscious, deliberate, and definite potentials."

Valéry's error here, and one he makes repeatedly, is the conflation of method with mind. He supposes that if the scientist or mathematician employs an objective method and pursues disinterested ends, that the mind so engaged must become objective and disinterested too. This is clearly not the case. One must play by the rules, but passionately by them; someone whose emotive system is switched off will hardly be able to think creatively.

Nevertheless, the strategy of withdrawal was shrewd. Let the poet continue to compose; let the man, Valéry, love if he needed to; let him entertain confused ideas—marry, work, worry; he, the other Paul, would observe carefully, allowing the value of each enterprise to detach itself from its original aim and fasten instead to the successive acts which the undertaking may have required and then finally to reach for something principled and abstract which, if it were mastered, would render writing unnecessary: namely, the method of composition itself. To have the power, yet withhold its use; to be divine, and not create, is to possess a double strength. It is to say: I could if I would, and I *can*, so I won't. It is also the ultimate in fastidious disdain.

Just as someone in training may run, not to win, to defeat time, or eventually to cool off in the sweet breeze of applause, but to improve his wind and strengthen his muscles, so the mind may come to problems interested mainly in the results on itself of the exercise (I was told this myself, by liars, about Latin, and it is frequently said of crosswords and chess). So Valéry looked for the chief rewards of his thinking and "poetizing," and found them in their effect upon himself.

The difficulty is that one may strengthen one's muscles or thicken one's head as well by losing as winning; it is hard to become intrigued by the successive acts of a hack's composition; quality dominates and determines everything; and it will not do to excuse yourself from that lonely, unromantic, even grubby struggle with the worst and weakest of yourself for the strength and excellence of the best of yourself by pretending, as Valéry invariably did, that he wasn't a poet; that he came to poetry by accident and might, just as well, have done something else with his mind; that he regarded poetry's arbitrary and useless forms as a few absurd hurdles to be leaped as gracefully as possible or altogether ignored; that, in any case, his works were merely exercises; that they were never finished; that it was the sheerest happenstance that they were published when they were and in the form they had, and that, in fact, the same was true of his plays, dialogues, and essays.

They were simply called forth by occasions, he claimed, and composed upon command; they were on any old subject and tailored always for a special audience; furthermore they often had to meet some extremely silly requirements in order to come into existence at all—for example, the philosophical dialogue, "Eupalinos," which had to be, for the purposes of an elegant book's regimental design, exactly 115,800 letters long. Consequently nothing he did could be regarded as really polished, finished, or perfect—didn't he say so all the time? Thus it wouldn't do to be intense, serious, or terribly puffed, and Valéry seldom was. He was eloquent, graceful, jocular, always personal, easily distracted, disarmingly indirect (this amateur at everything), and he regarded the too solemnly ambitious with a certain scorn (tragic subjects? dear me, what bore!). No, he was merely, he maintained, a modest man of mind, a student of consciousness during, particularly, its early fumbling moments; he took a few notes . . . oh, he kept his notebooks the way some people keep cows—perhaps there would be a little milk.

It would not do, except that it did do very well. These cavalier "English" attitudes soon outgrew pose and became fixed traits of character. After passing his critical night, Valéry did not give up poetry at once, nor did he leave for Aden or Abyssinia to run guns as Rimbaud had. Relieved of the burden of having to measure up to Mallarmé or, for that matter, to the very sensual, highly romantic poet in himself, and imagining that now his life was to follow a dedicated straight line as he felt Descartes's had (even though, at this distance, we can see that it was to transcribe two great curves across the axes of poetry and prose: away, then toward, then away from poetry again); and taking as his model another omnivorous mind, Leonardo, who—he conveniently believed—had the same interest in method, the same drive toward perfection that resulted in similarly unfinished and fragmentary works, Valéry began keeping notebooks in earnest, rising at dawn every day like a priest at his observances to record the onset of consciousness, and devoting several hours then to the minutest study of his own mind.

This scrutiny was as disciplined and severe, he often bragged, as the practice of poetry. It was coldly impersonal . . . wasn't the calculus? And it began to soak up all his energies. Soon he would be silent. But in the eight years between the night of crisis and 1900, and before ceasing to publish for about a dozen years, Valéry wrote two important prose works: "Introduction to the Method of Leonardo da Vinci," and "An Evening with Monsieur Teste," the first expressing the theoretical aims of his new labors, the second revealing their psychological value.

Odd, mannered, doctrinaire, yet exquisitely wrought, "Monsieur Teste," from its famous opening line ("Stupidity is not my strong suit"), has seemed to its critics to show Valéry at his most arrogant and exasperating. Scarcely a fiction, it is scarcely anything else. Certainly it contains one of the more curious, though forthrightly named, characters in . . . in . . . what shall we say? fictosophy? "Mr. Head?" is that the right address? No, the wrong resonances. "Mr. Headstrong?" No, that's out of balance. Taken from an old French form of *tête* (shell, pot, head), *teste* also means "will/witness/testament," and thus combines, with only a little distortion, three qualities Valéry valued most at the time. In addition, *teste* refers to the *testes cerebri*, the optic lobes, which are called the testicles of the brain.

Although Valéry treats him with characteristically amused and skeptical reservations, Monsieur Teste nevertheless represents the ideal man of mind. He is a monster, and is meant to be—an awesome, wholly individualized machine—yet in a sense he is also the sort of inhuman being Valéry aimed to become himself: a Narcissus of the best kind, a scientific observer of consciousness, a man untroubled by inroads of worldly trivia (remember Villier de Lisle-Adam's symbolist slogan, "as for living, our servants will do that for us"?), who vacations in his head the way a Platonist finds his Florida in the realm of Forms. Like the good analytic philosopher he also resembles, Monsieur Teste complains constantly about the treacheries of words and the salad-forked tongue wagged so loosely by language (while his own name, perversely, is an excellent example of ambiguity well used). Teste has become almost pure potentiality, and a man in whom knowledge has finally made unnecessary the necessity to act.

Watching himself, then, Valéry grew as comfortable with contradiction as the best Hegelian. He noticed that in time attitudes would turn themselves inside out like gloves, go from bug to butterfly. He could deprecate his labors, but he would also increasingly insist upon their worth: the notebooks were his great work and he would be remembered, if at all, because of them. He sought absolute clarity, he said, and in those thoughts which, like Monsieur Teste, he felt no need to record, he pursued his thinking through ruthlessly to the end. It is curious that many of those which he did put down, and indeed published later, pursue nothing through to the end, but reveal, instead, when they don't read like diary entries or blotter jottings, that same love of aphorism, apothegm, and smart remark that is such a frequent failing of the French mind.

It's not that the notebooks aren't fascinating or important (they have yet to be translated in their entirety, but portions of them are printed as addenda to several volumes of the Bollingen *Collected Works*), it is simply that they do not come anywhere near making any methodological discovery. There are notes on love, life, literature, morals; on books read, people met, thoughts exchanged. In the actual notebooks, not the translated bits, there are cryptic lists, algebraic dithers and geometric doodles, maplike mental layouts, and occasionally a watercolor sketch: boats, windows, costumes, rooms.

A poet of the utmost formality, an admirer of ceremony, of the rigors and several clarities of mathematics; in fact, in the early thirties, in the political sphere, a little too impressed by order, though at one time, too, one of the few not a philosopher or logician who understood how much the architecture of a thought—its form—is really in the richest sense the thought itself (as this is wholly the case in poetry and the other arts); Valéry was nevertheless suspicious of systems.

He dismisses Descartes's philosophy with the suggestion

(which he could have borrowed from Nietzsche) that a thinker's effort to make his ideas acceptable may lead him, inadvertently, to disguise his central thought and conceal from others the actual insecurities and confusions of his mind. Systems are like forms for writing letters: they insure that any content will be harmonious, temperate, and polite. It will be "professional." It will be correct. Thus Valéry refused to regiment his thinking (which is the ego's way of saying it is unable to), and even his essays are organized, mainly, on esthetic lines. His further reluctance to express what cannot be expressed gracefully leads him to seem to tease the reader, rather than, as Valéry desired, to be exceptionally honest with him.

Although Valéry himself regarded the poet's biography as an impertinent irrelevance to the work which was his real life, to realize that Valéry's long devotion to his "notebooks" was an elaborate Maginot, a barrier he lay quietly behind until he was ready, again, to let the enemy in, is, it seems to me, the most important thing to know about him. After such resistance, such abnegation of gifts, how surprisingly easy was the change. In 1912 Gide suggests he print his early poems. Although Valéry has already attempted this several times, he expresses reluctance. A typescript is given to him and he is, he says, appalled. A few revisions . . . then quite a few, whole new stanzas. He will go ahead. Perhaps an introductory poem might be composed, a few verses . . . It is "La Jeune Parque," a poem which grows from 40 lines to 512, which occupies four years of work—years of war—and, preceding the volume it was expected to preface by three years, makes him famous. Completed finally in 1917, he dedicates it to Gide. Long, dense, difficult, personal, obscure: these are the critics' words. More unsummarizable poems—masterpieces—follow to fill out *Charmes*, which appears in 1922. All exercises, of course, all experiments, all accidents, all unfinished . . .

It is now plain that when Valéry returned to poetry it was as an altogether superior man, for what he had loved during that muffled time was not himself but a true image, an inversion, an opposite: against the vague indefiniteness of the symbolist poetry he had begun by admiring, he had placed the precision and crispness of mathematics; against practice he'd put theory, exchanging the careless literary use of ideas for their cautious, responsible, scientific employment; from the forms for feeling and desire he had turned away to study the structures of thought, working—in the phrase of Huysmans, one novelist he allowed himself to admire—always *au rebours*, against the grain, and consequently correcting in himself a severe and weakening lean in the direction of the mystical and romantic.

This extraordinary straightening up produced a poet who was not only supremely skilled in practice, and sound in theory, but one who did not feel his work so beset by other subjects that he had to make a castle of himself and dragons out of everything else. Above all, it enabled him eventually to achieve poems that created in their readers strange yet richly integrated states of consciousness—the mind as the face of a Narcissus. They were indelible evaporations, works in which the shadows that words cast had more weight than the words themselves, and whose effects were—in his own wonderfully reflexive phrase—like the *"frémissements d'une feuille effacée,"* the shiverings of an effaced leaf.

2

Built slowly, with a patience appropriate to the pyramid it is, and the pharaoh who lies within it, the Bollingen edition of *The Collected Works of Paul Valéry* has now reached the twelfth of its projected fifteen volumes.[2] More than a dozen prefaces and introductions grace it (by Eliot, Auden, and Wallace Stevens, among others almost as distinguished); twelve translators,

---

[2] In 1972, when this was written. The edition is now complete.

most of them gifted, have so far contributed their labors; and if, since 1956, when it was the first to appear, the most successful undertaking has been William McCausland Stewart's inspired version of the *Dialogues*, works which now seem unimprovable in English as well as French, the most difficult task has been that of David Paul, who has done the major poems, in addition to an excellent prose rendering of *Idée fixe*—a kind of extended conversation insufficiently ceremonious and solemn to be a dialogue. Valéry's late, unfinished play, *My Faust*, is Paul's work, too, as well as the poet's relaxed and anecdotal pieces on the painters, *Degas, Manet, Morisot*. If I say that Mr. Paul has been only intermittently successful with the poems, that is praise, for Valéry's poetry, like Mallarmé's, is not translatable.

And not because Valéry was merely a mouthpiece for the gods—he despised that pretense—but precisely because, while courting chance, he left nothing to it. His muse was a domestic. What are we otherwise to think of the efficient, modest maid who comes to make the poet's bed, flit among the mirrors, find fresh water for his flowers?

"Une esclave aux longs yeux chargés de molles chaînes." Long, shall we say her eyes are? slow? laden or burdened? and shall we believe her chains are slack, soft, loose—what? "A slave girl, her long eyes laden with soft chains," Mr. Paul decides to render it; yet are these words and these decisions about her eyes, her soul, her situation, or the poet's mind? How elusive the line is, wound in music like a gift in tissue, both wrapped and wrapping fragile as a bibelot, one as precious as the other. The language is so precisely used that its object cannot be exactly seen, for nothing is easier than to paint a resemblance, follow a line a leg makes, let the world do your creative work.

Every word in the poem has a dozen causes, so that when the poet suggests that this slave, maid, and muse of his can busy herself in his room, pass in and out of his sight without disturbing its preoccupied "absence," as glass passes through sunlight (*"Comme passe le verre au travers du soleil"*) without having to set in motion the machinery of the mind (*"Et de la raison pure épargne l'appareil"*), it is painful to hear Mr. Paul say instead: "As a windowpane traverses the sunshine/Leaving intact the appliances of pure reason," because now only the bare "idea" remains, rather stricken and emaciated, too, as though it had lain sick in a cell for some time.

A maid straightening a room: all right, we can translate that. And to the extent a writer achieves his effects through the invention and manipulation of fictional things and people (a skill which is not a linguistic one), these effects can be suggested in another tongue or even in another medium.

Thus it is possible for me to tell you that in one of Valéry's poems there is a rower on a river. Rhythmically bending and straightening as he must, seeming to move the world rather than himself as he passes between the banks and beneath bridges, his eyes wander downcast in a landscape of reflection.

On the other side of the sky, philosophers—and others momentarily like them—are combining their concepts in amusing, instructive, or dazzling ways, and to the degree these concepts can free themselves of the language in which they were originally expressed, they can travel without too much wear and tear. Plato was an artist of ideas, as Valéry suggests all philosophers should be, and that the body is a prison for the soul is one piece of philosophical poetry with which you and I can fairly easily acquaint ourselves without knowing much Greek.

With regard to "The Rower," then, I can indicate how Valéry imagines objects and their reflections, like Narcissus and the puddle-picture of himself he loved, to be like the images of burning which smoked the walls of Plato's cave; I can describe how, in the poem, the boat's prow is urged to divide the world which seems painted in the water, shattering its calm so that of such a massive stillness no memory will remain.

But Valéry bitterly objected to this kind of poetic play with ideas in Pascal and in other philosophers because he suspected them, lest reason fail, of using the methods of poetry, like the welcome lies of politicians, to persuade, and in this way debasing both truth and beauty. In Pascal, because he was not only a splendid writer but a fine mathematician, this Jansenist unscrupulousness was intolerable.

Of course I don't need to translate the poem's exterior design because I can exactly reproduce it; yet rhyme schemes, stanza forms, and even meters, not to say the sounds of words, their multiple associations and other shades, the syntax of the language, the tone of the "voice"—detached or angry—shared techniques, shared subjects and concerns, with all their risks, his very personal quirks, like the crotches of trees, as well as the traditions which the poet is a human and historic part of: all these—and many more—make their claims, often quite stubbornly and without any evident justice.

Valéry liked to think of forms as arbitrary obstacles set up simply for the sport, and he was happy to believe that the sport itself was one of resolution, harmony, wholeness; one in which the poet, by consciously calculated and successive steps, creates out of artificial and even antagonistic materials an object as mysteriously complete, continuous, and beautiful, as the shell of a mollusk or a spider's snare. Yet not an object like theirs designed to trap or protect, but one simply *willed*— made to be because the soul is finally satisfied only by what resembles it in its supremest dreams, when it is invincibly principled, and consequently something so inwardly radiant that, like the contours of a resting woman's body, as he writes in one poem, it has to be, itself, alive . . . alive to return our gaze. And yet it must also be an object as theirs sometimes is, since it must seem, against the actuality of its contrivance, instinctive, seamless, easy . . . as though exuded through a tube or spun from a gland. But no words of mine can convey the loveliness of style and idea contained in his finer essays, "Poetry and Abstract Thought," for example, or "Man and the Seashell."

For the translator, alas! Valéry's verse succeeds. It's so fastened to the word, so confined to the tongue which expresses it, there's no remainder. Such was his intention, and to pretend, when all else fails, by freer, more expansive measures, to find some poetic corollary elsewhere is like hunting through the music of the Balinese for the musical equivalent of *Till Eulenspiegel's Merry Pranks*. Mr. Paul does not obviously wander away, but what is near and what far in this connection? Here is a poet so careful he seems always to be walking upright on his own life as though it were a swaying wire. To render him, then, as if he were forgetful and a bit careless about his budget: how shall we measure this departure?

"The Rower" is a poet struggling upstream against time and the temptations of a pleasurable drift. His oars part him from the repeated grip of the river:

> *Je romprai lentement mille liens glacés*
> *Et les barbes d'argent de sa puissance nue.*

Mr. Paul, who with the less famous poems has sometimes taken the first meaning to fly by, not troubling himself about the sense of the whole, construes this pair as follows:

> *Piece by piece I shall break a thousand icy bonds,*
> *And the silvery barbs of her naked potency,*

which is, first, careless (you don't break bonds "piece by piece"), and then incorrect (*barbes* refers to a *lappet*, a kind of apron, here), so that the consequence is confusion, and the central meaning of the line, the sexual exposure of the river by violation of its surface, is lost. In the final verses of the poem, too, Mr. Paul interprets the poet's critical concluding act of defiance as . . . well, it simply isn't clear. The rower is passing beneath bridges whose darkness oppresses him.

> *the mind*
> *Lowers its sensitive suns, its ready eyelids,*
> *Until with a leap that clothes me with jewels*
> *I plunge into the disdain of all that idle azure.*

You should have to have a court order to use "azure" in English. The early poem, "Helen," begins "*Azur! c'est moi . . . ,*" which Mr. Paul renders, "Azure, it is I!" Lowell quite properly avoids the word. "I am the blue!" his poem cries, which isn't right either, but—never mind—the poem that follows is a brilliant one, if not by Valéry.

Then to transcribe these famous lines of "The Cemetery by the Sea":

> *Midi le juste y compose de feux*
> *La mer, la mer, toujours recommencée!*

in which Valéry describes the light of the noon sun falling with the kind of impartial light we get in certain classical paintings —everywhere in a rain of right angles—so that the quiet sea has no slopes with which it can contrive a shadow, and consequently seems composed of fire; a fire, indeed, like that which is said to consume the phoenix, death and birth proceeding so continuously that nothing appears to change—to transcribe these lines as

> *Justicer Noon out there compounds with fires*
> *The sea, the sea perpetually renewed!*

is to replace a delicate balance of ideas with simple awkwardness. And as the poet's shining wine subsides in its glass, the remainder remains sweetly sticky still, like flat pop.

Valéry always insisted that his interest in poetry lay in the *work*, not in the poem: in the successive acts of composition which were, for him, like the moves of a dancer passing gracefully from one position to another. And if poetry stood to prose as dancing did to walking, as he liked to say, then it did so because, like dancing, its motions served no master but the mind at play which designed them; because it became a continuum: there was the art! by seeking minuter and minuter modulations, by the steady overlay of straight lines, to achieve the curve first, and then the circle—a visible summation of many nearly invisible steps and decisions.

Shatter a stone and the bits you make are simply further stones, but break a seashell or a poem and every piece will continue to declare itself a fragment of some whole. Dancing supervenes upon the serious business of walking the way a child's skip-a-longs and fence-balancings accompany him as he makes his imperfect way to school. Unlike prose, poetry is not a kind of communication, but a construction in consciousness. Words in ordinary speech and trade . . . they disappear before their messages do, disposable as Kleenex; but the cry of fire in a crowded room, if it is eloquently framed and sweet enough, will snuff all sense of burning. The form will hold us there.

. . . and we become a light white ash.

Through long years of patient dedication Valéry advanced by means of even detours toward the outline of a powerful poetic theory, and I am convinced, as Auden remarks in one of the several excellent introductions to *The Collected Works*, that "In his general principles . . . Valéry is right past all possibility of discussion."

Permanence and repeatability were two qualities which Valéry thought essential. Sensations are usually simply used, or canceled by others, and those which we wish to prolong belong, he said, to "the esthetic infinite." He only glimpsed another possibility: that as the demand for culture grew it would be necessary to create along other lines, for poetry is presently composed as the paper in picnic plates is shaped. When the beans have been consumed, and the plates scraped, they can be ditched or burned. New ones appear in the stores every day, some with dashing designs, and so sturdily constructed they can carry a glass. Tomorrow, too, there will be further festivals, clean blankets and new friends, fresh glass.

Perhaps Valéry rather naïvely believed the novelists when they announced (as Zola, for example, did every day in the press) their plans to make to the world a present of reality . . . believed, that is, in the sincerity of their pretensions, although shocked by their performance. Perhaps his commitment to excellence was too great, and in poetry the sacred purity of vocabulary, narrowness of subject, the neatness of small forms and the satisfaction of their palpable tightness, shut his eyes, as a cat's eyes shut, in self-centered satisfaction.

In any case he did not understand Flaubert; he took little interest in Proust; about the great works of Mann and Joyce he was very noticeably silent, and of such exemplars of oddity as Gertrude Stein I doubt he ever heard; but there were, in the works he did examine, so many pages of "information," so many events, traits, qualities, and verbal formulations which could just as well have been otherwise—so much invented gossip, so many inexpressive details—that he failed to observe what his own attitudes had helped make possible: how the techniques of the modern novel were rapidly becoming the strategies of the long poem, and that original forms were being designed for such extended breaths—new chests were necessary, and larger lungs.

Edmund Wilson once wrote that Valéry's prose, "in spite of the extravagant respect with which it is treated by his admirers, is by no means so remarkable as his verse," but I find myself unable to agree. The curve that carried Valéry away from poetry a second time, and plunged him, as it seemed, in notoriety (he threw open doors and cut ribbons, made addresses, lectured, wrote testimonials and prefaces, responded to requests, modestly discussed his own successes, and in 1925 accepted election to the French Academy), led him at the same time to create his dialogues, the "Eupalinos" among them, one of the most original and moving pieces of prose in any language.

The empirical distinction between poetry and prose is a wholly illusory one, a fact of which Valéry was at times perfectly aware, for the French have pioneered the prose poem; Valéry admired Rimbaud's, and wrote not a few himself; he also dabbled in the story, wrote "Monsieur Teste," of course, made jots of plots, especially fancying the kind of flat, weird, metaphysically menacing situations Lettau could find stimulating, as Borges certainly did.

Valéry could never quite give himself up to prose (prose as he had got in the bad habit of defining it), and this accounts, at least in part, for the flicker in his thought which one often finds in the essays. Perhaps his mind was too playful, perhaps it danced when it should have walked or harshly stomped, yet what is striking in even his most occasional pieces—let alone the famous ones like "The Crises of the Mind" or "The Outlook for Intelligence"—is his remarkable prescience, so that even brief asides ("Perhaps waste itself has become a public and permanent necessity"), made in 1940, or 1932, or 1929, fall further over and into the present than any wholesome shadow should. It's not just his style alone that sometimes causes the scalp to prickle.

I suspect that Valéry's success as a wise man was not due to his Leonardo-like ambitions, because his studies were not as universal or as thorough as he liked to let on, and the central concern of his life was a stubbornly restricted one; nor was it because he reasoned like a Teste, for his mind was essentially metaphoric in its operation (what he knew and liked most about architecture, for example, was almost wholly embodied in the very idea of "building"); and although his sovereign detachment certainly helped him and he was instinctively right about what to despise, he was particularly a master of the sidelong look, and the practice of composition over many years had taught him to attend to "little" things and small steps, for

there, in scrupulosities only a spider might otherwise pain itself with, were the opportunities for genius. It is Valéry, himself, who writes:

> Great events are perhaps so only for small minds. For
> more attentive minds, it is the unnoticed, continual events
> that count.

It was these small movements of which Valéry was such
a master, if we think of them as the movements of a mind
which has practiced passage to the point of total purity, com-
pressing those steps, those postures and attitudes which were
learned at the mirror so painfully, into one unwinding line of
motion; and as we follow the body of his thought as we might
that of an inspired dancer, leaving the source of his energy like
flame, we have presented almost to our eye other qualities in
addition to those normally thought vital and sufficient for the
mind, though rare and prized like clarity and rigor, honesty,
openness, interest, penetration and brevity, truth; that is to
say, lightness, tact in particular, and above all, elegance and
grace.

Sartre on Theater

Act One

The curtain rises, and Sartre, coming forward to address his audience, says:

> The chief source of great tragedy—the tragedy of Aeschylus and Sophocles, of Corneille—is human freedom. Oedipus is free; Antigone and Prometheus are free. The fate we think we find in ancient drama is only the other side of freedom. Passions themselves are freedoms caught in their own trap.[1]

Observe the speech and not the speaker. There is first the round unguarded expression of essence, and the little exemplary list, notable for what it leaves out, then the ritual invocation of freedom (better than *patrie*, *gloire*, or god), followed by an outrageous falsehood (Oedipus is free) which is rhetorically removed with one rub of a paradox put epigrammatically. There will be a lot of this.

But what should we expect from a character on the stage? Surely not argument, fairness to fact, or niceness of distinc-

[1] *Sartre on Theater*, edited by Michel Contat and Michel Rybalka (New York: Pantheon, 1976).

tion. Eloquent outcry, rather. Soft soap. Pithy remark. Snappy retort. Short shrift.

Four years earlier, in 1943, Sartre had described his own play, *The Flies*, as a tragedy of freedom composed in direct contrast to the Greek tragedies of fate. Using the same formula —that fate is inverted freedom—Sartre then said of his character, Orestes: "I have shown him as a prey to freedom, just as Oedipus is a prey to his own destiny." Sartre had not yet seen how to liberate Oedipus, but we can follow the maneuver quite easily now. Over the years the mind drifts, Sartre's most especially, and by philosophically freeing Orestes in his own play, Sartre came to feel that he had freed Oedipus in the two plays of Sophocles.

> For freedom is not some vague abstract ability to soar above the human predicament; it is the most absurd and the most inexorable of commitments. Orestes will go onward, injustifiable, with no excuse and with no right of appeal, alone. Like a hero. Like all of us.[2]

And beneath the weight of such flattery we rise like balloons.

The theater today, Sartre said, when interviewed in 1959, must be philosophical. Philosophy itself? It is dramatic.[3] And Sartre has always been theatrical. In this same interview, for example, we find the following stagey sentences: "If literature is not everything, it is worth nothing," and "What is the literature of an epoch but the epoch appropriated by its literature?" and "You have to aspire to *everything* to have hopes of doing *something*," again "literature finds its *initial* impulse in silence," or "Any string of words *whatsoever* . . . calls everything we have done into question . . ." He warns us that his long study of Flaubert is a kind of fiction. "It might indeed be called a novel. Only I would like people to say it was a true novel."[4]

---

[2] *Sartre on Theater*, p. 187. ·

[3] This and the quotes which immediately follow are taken from "The Purpose of Writing," in *Between Existentialism and Marxism* (New York: Pantheon, 1975).

[4] From "The Itinerary of a Thought," in *Between Existentialism and Marxism*.

Our complicity in Sartre's passions is presumed to be complete. We are embarrassed by psychology in the theater, he tells us. We are unmoved by inevitability. We are pressed into this "we" like the buttocks of a crowd on bleachers. Antigone's dilemma—the antagonism between family loyalty and civic duty—no longer makes much sense, Sartre insists. It is foreign to the Kennedys, we begin to ask; it was out of place at Watergate? But the act has changed; we don't want to miss the seals; our objections slip through the seats and disappear among the struts and props of our support. No indeed, it can't be the world we're in. It must be the theater.

In any case the formula is familiar enough: the duty of any drama is to unify its audience by depicting human beings in extreme existential situations: extreme because one outcome can be death; existential because choice, though limited, is unconditioned and unconditional; and situational because it is the context of challenge which counts, not the character or the character's fossilized past.

This is a dramatic disjunction indeed. We are compelled to wonder whether Macbeth, as he allows his lady to stiffen his resolve, is choosing what he will become or expressing what he is. He is not permitted to do both.

> Immerse men in these universal and extreme situations which leave them only a couple of ways out, arrange things so that in choosing the way out they choose themselves, and you've won—the play is good.[5]

As easy as talking on the phone. And so this performance begins.

Sartre on Theater is a beautifully edited collection of all the bits and pieces of opinion which Sartre has left behind in this place or that while he's had his show on the road: a sanatorium at Bouffémont or the main hall of the Sorbonne, a reel of

---

[5] "For a Theater of Situations," in *Sartre on Theater*.

tape here, another there, as though he had forgotten his coat in Tokyo or lost his left shoe in New York—feuilletons, fusillades, conversations, interviews, debates, book blurb, a bit of letter, record liner, squib, a casual talk, a few formal lectures —now raked together the way Isis gathered the body of her brother, and restored not to Sartre exactly but to us; for we might not have recognized the first time that these aperçus and appraisals were gifts, we might have naïvely thought they were merely left shoes.

The earliest piece dates from 1940, but except for the most recent, which consists of a few short selections on "the paradox of the actor" from Sartre's study of Flaubert, *L'Idiot de la famille,* these are responses to specific questions or occasions, directed toward particular audiences, the shots of an author zigzagging under fire more than the reflections of a philosopher calmly waiting on his stool to be dunked, and in that way they partake of the theater in terms of form, occasion, and delivery, as well as subject.[6]

So these are the notes of an old campaigner; they focus on present issues as if the present were of more than passing importance; theories are regarded as presented with three-line simplicity; slogans are flashed; there is much easy assessment and plenty of name-calling; and it is thought very important that the masses think alike and rightly.

The distance between Sartre's serious work as a philosopher (in *Being and Nothingness,* say, or the *Critique of Dialectical Reason*) and the mainly momentary verbal encounters recorded here is more than customarily enormous. Sartre's changes of mind are legendary, and he now confesses to being shocked by some of his earlier opinions.

---

[6] Commenting on "Forgers of Myths," one of the essays collected here, after it appeared in 1946, Eric Bentley wrote that it was "the typical Sartre compound: bold to the point of temerity, confident to the point of cocksureness, magnificent to the point of pretentiousness." Bentley's paper is reprinted in *Sartre: A Collection of Critical Essays,* edited by Edith Kern (New York: Prentice-Hall, 1962).

The other day, I re-read a prefatory note of mine to a collection of these plays—*Les Mouches, Huis Clos* and others —and was truly scandalized. I had written: "Whatever the circumstances, and wherever the site, a man is always free to choose to be a traitor or not . . ." When I read this, I said to myself: it's incredible, I actually believed that![7]

Sartre will doubtless find some of his current opinions equally extreme, since he likes to look over the edge of an idea like a tourist at a canyon; and his mind has always been both centrifugal and parochially sensitive to the present; so when he uses the word 'universal,' it most often means, "generally obtaining at the time." That's why the Greeks grow out of date. And why the conflict between clan and city can no longer interest us. That's why the recurrent word in these interviews and statements on the theater is 'now,' though in this volume "now" lasts thirty years; why it made sense to devote a half of *What Is Literature?* to "The Situation of the Writer in 1947," and why, in reply to criticisms, Sartre can calmly say: "I wrote *L'Etre et Le Néant* after the defeat of France, after all . . ."[8] or respond to the suggestion that *The Flies* is perhaps not the best play to perform before Germans because it "bestows a gigantic pardon," by admitting that the issue turns "on the question how far a play which may have been good in 1943, which was valid at that time, still has the same validity and, in particular, validity in 1948. The play must be accounted for by the circumstances of the time."[9]

So throughout these pieces he serenely repeats the collec-

---

[7] "The Itinerary of a Thought."

[8] There is a wholly minor but amusing indecision about how to print the title of this book—as Hazel Barnes has it in her translation, *L'Être et le Néant?* or as Danto does it, *L'Être et le néant?* or as Jameson spells it in *Marxism and Form*, *L'Etre et le néant?* or finally as *L'Etre et Le Néant* as it's done in *Between Marxism and Existentialism?*

[9] The problem is placed before Sartre by Professor Steiniger following a performance of *The Flies* in Berlin in 1948. Recorded in *Sartre on Theater*.

tive "we don't think that way now" when he means that although most of us are always out of step, we ought to keep up, perceive the immediate situation, just as, when existentialism became *passé*, Sartre nonetheless kept *au courant* (in 1943 anxiety was a universal sickness of the spirit, but mankind had so recovered by 1947 that the disease was confined to the bourgeoisie), and who can predict what character will follow the letter Mao?

It is this recurrent certainty, this calm acceptance of the nonce, this franchising of fads, which has made his readers morally uneasy.[10] There is in the reduction of ideas to praxis, in a too noisily vibrating intelligence, a not very carefully concealed determinism of circumstances like the song of the windharp; just as one might praise or excuse Plato by saying that after all, the *Republic* was written after the disgrace of Greek democracy, the fall of Athens, and the death of Socrates— facts which no one will dispute, and facts which remain philosophically irrelevant. To suggest that a work is principally a reply to local conditions is to suggest that it is unimportant.[11] Ideas have their sordid grounds and conditions, their secret social motives, a private itch they are a public scratch to, but what is exactly central to philosophy is the effort to propose

---

[10] John Weightman, who is favorably disposed toward Sartre, recently wrote (in *The Times Literary Supplement* for June 25, 1976): "If I have a reservation about him . . . it is that he is always so imperturbably sure that he is now in the right, even after changing his mind so many times. All the criticism levelled against him runs off him like water off a duck's back . . . what they [critics] say, or have said, has no relevance to Sartre's intimate conviction that the only relative truth is represented by his own ideas, as they can be formulated at the moment . . . He is a changeable dogmatist, and an ideological authoritarian who does not really accept *le dialogue*." Etc.

[11] Many of Sartre's current commentators understand this, so they are busy establishing continuities between the master's early, early middle, middle middle, late middle, and early late periods. Fredric Jameson rereads *L'Être et le néant* through the enlarging lens of the *Critique de la raison dialectique* in *Marxism and Form* (Princeton, 1971), and does so brilliantly, while Mark Poster argues that "*Being and Nothingness* does provide a concept of freedom adequate for a renewed Marxism" in *Existential Marxism in Postwar France* (Princeton, 1975). Unfortunately some critics, most of them Marxists, measure everything in terms of Sartre's approach to or departure from their own jargon-draped dogmas, which is like measuring the extent of a flood by how close the water comes to your foot.

and argue views whose validity will transcend their occasions, and not to manufacture notions which, when squeezed, will simply squirt out causes like a sponge. If that effort cannot succeed (as we know in many cases it does not), then philosophy becomes a form of conceptual fiction, and new determinants of quality, equally harsh and public, must be employed.

As a space, the present has been oversold. It is simply what the future, pushed roughly by the past, falls flat in. That's rather nice, I think. So shall I say that I believe it?

The moment overwhelms in other ways. The lively force and narcissistic drama of one's situation, like a passion or a toothache for which the world shuts shop, so only one's wound is open, only one's pain is beating, easily leads to the conviction that the rush of lust through the loins, the ache, the ear which won't stop ringing, are universal conditions of consciousness, and that the utterly personal solutions one has adopted constitute a program of relief and reform.[12] What a change being out of love brings; what a blessing silence is, or the departure of pain; and what a rush, then, of opinion in the opposite direction.

One is reminded of similar contradictions in Sartre's great opposite, Bertrand Russell: the careful, profound, and creative logician displaced by a careless and unoriginal historian; the shrewd and sophisticated epistemologist coupled with a naïve social critic and marital adviser—one pictures a unicorn hitched to a beer wagon—so that cautious investigation alternates with a pellmell rush into opinion; the genuine lifelong though abstract concern for humanity unbalanced by an occasional personal indifference and even fickleness and cruelty;

---

[12] A beautiful example of the way personal exigencies can be given the dignity of radical purpose is furnished by Simone de Beauvoir, who remarked, after she and Sartre had established a *ménage à trois* with Olga Kosakiewicz, "we thought that human relations are to be perpetually invented, that a priori no form is privileged, none impossible . . ." Poster quotes this (p. 76) and then says, with a naïveté I had thought gone from the world: "Although these arrangements cannot be identified with socialist politics, at least they indicate a self-conscious refusal of conventional mores." The refusal took a solidly bourgeois form. If Olga had been Fred Kosak, a sandhog, however . . .

the deeply private work and pure reflection which is weakened
by the need to embrace popular causes and at great cost fight
the good fight when from the public there is nothing to be
caught but the clap; the adversary psychology, the small boy
who will suddenly dash from ampersand and implication, an-
guish and *en soi*, to pee on a bed of pansies (in round: the English dervish and the French hoop); however, it is symptomatic
of their profound difference as philosophers that when Russell
tells us he has a passion for knowledge, it is easy to believe
him, because Russell wanted desperately to discover the real
way the world was, while Sartre's concern has never been for
reality as such, but for his own relation to it, and consequently
for the quality and character and content of what he would
eventually come to think about it.

Act Two

Imagine that I am a man who eats his dinner daily and that I
am in a restaurant, gazing at the menu. If I ask for something
not on the carte, chances are I won't get it, but I've no grounds
for complaint since I could have gone to *La Bête Noire* where
the *bête à laine* is always superb, as are each of the other
bêtes; however I wanted the fine view of the square one has
from *Café Cul de Sac*, and all the girls. I feel the weight of custom, too: not to order soup as a side dish or begin with pie.
Some of the entrees are too expensive for me; the chateau-
briand is for two; I hate tongue; the last time I was here the
stew gave off a pale gray taste like Auschwitz smoke, an experience I'd just as soon not repeat; a newspaper review has described the *culotte de boeuf* as a gourmet's delight. All of these
factors, in varying degrees, limit and condition my choices. I
can decide to impress the waiter, pamper my ulcer, defy my
childhood training, overcome my horror of beets, ignore religious taboos, or honor my vow to remain a vegetarian until my
first poem is published.

Or I can choose as the kind of man I wish to become would choose, for no matter how loose or straitened my circumstances, there is always an alternative for my future self to select, so when I indicate to the waiter that I shall have escargots and salad with perhaps a half-carafe of quiet white, I am arranging my meal as a part of a *project* (a series of acts with a unifying aim), as a dancer might diet or a weightlifter gorge on meat.

Since the act of ordering is itself a mere snip from a lengthy trajectory, it cannot possibly be the simple sum of my present limitations and my past conditioning, as the bourgeois would prefer to describe it, because my act would then be deprived of both freedom and purpose, and I should be relieved of any responsibility for it. But I do not fly south as blindly as the birds; I choose to be a person of a certain sort: saint or sinner, ruler or servant, philosopher or fool. I can justify my diet on the grounds that I want to be a dancer, but the final self I desire to be is simply chosen—I am free—and there is no rational way to justify picking one long-term project rather than another.

As for myself, well, I'm in training to be the ultimate gentleman, a man of supreme refinement like white sugar, and so I order escargots. I am engaged and mealtimes are a part of my situation; that is, all my surrounding circumstances are seen and weighed and evaluated in the light of my long-range plans. Not for me is life a meaningless scatter. The café gives me another opportunity to discriminate further among garlic butters. It is my projects which bring values into existence. They make my perceptions particular, and it is my particular perceptions which make me. Some projects are plainly less encompassing than others, hence the great advantage in choosing to be a novelist or philosopher: nothing now falls outside my situation.

"I am the self I will be, in the mode of not being it," Sartre explains, rather badly, in *Being and Nothingness*. The paradox of purpose to which he refers is best exemplified by Aristotle's famous teleological proof for the existence of God. God is that condition of complete actuality or self-absorbed thought toward which the material world is continuously straining, but of course if this is so, as the proof claims, then God's existence lies ahead, around some bend in Becoming, and all we have at present to consider divine are small as droplets, though one day they'll be parts of a sacred sea; here or there the whistle of pure thought through a soul, this or that Russell-like mind brooding on the structures of argument and looking for interstices in demonstrations. "The decisive conduct will emanate from a self which I am not yet."

Although modern biologists have washed purpose out of nature the way we scrub down walls, they have never denied what Aristotle had so carefully observed and documented: that among plants, animals, and men (if not among things), there were very predictable patterns of growth and development: that each growing season carrots pushed themselves like pegs into the ground, onions layered, the dogwood fought its way through the raining air; that flowers did not bloom before bursting into bud and then sow their petals like seeds, sometimes on sand, sometimes on snow, or the maples burn with colors hitherto unseen, and then, having lost their leaves, commence to grow; that human infants became men and women of much the same color and configuration as their parents on a rather regular basis, though with generally discouraging results.

Aristotle tried to explain these interesting but he thought innocuous phenomena by supposing that living things could be more than merely described (which is all Sartre seems ready to allow is possible for persons); they could be defined. There was a discoverable list of interrelated characteristics which earned any individual its place in a species, and Aristotle quite reasonably believed that some of these characteristics were developmental, so that the essence of a human infant included not only the baby it was but the adult it would become.

In a sentence with considerable Germanic presumption, Sartre tells us how he wants that relationship (of present to future self) understood:

> Thus the self which I am depends on the self which I am not yet to the exact extent that the self which I am not yet does not depend on the self which I am.
>
> *(Being and Nothingness)*

To display the relation in other words: I shall love you only if you do not love me . . . an odd but not unheard-of arrangement, one which exists so long as it is not symmetrical. But that is odd indeed, because the relationship constitutes and sustains itself. Fatherhood is asymmetrical too, but I am not the father of my children precisely to the extent that they are not a parent of mine.

My table in the restaurant seats me in the center of a real situation because the entire meal is eaten in a context of significant action, action which will in part alter the world and move me closer to the fulfillment of my project—the realization of a value. Sartre sometimes writes as if one's project involved the wholesale rejection of the present, but this is clearly not so. One sometimes acts to slow change, or to employ the present the way one uses a library, reaffirming values while bringing about others.

In all this my essence is hardly my enemy, although Sartre acts as if essence were some dark blot on the family past which ought to be kept secret. In fact, Aristotle's definition of man limits his behavior about as much as a mesh fence around the solar system, and the ends ascribed to any class are so general I should never think to mention them if someone were to question me, for the purposes of my *species* are rarely *mine*. I do not exist to breed, but from the point of view of biology, what else am I fit for?

Camus's Caligula chooses to be a tyrant, Macbeth chooses to become a murderer and usurper, I choose to become a connoisseur. In effect, to choose one's destiny is to choose not to be free, even if Sartre would dislike this formulation. It is either to create a character and then to insist on acting within it (that's the way I am and the way I intend to remain), or it is to set in motion causes whose consequences increasingly compress the future into a narrow channel, as one who robs or kidnaps finds the rituals of chase and capture, courts and confinement, quickly close around him like fingers in a fist.

To choose a destiny, however, as Sartre insists, is not to obtain one, because I must continuously will my future. I can have them clear the snails away and bring me franks and beans. You must call yourself a saint again tomorrow and suffer another nail. The intellectual's position is both easier and more perilous than most because writing effects little (Sartre sometimes says),[13] and is normally accompanied by fewer risks, while crimes and coups can box you in. At the same time, a blow struck today may require another be struck tomorrow. The violent man will always find public support for his conception of himself. But opinions do nothing but implant in others the expectation that their owner will continue to cherish them like children. In short, every free act imperils its own base by creating conditions that encourage its repetition, a trap which Sartre has so far managed to avoid. Yet if I am to carry out my project, what else can I do? The existentialist wants to will himself . . . no . . . the existentialist wills to want to will himself: "I choose to be such and such a sort"; but he hates it when others say of him: "Oh, he's such and such a sort"; because he knows it is his will which daily denies the flesh, and

---

[13] "After the war, we felt once more that books, articles, etc. could be of use. In fact they were of no use whatever. Then we came to feel—or at least I did—that books conceived and written without any specific relation to the immediate situation could be of long-term use. And these turned out to be just as useless, for the purpose of acting on people . . ." ("The Purposes of Writing," in *Existentialism and Marxism*). This was said in 1959. Notice how short Sartre's long-term is. Already over. Unlike Stendhal, he does not regard his works as lottery tickets and count only on being reprinted in the next century.

my will which impels me from escargots to Dobosch Torte, whereas others see him as a fearful neurotic and myself as a gluttonous gourmet, a slave to the snobbery of my stomach.

Aristotle had argued that virtue ought to be a habit; that honesty was second nature to the honest man (who thus has, after all, a created essence), but Sartre prefers the Christian position: that virtue consists of a continuous self-conscious triumph over temptation; and it would appear that in order to prove that the temptation is there, it is periodically necessary to succumb to it. How will *les autres* know I'm free, if my behavior is consistent?

There is no such thing as an isolated freedom—any circumstance will contain the intersection of my projects with others—and the new religious theater of the folk which Sartre speaks about will give us *agons*—conflicts of right in the form of reenacted clashes of passion; because only by means of passion can we portray the whole man. In 1944 Sartre was saying that "anyone performing an act is convinced that he has a right to perform it." In 1960 he is making this claim about the passions: "passion is a way of finding oneself in the right, of referring to a whole social world of claims and values to justify the fact that one wishes to keep, take, destroy, or construct something." I happen to agree with Sartre that feelings are cognitions (though frequently faulty) and that values are fundamental ingredients of them, but Sartre draws a thick line between feelings and passions and rolls with characteristic unconcern over an entire series of faulty implications like a train over a bad track.

> For what is passion? Does a jealous man, for instance, emptying a revolver into his rival, kill for passion? No, he kills because he believes he has a right to kill. . . . jealousy implies a right; if you have no right over the person with you, you may be very unhappy because she does not like you any more, because she is deceiving you; but there will be no passion.   *("Epic Theater and Dramatic Theater")*

Let us take a case and see what we can discriminate within it.

I am furious because this nigger's dog has just shit on my lawn. I strike him smartly across his sassy black face with a length of sprinkler hose. Then it turns out that it was not his dog but a neighbor's. Man . . . am I mad at that nigger now.

First, when I strike anyone, I usually strike those whom I dare to strike. Second, those whom I dare to strike are rarely the ones whom I should like to strike. So I frequently strike substitutes . . . like my children. Do my feelings claim the right to do that? Or I mistake my enemy and call the wrong dog to a duel. Do my feelings claim the right to revenge myself in the wrong way, at the wrong time and place, toward the wrong persons, and with respect to the wrong things? Third, even when it is really the person who has wronged me whom I've struck, and even if I feel I have then a right to my anger, does it follow that I have a right to the blow? If, frustrated, tired, and angry, I beat my baby, will I want to claim my feelings claimed a right? Anger often arises from the recognition that one is in the wrong, and it is the wronged one I blame and beat. This person has been the instrument of my mistake, so I hate him all the more. He has made me look bad.

What Sartre's language unwittingly suggests is this: I come home unexpectedly and find my wife in bed with the black man I had beaten with the hose. As soon as I assess the scene, I realize no jury will convict. I have a right to kill my rival. So naturally I do so. Of course this is a travesty of Sartre's intention. When he says that the jealous man kills "because he has a right" he means that the man is free of moral scruples.

Observe not the speaker or the speech then, but the techniques. Sartre first locates something that may sometimes be true of some feelings (and perhaps *ought* to be true of them all). This is universalized. Then objectified. We may begin with a claim, but we end with an implication. The ontological proof got along on less. Finally, if someone produces a case where there is a feeling but clearly no right, let alone a claim of one, as in the case of the mother who beats her child, he points out that he was not speaking of mere feelings, but of passions (which always do claim a right). In short, he turns his statement into a definition and begs the question.[14]

The point I am belaboring is essential to Sartre's theory of the theater: it is an arena in which we perceive ultimate projects in collision, these represented to us through the display of passions which claim a right to the acts which express them. These actions, furthermore, are irreversible and must be ridden like a bobsled to the end, becoming more and more radical, picking up speed. Language must be seen as a kind of action, too. Its function is not to describe conditions or reveal character, but in effect to do battle.

We are once again confronted by an emotional definition like still another snake on the trail. "A real action is irreversible," he says. Then the following are not real actions: (1) I write "phooey" in the margin of a book and then decide the word is too adolescent so I erase it; (2) I buy a TV but return it to the store when I find that it's defective; (3) I sign your death warrant but countermand the order before the soldiers reach your cell; (4) I swallow rather too many sleeping pills but help is at hand and they pump out my stomach in time. Of course there is a trivial sense in which nothing done can be wholly undone, and there are always varying degrees of doing and undoing, but that is not what Sartre has in mind.

I think we can detect in Sartre's attitude here, as elsewhere, a contempt for common sense, as though it were the condition of a cowardly mind. There is the need to push a thought toward an extreme formulation, and to hurtle every obstacle, logical or otherwise, which may lie in the path of that push. The free act may be irreversible, but the theatrical act must be irrevocable; the free man can always stop, abandon

---

[14] In context, the argument is even worse than this. Sartre begins by distinguishing between good passions and bad (blind) ones, but within the space of a few sentences, he has forgotten the difference and is talking generally again.

his project, change direction, for actions do not stay up to party after their agents have gone to bed, but Sartre is perfectly aware that an aborted tragic action will not look well on the stage; that we cannot have Macbeth decide he's had enough of the usurpation business and refuse to murder Banquo, who, after all, is a fine brave fellow. The theatrical act, as he says, "wipes out the characters who were there at the beginning" in its demand to express itself. Yet this dramatic necessity gives us a Macbeth who is overpowered by his passions, who is weaker than his wife, who is increasingly constrained by circumstances, who is ridden by the actions he once rode.

Antigone and Creon represent opposing terms of a fundamental political contradiction which rent but also animated Greek society. According to Sartre, the contemporary theater places such conflicts inside the protagonist, and the action of the play arises from and reflects these contradictions. However, Sartre immediately slips from the stage into psychology. "A man," he says, "only acts insofar as internal contradictions are the driving force of his action." By his action he severs himself from these contradictions (how this happens isn't clear), escaping them to achieve an end, but the act itself must continue to embody contradictions (whether the same ones or others isn't clear).

Freud provides us with many examples of such acts—the inappropriate gift, for instance. You can't drive, hate every shade of red, all ostentation, and own a house with a dinky garage, so I give you a pink Cadillac. This gift beautifully blends my generosity and my meanness, my knowledge of your likes and my disdain for them, my sense of indebtedness to you and my dislike of that situation. But Sartre's principal case (Brecht's Galileo, who both pioneers a new science and abjures it) reveals the contradiction by successive actions, and furthermore the conflict is not truly an *inner* one. Left to himself, Galileo would have continued to advance science. Left to himself, he would not have abjured his doctrines.

The bourgeois theater tries to persuade people (for its own foul purposes) that all acts are failures, and so the People's Theater, which Sartre supports, must show that this simply isn't so. The tragic action achieves success in the radicalization of itself, but it is hard to imagine what the success of inherently contradictory acts would be, for the various aims are likely to inhibit one another, making it impossible for any one of them to fully express itself—neither my meanness nor my generosity. They are crippled by the conflict which gave rise to them, and of which they are an expression.

Act Three

We may understand what this flummery-mummery on the stage is all about, but what is it for? It is for the good of the Folk, and the reformation of the Bourgeoisie? O dear.

There are two kinds of theater which are satisfactory to Sartre: dramatic theater and epic theater. The difference lies mainly in the relation established between those on the boards and those in the seats. It is characteristic of epic theater to put the audience at an esthetic distance from the action, as Brecht famously does; to insist that what is being seen is a performance; and to inhibit participation and identification. In dramatic theater the audience is presented with an image of itself which it recognizes and joins, but bourgeois theater also does this, and Sartre begins by rejecting the idea of participation because the bourgeois use it so effectively as a weapon.

The distinction is a general one, and can be drawn between novels with equal ease. I can identify with David Copperfield, regardless of my sex, and participate in his growing up. Dickens certainly does nothing to discourage this identification. In the first place, Copperfield's life transcribes a successful arc, as I should like mine to, and passes through socially defined and acceptable stages which I have traversed or can expect to. His problems are those which anyone might have. In the second place, Copperfield has only soft or sympathetic vices; evil occupies itself with other people; and there is no ambiguity about values. I can fling myself wholeheartedly into his life, share his joys, his griefs, mistakes too, without danger to my self-esteem.

Humbert Humbert, on the other hand, is clearly a fabrication; he is scarcely nice; he is embarked upon a most dubious sexual adventure; he is subtle, devious, complex; there is no telling what will turn up. Certain sexual titillations may invite my deeper participation, but I cannot trust the style. It is cold and cutting, too careful, intellectually too superior, too self-conscious. It obtrudes itself like a head in the beam of the projector, and my satisfactions are short-lived and uneasy.

As Sartre sees it, the advantage of dramatic theater is its greater emotional effect. It fashions an image of my situation. It plays my song. I sing along. Dickens can effectively expose the Victorian exploitation of children, for example; but he can also encourage me to be sentimental about poverty and find the poor in some ways privileged. It is difficult, furthermore, to limit identification. A bourgeois can worm his way into the soul of a militant radical who dies for his cause, because "while he rejects the *substance* of the play, he will be attracted by the formal design of heroism." In any case, when I am singing my song, I do not quite hear it, and epic theater forces me to listen as if I were hearing my voice on tape. It is a pedagogically superior technique. *That's* how I sound? My god.

Another reason why Sartre waffles on this issue is that he really wants a religious theater. He longs for the interpenetration of values characteristic of the Greek arena. Sartre certainly approves of Brecht's effort to educate his audiences concerning the social determinations of individual action, but Sartre wants to involve his audience in myth, to touch them at their deepest emotional level, while showing them their common situation (and, in later Sartre, the contradictions which comprise it). He wants to enlist the people's participation in breaking the chains which the system has fastened around them and which the play has shown are there. Brecht's theater is not sufficiently kinetic. It informs, it does not energize, its audience. It does not create a true community.

Common interests don't necessarily unify. If six of us have flu, we have indeed the same disease, but we aren't sharing an illness like a blanket, and our common desire—to recover— may be quite divisive; thus if I am brought to realize that my interests are the same as yours, I may be recognizing you as an enemy. Diverse and divergent aims often promote peace. Separation and indifference are frequently as benevolent as openness and quiet. The recognition, then, that you and I are in the same boat may please neither of us; common descriptions do not signify common interests; common interests do not necessarily unify; unification is not always desirable.

So the drama cannot rest with revealing a mutual plight, nor is any play able to appeal to human universals of whatever sort (sin and salvation, for example, happiness or entelechy), because for Sartre there aren't any; therefore the appeal must be to a concept of collective action: the need to hold property in common or to unionize, to seize the utilities or run the railroads. The formula for successful plays of this kind consists first in revelation: this is your situation and here is the enemy mainly responsible for it (early Sartre might have bravely blamed the masses for their own enslavement); second, the individual's only hope lies in collective action; third, there is value in collective action which transcends utility: cooperation becomes brotherhood. This last part is vital, because in establishing a common cause through a common enemy, one must be careful that the joint venture isn't nevertheless still held together by self-interest, in which case the collective will dissolve like a team at the end of the season, or incorporate itself and become a business. In this country at present, government, business, and labor are each agents of reaction.

One of the qualities which make a great play, especially

a great tragedy, is (exactly contrary to Sartre's formula) that justice be done every opposition, all aspects, each element. When a pie is cut there is pie on both sides of the knife. Brecht regularly wrote plays which were too artful, too original, too *just*, to be acceptable to the narrowly political mind which invariably expects the poet to condemn other wars than his, other lies than his, other necessary disciplinary actions, expediencies, confinements, interrogations, tortures, murders, than his—and never wars, lies, secrecy, or tyranny in general.

In play after play, even the most dogmatic and didactic (*The Mother* or *The Measures Taken*, for example, *The Trial of Lucullus*), the text undermines its intended message, and the party growls its displeasure, admonishes and threatens.[15] One part of Brecht wanted to sell out to discipline, order, and utility, to replace religion with politics, to take a belief like a Teddy bear to bed; another part wanted to compose great plays and have them properly performed. And while that first half tried to submerge us all in the collective, the other continued rather shrewdly to define the special divided self that was Brecht.

Sartre is himself a sufferer from this saving split of feeling and value. His own play *Dirty Hands* was "misunderstood" because the characters for once escaped the program they were tied to and became problems.[16] Sartre, at his deepest point, is anarchistic, playful, ironic, proud, lonely, detached, superior, unique. It is a painful position and it is not surprising that the surface flow of his life and his thinking should run so strongly in the direction of humorless moralizing and the obliteration of the self.

---

[15] Beckett's work continues to ooze from the pedantically gloomy romantic mold critics persist in seeking for it. Dogmas end up fitting the same conical cap to the same cornered dunce. Claudel's difficulties are little different, in this respect, from Brecht's.

[16] Camus was one of those who stupidly "misunderstood." Camus's attitude and the general reception of *Dirty Hands* provoked Sartre to some interesting comments on

Hugo von Hofmannsthal, writing about Brecht's play *Baal* in 1926, anticipated the future as he summed up the past:

> Our time is unredeemed; and do you know what it wants to be redeemed from? . . . The individual . . . Individuality is an arabesque we have discarded . . . I should go so far as to assert that all the ominous events we have been witnessing in the last twelve years are nothing but a very awkward and long-winded way of burying the concept of the European individual in the grave it has dug for itself . . .[17]

How can consciousness, that emptiness in Nature of which Sartre has spoken so eloquently and so often, be a curse? Nietzsche warned us of its weight, of the difficulties in being human, of the temptation to throw down the soul like a rucksack to lighten one's flight. Consciousness is like the shadows cast by bodies on a summer's day, and such evanescence, such Nothingness (it is poetic to report), is more burdensome than Being itself. "The dark was heavier than Caesar's foot."

The key concept again, as in all of Sartre, is freedom; but there are as many freedoms as there are threatening pairs— like frying pan and fire. Do we avoid essence only to fall victim to accidents? And in our escape from sufficient reason will we wind up in the arms of chance? Is our freedom going to be metaphysical, physical, psychological, economic, or political? Sartre has bounced the same word off each of them like a yodel from a mountain. These echoes don't sing harmony.

---

the relation between morality and any behavior aimed at realizing an important social project: "Morality is nothing but a self-control exercised by praxis over itself, but always on an objective level; consequently, it is based on values which are constantly becoming outdated because they are posited by previous praxis." Can one imagine a more essentially Nixonian proposition? And note the "nothing but." Yet, according to Sartre, those who oppose this doctrine are—again—bourgeois. The entire conversation with Paolo Caruso about *Dirty Hands* in 1964 is epiphanous. See *Sartre on Theater*.

[17] Quoted by Martin Esslin in *Brecht: The Man and His Work* (Garden City, N.Y.: Anchor, 1961), p. 31.

Metaphysical determinism, like the will of Allah or Calvin's God's forechoosing, maintains that what will be will be, but only well after it has been. Psychological laws do not limit acts, only our motives for them, so if Hobbes says we always act to preserve our lives, then even if we sacrifice ourselves for others like a lamb who loves the knife, it is probably a life everlasting we're after rather than this brief, miserable, and threatened one; or if Epicurus claims we are always on our knees to lap up pleasure, then even if we lacerate ourselves, we shall find our flesh in happy tatters.

Behavior seems a still center compared to the whirligig of explanations we have Disney'd up around it.

It is obvious, however, that if I am macerated by the NKVD or any other malicious alphabetical agency of police, I am as unfree as a canary, sing as I must and they please, and it's *that* determinism I don't like; the determination of outsiders that my determinants shall not be permitted to determine me; for freedom does not begin—is not an applicable idea—until all the necessaries are out of the way. One does not wonder whether the clam is free to be a bee. Why did Aristotle labor to show that change can only take place along a specific line of march (what's white cannot become musical, he said), if not to instruct posterity?

So shall we deny the hindrance of the genes? Are we ready to defy the fact that human seeds make babies? And when we survey the range of human accomplishment, what has destiny deprived man of, or nature held him back from, which he wishes were in his reach? . . . besides omnipotence and immortality. Such views of man as Aristotle had, or Hume, or Hobbes, such laws as Spinoza laid upon him, or Kant or Marx, are not designed to limit behavior but to enable and explain it.

Sartre's examples inform us that it is the determinism of the family and the state that troubles him most: character and government—the clash of classes—the constraints on man placed there by man himself, not selfish cells or designs depicted in the stars; yet he has made his objection to social and political coercion into a freedom from human *physis* as mythological as the *Moirai* themselves. Against *Ananke* not even the gods fight, Simonides says, and it makes desperate good sense to distinguish between physical necessities and social constraints, and to kick against the pricks and not against the laws which enable us, as Aristotle says, to be an ensouled body rather than an unarticulated boneless ham or silent pitted stone.

Freedom is a wonderful dream, but Sartre's defense of human freedom has been too strongly asserted, too badly stated, too weakly reasoned, too plainly *caused*, and by now the freedom he speaks of has been reduced to a blind Lucretian swerve within a steady rain of atoms.

> This is the limit I would today accord to freedom: the small movement which makes of a totally conditioned social being someone who does not render back completely what his conditioning has given him. Which makes of Genet a poet when he had been rigorously conditioned to be a thief.[18]

Yet Genet could become a poet because he possessed his enormous talent from the beginning. The fact is that social and political categories of this kind (God and His Dominions and His Powers) don't adapt well to the rarefactions of metaphysics . . . unless Denmark's a prison, of course, and the world's one.

---

[18] "The Itinerary of a Thought." A number of recent books have had to tackle these problems, as almost any work on Sartre must. Many of the points I have brought up here are sympathetically treated in Chapter Two of *Existentialism and Sociology*, by Ian Craib (Cambridge University Press, 1976). "Consciousness is a *lack* of Being and a relationship to Being and at the same time a desire *for* Being. It seeks to become Being. . . ." (p.19). Existence wants to become a part of essence, as was once alleged of God. One can also find an account of Sartre's notion of freedom in Phyllis Sutton Morris's *Sartre's Concept of a Person* (University of Massachusetts Press, 1976). She narrows it finally to our choice of an ideal self; however, I am not wholly free even there. The success of my project is not essential, but my choice must be realistic. I cannot choose to be a dancer like Nijinsky. In my case there are no means to this end.

Sartre explains that Beckett's plays are admired by the bourgeois because the bourgeois enjoy being told that man is a depraved lost vicious lonely bored but frightened meaningless creature. Such a view will justify the severe social order they favor: the cage man is to be safely kept in. Yet the bourgeois do not like Beckett. The vast mass of the middle class like *The Sound of Music*. Those few self-selected members of the class who respond to *Waiting for Godot* are hardly characteristic of the whole. They are, furthermore, the same intelligentsia who provide Sartre with his audience and readers. It was a collection of *clercs* who nearly made existentialism commercial.

It is the word "bourgeois" which Sartre brings down like a club on most of his traditional opposition. Wouldn't we all like to have such a weapon? All right. We can invent one. Some time ago there separated from the mass of men like cream in a bottle a group I have chosen to call (after consultation with Dr. Seuss) the Snerls. A snerl is a real or fancied aristocrat who repudiates his origins to play Papa to the masses. (There are a few Mama snerls now, but for a long time the group was almost exclusively male. This did not threaten its existence.) Not all snerls are literary men, though many are: Yeats reaching out through myth to the peasants; Tolstoy, as a young man, shutting himself in his room after witnessing the whipping of an erring coachman, and resolving, so he tells us, to change the world so he would not have to see such unpleasant things again; Mailer running for mayor; and Sartre's many games of principle and conscience, pronouncement and cancellation, where, quite contrary to Russell's case, the price is usually paid by others.

Yeats grew peevish with the peasants. From the seat of the righteous, Tolstoy hurled thunderbolts at Baudelaire. Dos Passos crossed nothing to reach the other side. And Mailer's cock flaps both right wings now when it crows. Sartre is far more subtle. The writers with whom he has had some of his most remarkable differences (Baudelaire, Genet, Flaubert,

Mallarmé), he surrounds with his own words like a swelling around a wound, and one of the aims of all this inflammation is to make it impossible their texts should reach us without passing, on their way, through his; although, of course, he also wishes to prove that Flaubert, for instance, was politically engagé, that he hadn't that purity of esthetic purpose frequently pinned on him like a medal (all true); yet none of this changes the fact that Flaubert could accept his loathing of the middle class (and himself) only if it were contained in the most rigorously articulated and profoundly beautiful forms. Flaubert was not a snerl (nor in the long run was Yeats). He was a crabby aristocrat.

Sartre insists that "you always have a right to speak evil of the bourgeois as man, but not as bourgeois," but I should have thought that no one spoke well of the bourgeois . . . not under that rubric. Of course everyone has his own bourgeois (Sartre his, I mine, you yours), but to prefer content to form— what could be more bourgeois? to think of art in terms of social utility—what could be more bourgeois? to be an intellectual good Samaritan—what could be more bourgeois? to dislike plays that are too gloomy and pessimistic—what could be more bourgeois? to believe that the artist holds some sort of mirror up to nature, or like Taine that a successful work must be in harmony with its era—what could be more bourgeois? and then to feel that plays ought to do you good, that the aim of theater should be "telling the truth"—what could be more bourgeois? to hector, to teach, to drag morality into everything like the worst Victorian Pa—what could be more bourgeois? above all, to put on plays which will be eaten like ice creams at intermissions (and for new times there will be new plays, new plans, new truths, and new demands)—what could be more bourgeois, or more in keeping with our consumer society, where long novels burn like cigarettes, poems don't outlast their speaking, paintings fade into the walls they hang on as though the sun were their only patron, and sculpture is made to look as if it had already been thrown away? to use up the whole of the present and dispose of it in history like trash thrown in a can—what could be more bourgeois, more vulgarly commercial, more nightschool, more USA?

Sartre admits that a revolutionary movement needs a reactionary esthetic, and it is perfectly true that if Sartre entered stage left, he is leaving stage right, for he has managed to forsake every esthetic norm in favor of a praxis about as effective (though no doubt immensely satisfying) as spit on a wall. The editors inform us in their introduction that Sartre has given up writing plays because "the time for individual creation is over and . . . the dramatist's new role is to share in a theatrical company's collective work." One can readily imagine the excitement of working in the company of gifted and committed people toward a cause which confusion allows everyone to believe is common. Once perhaps men were more like ants and toiled at cathedrals as if they were hills, though I don't believe it. In any case, the individual, in-formed, isolated, and sometimes lonely consciousness which wrote Sartre's books and (like Rilke) wrote the rest, is the supreme achievement of our tradition in the West, and if (which again I do not believe) the creative consciousness has become too expensive and in any case rather useless to the struggle of mankind for general animal ease, then general animal ease is too expensive and in any case rather useless to accomplishment, which is the task at hand. Groups feel with a shallow though terrifying strength like a wind over an inland lake; they *cause*, but they neither think nor create, nor did the Greeks suppose their many gods together jerrybuilt the world. I've had to say it before, but even in a gang bang, the best sperm gets the egg.

Upright
Among Staring Fish

The memory seems to me now like a clipping I'd forgotten cutting and sometime later rediscovered in a book, or perhaps inside the sexual section of my wallet, coming apart in its yellowing creases, the paper as fragile as its message; but I did once glimpse Nabokov at a Cornell literary club afloat in a room of brutes, bores, snobby Philistines and shabby quacks, with here and there a Sigmund Freud, a Karl Marx, several slowly ticking thought machines, a school of puffed-up poets, languids, frauds and sharks. There was a tilted bookcase of amateur shellac, sloping sherry, shelves of toppled books, and if the meeting was held in the fall, the fall was wet.

I was a graduate student in philosophy then, and he was . . . well, to me he was the author of *Bend Sinister*, a work of lurid promise which I had by chance begun that week. There were leaves on my feet. Alas, memory has never served me, not the way it has served V. Sirin or any of his other nims and nibs. For them it has always come at call. I remember at Hourglass Lake sitting down beside my wife so silently—no, so noiselessly—she started. I remember many conversations in cafés, unsteady beds in rented rooms, parcels left on seats in trains, visual impressions, mountain cold. And murdering, and loving, and dying several times in the course of a malignant design, the only source of final silence in either Nabokov or Wittgenstein. My memory of *Speak, Memory* entitles me to see a resemblance between it and the hole that opens just inside his latest . . . to see, in fact, that it composes an elaborate intertext, not only for the great N's books themselves but for selected others. *Transparent Things*, indeed. Aquaria with impenetrable glass sides. Death by drowning, in Nabokov, is a common contemplation. Strangulations, dream deaths of several kinds, including removal by eraser: these are frequent. Even those who die in fires die first of asphyxiation.

We were inside a hollow object—true enough—but there was no whirl of colored images around us, no incandescent wall like that which folds about the master's readers when, for them, he dreams. It was a room of . . . well, I was myself a bore and Philistine—no more were needed—sometime Freud and swollen poet, slow ticking clock. I'd never have the biceps of the brute or possess the shark's incisive honesty, and my genes had guaranteed I should never in my life commit an act of Marx. Still I was crowd enough, and knew us all, and so I remember seeing him with some surprise. How was it he was here among so many of me?

There was a certain weight to his name, but it was the kind that attaches to kings of Persia and other far-off figures about whom not even rumors are very directly encountered. Awkward among strangers, I'd managed to wet my sherry hand with sherry. It was a mercy that I could not wonder, in the inflated terms of my type: is it my lifeline from which this sherry seeps like sap from a wounded twig? Such reflections I reserved for a better mind than mine, the one I believed wrote my journal at the time. There was the usual ruck, then: thoughts unthought, acts unacted, clutter and confusion, reviseless speech. The Important Man was next seen shutting his back like a door in the face of a tradesman (a Balkan-faced but German-tongued librarian), the sort who seem to be, without benefit of photos, phonographs, or mirrors, multiple. I left a leaf and one damp half-shoe footprint on the rug. I wiped my sticky moist palm on my trousers. Later we were introduced but didn't meet.

I shall explain. A thin veneer of immediate reality is spread over natural and artificial matter, and whoever wishes to remain in the now, with the now, on the now, should please not break its tension film. Otherwise the inexperienced miracle worker will find himself no longer walking on water but descending upright among staring fish. More in a moment. *(Transparent Things)*

Sinking slowly inside a syllable, we do discover distinct connections of another kind, and I suppose it was that which first impressed me about Nabokov's novels: an object taken from a drawer, as a pencil is shuddered from its rest in an old desk, has not been held there by wood and physics through the years, nor does it appear now in obedience to our hero's rough tug, as some worldly pencil might. It comes to light because it has a place in the Divine Plan, otherwise a dead moth might have slid to view instead . . . a matchbook, bridge tally, or a medal. Once we make that move which Nabokov, in *Transparent Things*, so movingly describes, and pass into the state of being of his books, forgotten pencils, mislaid memories, discarded persons, all the meaningless moments that make up life (each day nothing but a noisy rain of accidents like a spill of beans) are transformed, for now every item is a passage . . . is a peephole where eyes can be seen staring at staring eyes.

"More in a moment," Nabokov writes. And there *is* more: there is Jack Moore, fellow student, with whom our hero rooms at college, and who separates him from the tiny table he's attempting to strangle in his sleep. He knocks books off, coughs drop. There is Julia Moore, a woman with whom he has a brief affair, although she figures largely in the plot. And then there's Giulia Romeo, a whore who motivates the nightmare which will wrap itself so fatally around the neck of our hero's wife. Another table tips on that occasion. A lamp, a book, a tumbler: tumble. So there's Romeo and Juliet, who die of error together. Etc. And there is the Moor. Connections of another kind.

How could I know, when I was mismeeting Nabokov that single time, that immediately inside his books I'd find such sentences as heretofore had not been wrought? Cunning paragraphs enclosed them; swallowed them, smiling, like benevolent whales; while around these, darkening as you descended, upright as it was best to try to be, in layers like blankets, there were several seas. Characters were inserted into scenes as one might, making love, contrive a cry to fit each likely mouth, or with one finger sled a thigh to somewhere warm as winter. "I delight sensually in Time," the Master has written,

> . . . in its stuff and spread, in the fall of its folds, in the very impalpability of its grayish gauze, in the coolness of its continuum. I wish to do something about it; to indulge in a simulacrum of possession. I am aware that all who have tried to reach the charmed castle have got lost in obscurity or have bogged down in Space. I am also aware that Time is a fluid medium of the culture of metaphors.

And I have come to think of his novels as clocks, each marking and making its own sweet time. *Ada*, for instance. Wit-wit-wit, they go when they go round. Slowly I saw what was artistically right: how they were themselves, not imitations; they were constructions to delight the heart and stir the mind. They were not stuffed, like geese, with journalistic observations, determining and moralizing milieus, intensely instructional entanglements, those shifty banalities that do credit to their authors and also to mankind, details like so many jawless clothespins, or sentiments that bless the belly of the reader for whom they are prescribed like simple soothing syrups and bready pudding. One did not hear the tinny click and whirr of toy psychologies as the eyes and loins of the characters lit up, wet, or otherwise expressed themselves, or find the weight of sex and class was heavier than shoulders.

Thus that firm turn of Nabokov's attention, which really was my only observation of him, although the life that occupied the gesture has escaped, remains for me a sign, like the hollow changing chamber of the butterfly, of what it is to write and to create these stillatories, metaphors, transparent things: to unfold from within what is within—fragrant petals of pure relation.

The Anatomy
of Mind

How
It
Began

*Nuns
Maids
Virgins
Barren Women
Widows*

Robert Burton has set it down in Part. 1, Sect. 3, Memb. 2, Subs. 4 of his *Anatomy*, with respect to the melancholies of maids, nuns, and widows, in a way unimprovable, thus:

. . . the most ordinary symptoms be these, a beating about the back, which is almost perpetual, the skin is many times rough, squalid . . . The midriff and heartstrings do burn and beat fearfully, and when this vapour or fume is stirred, flieth upward . . . Their faces are inflamed, and red, they are dry, thirsty, suddenly hot, much troubled with wind, cannot sleep, &c. And from hence proceed a brutish kind of dotage, troublesome sleep, terrible dreams in the night, a foolish kind of bashfulness to some, perverse conceits and opinions, dejection of mind, much discontent, preposterous judgment . . . Now this, now that offends, they are weary of all; and yet will not, cannot again tell how, where, or what offends them, though they be in great pain, agony, and frequently complain, grieving, sighing, weeping and discontented still, without any manifest cause . . .

And with such observations it may have begun: at Charcot's clinical theater, Brücke's Physiological Institute, Meynert's neurological lab, whatever *it* was: a thought, a therapy, a theory of nervous diseases: in the consulting room, at the bedside, on the dissecting table, where gradually whatever *It* was became *Es* and *Id*.

There was the case of Anna O for a start (she threw cushions); there was Frau Emmy von N, who emitted curious clacking sounds like those of the wood grouse, Fräulein Elisabeth von R, then, who slept in her father's sickroom (the good doctors gave to each a discreet and ladylike letter of the alphabet, an altered place, and a rubbed-out year); there was a Miss Lucy R too, one Katharina (otherwise letterless) whom Freud encountered on the summit of a mountain. Fräulein Rosalia H, Frau Cäcilie M, women whose illnesses now enliven patches of our modern faiths and fictions the way the peccadilloes of the gods once did, whatever their troubles were.

Yes, whatever these troubles ultimately were, in lives full of sabbaths and sacrifice which nevertheless displayed all the menacing emptiness of abandoned buildings, they were tribulations marked and occasioned by severe anxieties, odd and naughty behavior, hallucinations, facial paralysis, a compulsive cough in some cases, leg pains, loss of breath in others, by unbearable disappointments in love, profound yet groundless feelings of unworthiness, perhaps the persistent odor of burned pudding or noises like Captain Hook's ticking clock which followed the ear or nose about, embarrassing compulsions, irreparable losses, suspiciously many importunate uncles, frustrations like those of a fly abuzz in the pane of a window, constrictions of every kind, boredom beyond description; and as these symptoms accumulated like trash in a can and Freud waited for them to say where they came from or what they meant, he found among them many of his own queer tics and quirks, the same bugs biting in his own bed.

Hobgoblins—urinary incontinence for one, chronic consti-

pation, migraines, other bugbears and glowghosts, upsetting
insecurities about travel combined unwisely with spells of wan-
derlust, superstitions regarding dangerous dates and fatally
significant numbers, as well as wild and sometimes sudden
swings of mood—followed him for much of his life.

Freud also had his share of fixed and foolish ideas whose
protective function we can now readily see since he himself
taught us this kind of alertness: that Shakespeare was the Earl
of Oxford, that there just might be something to Fliess's nasal
theory of sexuality, or to thought transference, and so on. With
all Freud's luminous self-knowledge and characteristic control, he was still of course capable of slips and unintentional
epiphanies. Like the muscleman's ripple, his ability to hate
was perhaps too finely developed to be counted a strength, and
when he took his theories touring through foreign areas of information, it was sometimes with a bit more ease and arrogance than was altogether wise. Freud's dislike for Americans
was founded as much on guilt and ingratitude as on reasoned
judgment, and the book about Woodrow Wilson which he
wrote with William Bullitt is oddly and nervously bad.

Freud believed and wrote a lot of twottwaddle too, and had
illusions about the love of mothers for their sons, for example,
or of the virgin for her husbandly penetrator. He suffered fits
of fainting as well as other similar attacks of anxiety, tobacco
addiction, a premature slackening of the sexual urge, and
those fairybabes of tombs and graves, as Burton has it: fears
for his heart, of open spaces, debilitating illness, death.

It would be too simple to say that Freud was driven into
medicine by poverty and to the study of neurological disorders
by a dislike of blood, although these were factors. He was, like
the psyche, an opportunist. He would make his mark, if not on
this tree, then on that wall; if not with claws or teeth, then with
penknife and razor.

Freud's patients, as it happened, weren't all women or exclusively strangers, but they each had problems picked up at

home like lint on a trouser. They suffered from their fathers, their brothers—from family, the repeated scuff of culture—the way miners do from black lung, because the job of being a son or a daughter in our day has never been easy, no one is born for it, not everyone is up to it, there's nothing about it in the genes. Unlike the enervating injuries of poverty and economic exploitation which occupied the mind of Marx, these were illnesses of education and economic ease—cases of parlor scent and sofa sickness—not that money didn't matter to the middle class or penis envy occur among the proletariat, but only the Unconscious of the relatively well-to-do could afford to equate shit so simply with gold and silver.

There were the thoughtful exchanges with Breuer, the letters to Fliess, etc., but there was no one who could help Freud draw the remarkable parallels between his patients and himself which were so essential to his own analysis; there was no one who could hypnotize him or put a palm upon his brow or order his eyes to close and his mind to associate and conjure. He had his deep stubbornness and courage, of course, and his almost perfectly formulated ambitions, to drive and guide him, while his fierce delight in opposition, and the compulsion then to overcome every obstacle, would supply his theories with many of their central concepts.

Freud had the hero's need to be self-made to such an extraordinary degree he replaced his father first with Fliess and finally with himself.[1] Will and work were his personal gods. Weakness was for others. His attitude toward suicides was severe, even brutal, and although he believed, and had chewed many a cigar while endeavoring to prove it, that character was inescapable and frequently fatal, he was often exasperated by the fact that people would not simply pull themselves together and behave like free, disciplined, and purposeful adults.[2] Soon

---

[1] Paul Roazen discusses this aspect of Freud's personality himself in his first book, *Freud: Political and Social Thought* (New York: Knopf, 1968).

[2] In regard to Freud's feelings about suicides (not his theoretical views), two letters

he thought he'd seen every kind of frailty and failing, and understood a good many of their causes; nevertheless, he really could not approve of his patients, or even the talented students and supporters who spanieled about him later, and his opinion of mankind grew progressively poorer as a consequence.

In the development of psychoanalysis, Freud's literary skills and interests, peculiar as they were, are not to be discounted either, for he saw everything extraordinarily as if it were taking place in a book, and in the same way his Jewish heritage touched everything he touched. He had the precise Jewish instinct, HD says, "for the particular in the general, for the personal in the impersonal or universal, for the material in the abstract . . ."[3] Deutero-Isaiah had had the wit to interpret the plight of the Jewish people in terms of a determining history, and Freud would do the same. The past was a parent, and he was fully mindful of every begetting, so he admired in the little antique figures he collected the appearance of something perfect from the past which was also perfectly expressive of its period, an object recovered from the burials of time the way his interpretive techniques made ancient artifacts uncave themselves like roused bears.

There were in addition—never secondarily—philosophical presuppositions which varied very little through a lifetime;

---

are particularly important: the famous "heartless" one to Lou Salomé concerning the death of Victor Tausk (the dramatically central moment in Roazen's account of their relationship in *Brother Animal* [New York: Knopf, 1969]), and an earlier letter to his wife-to-be about the career and character of a colleague, Nathan Weiss. This last *is* a sensitive letter, as Roazen says, but Freud's interest is psychological and even novelistic. Freud describes Weiss as "madly vain" and declares bluntly that "he died from the sum total of his qualities, his pathological self-love coupled with the claims he made for the higher things of life" (*The Letters of Sigmund Freud*, edited by Ernst Freud, [New York: Basic Books, 1960], L22). The tone of the Tausk letter ("I confess I do not really miss him; I had long taken him to be useless, indeed a threat to the future," etc.) is the consequence, of course, of many causes; it is, in fact, almost desperately "over-determined." For more on this point, and an informed assessment of Freud's ailments, see Max Schur's *Freud: Living and Dying* (New York: International Universities Press, 1972).

[3] HD, *Tribute to Freud* (Boston: Godine, 1974).

philosophical ambitions he sometimes cautiously hid, and certainly discouraged in others, but would uncover under comfortable conditons.

Freud has published some scientific papers, unwisely advocated the use of cocaine,[4] translated Mill, persuaded Breuer to write with him a work on Anna O and the others, when he writes in the present tense to Fliess as follows:

> I see that you are using the circuitous route of medicine to attain your first ideal, the physiological understanding of man, while I secretly nurse the hope of arriving by the same route at my own original objective, philosophy. For that was my original ambition, before I knew what I was intended to do in the world.[5]

And now at forty, having begun at this symbolic age his own self-analysis, and just completed the impressive "Project for a Scientific Psychology" (though eventually it will be cannibalized and banished), Freud has the necessary data warmly under his belt like a wholesome English pie; he is no longer a mere sense-struck boy but a man of analytic enterprise who is ready for smartly stepped formations, ordering and philosophy.

It is at an exactly similar breath in life that Thomas Hobbes, with whom Freud will share matter, motion, reason, cause, some first principles, and certainly the ideal of a unity of science, glancing through Euclid, cries out, "My G—, this is impossible!" only to be persuaded otherwise when he tracks the offending proposition back to its grounds.

When he is seventy-seven, Freud's spectacles are black round lines against his pale beard, face, and head; cancer has

---

[4] All of Freud's articles on the drug, as well as letters to his wife, notes on his coca-induced dreams, and so on, have been collected by Robert Byck in a volume called *Cocaine Papers* (Stonehill, 1974). Anna Freud has contributed a few notes, and many relevant papers from the period are included. Everything in this excellent volume supports a belief in the neurological origins of psychoanalysis.

[5] Letter of January 1, 1896, in *The Origins of Psychoanalysis*, edited by Marie Bonaparte, Anna Freud, and Ernst Kris (Basic Books, 1954).

bitten through his lip and robbed him of his public eloquence; but the tense remains present though the task is past when he says to HD one day during her analysis:

> My discoveries are not primarily a heal-all. My discoveries are a basis for a very grave philosophy. There are very few who understand this, *there are very few who are capable of understanding this*.[6]

There is no question that Freud used philosophical language loosely, and that, for example, he was apt to describe thought's functional dependence upon the brain (a condition far closer to epiphenomenalism, the belief that consciousness is a material by-product of the behavior of the body) as if it were really a case of psycho-physical parallelism (the notion that mind and matter run on independent but fortunately synchronous tracks).[7] He drew, in an undisciplined way, from everything that struck him, and many of his sources were derivative. He was one, as Henry James had hoped for his heroines and himself, on whom little was lost, and so from the beginning the theory which would eventually emerge from all his endeavors would be the consequence of a veritable synagogue of causes, including the fact that like Nietzsche he grew up surrounded by women, an eldest son with five sisters; that his first competitor was slain by omnipotent wish at eight months, while the arrival of others, always threatened, was put off ten years, every growl followed only by girls, until he was able to

---

[6] Perhaps the best general treatment of Freud as a philosopher can be found in Paul Ricoeur's *Freud and Philosophy* (Yale, 1972), a work brilliantly suggestive on every page. Ricoeur has his own ax, of course, but it is sharp and well swung.

[7] In *Aphasia*, 1891. Freud contended that psychic states were not reducible to physical ones, but he also believed (a) that although physical events could occur without corresponding mental ones the reverse was not the case, and (b) that all conscious states were initiated by and passed between the fibrous interstices of the body. See Ernest Jones, *The Life and Work of Sigmund Freud* (Basic Books, 1953), Vol. I, pp. 367–68.

name his ultimate brother, calmly, Alexander. Instead he took a nephew for his sibling rival.

As in a fine poem, so in a creative and productive life, relevance is the rule: he once incontinently peed in his parents' room and was informed by his father that on this account he would surely amount to nothing; he was forty and halfway to his own death when this father died (again that fatal age); he played catch-up-and-get-even, had heroes like Hannibal and Leonardo, Moses and Napoleon, was Viennese, knew Mach, read Schnitzler, and attended the lectures of Franz Brentano.

Then inside Freud's female melancholics, who were, as Burton had said, "cholerick, and soon hot, solitary, sad, often silent, watchful, discontent," there were the actual cortical lines, the wrinkled fruit in the skull, and somehow active within these lines energies of an electrical kind passing to and fro, accumulating as a battery does, discharging sometimes with considerable zap, or influencing neighboring areas like urban blight, the rise around a wound, cathecting, magnetizing maybe, establishing fields . . . how or why or what wasn't then clear, nor is it now.

Still, a lesion could be seen and studied. The damage was visible, like flaking paint. Freud's patients put on behavior that was particularly nerve-wracking and upside-down. Their bodies were booths in an exhibition hall where nothing was immediately for sale. When an ordinary cold compels the chest to squeeze air through its throat like the bulbous honk of a horn, the victim's miseries are caused by that closing chest and forceful cough; they are centered on that throat and nose. Such sicknesses obey the geography of the body. They understand and are respectful of anatomy.

However, the illnesses Freud grew concerned about were those in which the behavior of the body became expressive and symbolic in a way no measle ever was, or runny nose, so that an hysterical paralysis might define an arm by means of the shape and limits of a sleeve. The infection, in short, was that of an idea, not a common germ or fancy virus. A thought had invaded the body. Anna O, Dora later, the Wolf and Rat men, were cases in which the puzzling (perhaps impossible) meeting of mind and body had been so rudely and raucously announced, and had taken place with such sordid and raunchy results, that all the skid-and-squeamy issues of ontology seemed to solidify inside them like grease in a cold pan. Was it like the noisy mating and scratch of cats, or a holler across a chasm, this connection? Beckett's man astride his bike? independently orbiting satellites? romantic strife or classical harmony? the apparently purposeless flutter of a thousand bats, for example, or something like the gargle made by turbulence in pipes? Whatever the eventual outcome, I daresay since the Greeks no discipline which aimed to become a science began with data so outrageously metaphysical.

It aimed to become a science, yet if there was ever a target which the phallic arrow of analysis fell no way near, it was this one. It is even likely that psychoanalysis ended more metaphysically than it began. Freud knew, of course, that the territory was strange. He knew that his theories would meet with irrational resistance. He wanted his work credited with being truly observant, yet what he *saw* was not a half of what he *heard*, and the subject of his science soon became the story in the voice, in reported scenes of nightmare and daydream, in what could be inferred from his patients' feelings about words and their inadvertent play with language, the total history of a case . . . *eros* through *logos* . . . by the light of the sun to find the entrance to the cave. Since his reports would seem bizarre, his "situations" delicate, the analyst's behavior had to be severely objective, his aims rigorously professional, his mind tough, his facts hard. He had to say "science" fiercely and firmly, firmly and loudly, loudly and often. And since he was a doctor, he had to cure. And since he was a husband and a householder (so surely a "he"), he had to be paid.

Nevertheless, the therapeutic success of psychoanalysis

has been dubious; its empirical base remains weak; its testability is nearly nil; its openness to quantification, despite Freud's early predilections, is precisely that of the latched lid. In addition, it has remained suspiciously tied to its founders, and has shattered like a clumsy beaker into faddy camps of every conceivable Californucopial kind, rival schools whose appearance could have been anticipated if Freudianism had been perceived as a philosophical or religious undertaking instead of a scientific one.[8]

But no real science cares to remain so culture-bound and value-laden. There's none which delights in cultist spin-off either. Analysis has felt too national, too personal—too remedial—too racial, even, to its followers, in whom it has provoked a passionate interest in orthodoxy, and from whom we have received volumes of gossip principally about the passage of power and the true chain of leadership. I think one can reasonably doubt the scientific status of a theory it feels too good to believe. Whatever it once was or was meant to be, Freudianism is now no more a psychology than Marxism *is* an economics.[9]

In the midst of the master's own misdirections, the cries of plagiarism and betrayal, charges of heresy, simony, and

---

[8] Perhaps the most vigorous and valuable examination of the scientific claims of psychoanalysis is Ërnst Nagel's "Methodological Issues in Psychoanalytic Theory," a contribution to *Psychoanalysis, Scientific Method and Philosophy*, edited by Sidney Hook (NYU Press, 1959). Richard Wollheim's excellent anthology (*Freud: A Collection of Critical Essays*, [Garden City, N.Y.: Doubleday, 1974]) contains Wesley Salmon's somewhat kinder study from that collection, as well as Thomas Nagel's useful essay on Freud's anthropomorphism, in which he reasonably concludes that "psychoanalytic theory will have to change a great deal before it comes to be regarded as part of the physical description of reality." See also William I. Grossman's and Bennett Simon's paper, "Anthropomorphism: Motive, Meaning, and Causality in Psychoanalytic Theory," in *The Psychoanalytic Study of the Child*, Vol. 24, 1969, cited by Nagel.

[9] If Freud did not create a science, he maintained a scientific attitude: cool, rational, skeptical, objective, mature. His therapy, like the methods of those philosophers he most resembles, consists in the clarification of consciousness by the removal of illusions. Jung himself wrote that "if Freud is viewed . . . as an exponent of the *ressentiment* of the incoming century against the nineteenth, with its illusions, its hypocrisy,

lewdness, occasional canonizations and frequent courts of excommunication, the capture of the theory by literary critics,[10] mentalists, and religious mountebanks, the promises of cure and countercure, as though the analyst's office were Lourdes, the anti-Semitic insinuations, the creamy work of the popularizers . . . after the parlor games, clever seductions, the jokes . . . it was difficult indeed to get one's bearings, hear a single sane word, perceive a great philosopher inside that medicine man, messiah, and mischief-maker, who seemed to some the ultimate Asclepian, a miraculous cathartic in human spoon, a god made of good gritty soap, while to others he seemed equally an arch-defiler, sick Jew, god-poisoner—the thick and sticky dirt itself.

	Matter	From the first, Freud hoped to place his
What	*Quantity*	psychology on a firm scientific footing. If
It	*Conservation*	we were not like a waterworks, perhaps we
Was	*Cause &*	were complex electrical systems or places
	Reason	for the barter and exchange of heat; but he

was not really aware of how little or how much the science of his day was truly empirical or to what degree the commitments of Herbart and Helmholtz to materialism were acts of faith,

---

its half-ignorance, its false, over-wrought feelings, its shallow morality, its artificial, sapless religiosity, and its lamentable taste, he can be viewed in my opinion much more correctly than when the attempt is made to make him out as the herald of new ways and new truths . . ." (*Character and Personality*, Vol. I, 1932)."

Although they may otherwise differ as much as Plato and Bacon do, or Spinoza and Nietzsche, Hobbes or Wittgenstein or Marx, philosophers like them have always been concerned not only with the creation of consolations, but with their critique, even their removal, and to this end have provided us with the most unrelenting exposure of the mythsmiths who design and manufacture these idols, as well as the salvation salesmen who hoop-huckle-and-hawk them. See Philip Rieff's *The Triumph of the Therapeutic* (Harper and Row, 1966) as well as his earlier *Freud: The Mind of the Moralist* (Doubleday Anchor edition, revised 1961) for an excellent defense of Freud's disillusionist aims.

[10] See Frederick J. Hoffman's *Freudianism and the Literary Mind* (Louisiana State University Press, 1945), for example.

how far the principles of motion or the laws of thermodynamics exceeded the evidence.

It was distinctly in a cautious speculative spirit that in the fall of 1895 Freud began the "Project for a Scientific Psychology," because in the area of neurophysiology, at least, he knew very well how little was known; nevertheless, with extraordinary daring and considerable elegance, since caution excludes neither, and with his almost genetic gift for guessing right, he set out to provide us with a purely physical account of the operations of the mind. Except perhaps for Ivan Sechenov's beautiful little essay *Reflexes of the Brain*,[11] which was written in 1863 and falls short of Freud in numerous ways, there is nothing like it in the entire history of philosophy.

Although Freud's own clinical practice defined his problem, it was left to physics to suggest those first fine few general principles (laws of heat and motion) from which a solution might be drawn, and to neurology to provide the pieces (neurones) which would play the game. Freud's own basic assumptions (that reality is entirely material; that matter is best described in quantitative terms; that it is governed by the principles of conservation; that it operates through causation and can only be understood through reason) are hardly empirical generalizations. Once securely afloat, however, and the consequences of his "laws" derived, Freud descends on the facts from above the way the fisherman descends on his fish, and of course there is always the danger that the theory will seine too efficiently and capture only the kinds it wants. It is at this point that one must ask whether the explanation is satisfactory: whether all the data has been economically, even elegantly, interrelated; whether new material can be correctly anticipated; and whether surprises can be ungrudgingly welcomed and made to feel at home.

---

[11] English translation, MIT Press, 1965. This work was kindly called to my attention by a colleague, Professor Richard Watson.

So let us imagine for a moment the simplest organism in the animosities of its environment, and ask ourselves about the value of its sensitivity. Wouldn't every cell be better off as sand, and isn't any animal easier in the management of itself than a man? Then why accept messages? Let the dah-dits drone into wirelessed space, send the bellboy away when he knocks, ignore both the frothy tumult of events and the dull settle of sofas on their springs, put out all eyes in order to endure, hold tight—that's it—hang on, sink out of sight in blank and silent depths—the oyster has the secret—stay, remain, survive . . . though staying, as Rilke wrote, is nowhere; still, staying is all we want. It is that equilibrium or balance which Spinoza once proposed to us as the innermost law of our nature, even as Leonardo earlier observed, "every body has a weight in the direction of its movement," and Galileo, too, unsweetened Platonist, by measuring mass with inertia, revoked the ancient privileges of heaven and made the moon a stone; for which no thanks were given to him, or Hobbes, or finally Freud, who worked against the most presidential of our mental friends: Received Opinion.

The old stories tell us how Matter struggled, pointlessly or not, to become Mind. They weave a wondrous tale, rather reminiscent of the rabbit who tried to tie down the sun with string. Furthermore, these same myths relate how man escaped from his cave to club his skinless way to culture—most moving, most brave; still others describe his history and his fate, a pageant only Providence has so far found the funds for or had the fortitude to watch, while in addition Bergson's given all of us a Rotarian's upward fizz. What more could we possibly want?

In the face of such persistent flattery it is natural for us to think of evolution as a kind of growth, and growth as a kind of groping for sun and air in one direction, food and water in another, an open and honest reaching out, healthy and English as mountain climbing, full of fresh air and German joy, the happy rush of life into every nook and cranny like the scatter of roaches from a sudden light. But suppose that another rule prevails, the one that in logic is called Identity, in physics, Inertia, and among living beings, Self-Preservation; suppose that the instincts invariably seek to reinstate a previous condition, that the essence of things lies in the profoundest reluctance, in *Widerstand*, resistance; and suppose that in the same way that we go paradoxically to war to preserve the peace, we send out emissaries and take in guests—in order, ultimately, only to be alone. What of the inner impulse, then? the upward strive? the Life Force and the biological hurrah? [12]

"I do not believe in the existence of such an inner impulse," Freud said, "and I see no way of preserving this pleasing illusion." If Galileo required that the heavens turn on the same cogs as the earth, and Darwin found one law alike for every species, Freud would make a similar demand concerning the mind and consciousness of man. If it is to sustain itself as a discipline, psychology must manage to be but physics and physiology respelled. Freud's earliest commitment was to a regulative rule for reason which commanded him to seek a uniform order of explanation and a unity in science. It was a faith as Viennese as Sacher torte and strong coffee, and it implied that the concepts of every special area of investigation were logically coherent; that there was, thus, one language for science as well as one set of laws. Psychic processes had to be regarded as quantitatively determined states of specifiable material particles. [13]

As his work went on, Freud found it increasingly difficult

---

[12] What I want to point out here is that in Freud the rule *prevails*. There is of course a great deal of opposition to it. See Margaret Boden's paper in Richard Wollheim's collection: " . . . drive-reduction or purely homeostatic theories of motivation are clearly inadequate to the psychophysiological reality." She cites a number of opponents. Unfortunately, most of the objections to the constancy principle fail to understand its *a priori* postulational status, which I've just suggested it has, and approach it as if it were an empirical conclusion of some kind. That's a little like asking about the evidence for the rules of chess.

[13] From the opening sentence of the "Project," in *The Origins of Psychoanalysis* (New York: Basic Books, 1954), p. 355.

to retain his quantitative materialism in undiluted form, but I should like to suggest that, although he weaseled and he waffled, although dualisms bent him and mentalisms encouraged another language, at least every other heartbeat was for the work he set aside and never published, the "Project for a Scientific Psychology," and that his later romance with destruction and death is a disguised return to the old and drier flame. In his resourceful and devious way, Freud was as constant and resistant to change as his central principle.

The importance of the "Project" is now generally recognized and appropriately stressed.[14] One of the best essays in Richard Wollheim's anthology, Robert Solomon's "Freud's Neurological Theory of Mind," is devoted to it. Solomon quotes Karl Pribram, one of the world's leading neuropsychologists, to the effect that "the *Project* contains a detailed neurological model which is, by today's standards, sophisticated . . . The *Project* is very much alive and not just of historical importance." Solomon also notes that Thomas Kuhn calls the "Project" a paradigm of psychoanalytic theory; reminds us that the editors of the Standard Edition describe it as a ghost which "haunts the whole series of Freud's theoretical writings to the very end"; and himself concludes that "as in so many other instances, a work of this outstanding genius of our century has been abused for 'naiveté' only because it was too radical to be appreciated in its own time."

---

[14] By Richard Wollheim, for example, in his fine introduction to Freud in the Modern Masters series, *Sigmund Freud* (Viking, 1967), and there is an excellent exposition of the main ideas in this closely reasoned and sometimes difficult work in Raymond Fancher's *Psychoanalytic Psychology* (New York: Norton, 1973). The arc reflex model of the mind is considered one of the three basic models Freud employed by John Gedo and Arnold Goldberg in their *Models of the Mind* (University of Chicago, 1973). The other two are called "topographic" and "tripartite." Paul Ricoeur (in *Freud and Philosophy*, Yale, 1970), who wishes to budge Freud from the "Project's" broadly positivist base, admits nevertheless that " . . . in any event Freud will never disavow its fundamental convictions." But in Ricoeur's judgment "nothing is more dated than the explanatory plan of the 'Project,' and nothing more inexhaustible than its program of description" (pp. 72–73). Like Aristotle's *Metaphysics*, the "Project" has an editor's title.

If the first, second, and final act of every constituted system is to maintain itself, as Freud's "Project" assumed, then it will only be for the sake of such commonplace salvation that some systems will find a use for the sensitivity which genetic chance and circumstance have conferred upon them. Still, every system will seek to limit this sensitivity as far as possible, responding simply to what seems necessary to sustain it in any situation at the lowest possible level of stimulation. The boundary of a body will be built up principally as a barrier, so we shall soon have a hide to hide in, legs to flee, eyes with which we can preserve our blindness. Energies which penetrate the organism must be passed through as harmlessly as possible, conducted like lightning to the ground. "This process of discharge," Freud wrote, "is the primary function of neuronic systems." What we cannot shit out in a clear stream, what we cannot harden ourselves to, what we cannot flee from, is our own continuous demand for energy, since all our acts require supplies we must appropriate from somewhere.

The "Project" treats us as rather callous Cartesians, satisfied we understand things only when we can actually imagine how they might be fabricated, and since we make things of discrete and harmonious units, according to clear directions and specifiable rules, in successive steps through definable stages, the "Project" assumes that we shall feel we understand the human mind when we finally figure out how to manufacture one.

Freud naturally supposed that the nervous system was composed of a network of neurons through which electrochemical energies rushed at roughly ninety feet per second, although that was only the speed of life through a frog's leg, as Helmholtz had measured it. The neuron had only recently been established as the basic unit of neurological activity. Freud asks us to imagine them as containers that discharge their contents the very instant they are filled, in an elegant and economical response which uses the occupying energy, just as judo does, to trigger its own release. Nothing leaks or spills, but suddenly the restraining walls unglue. Whereupon, neuronasm over, the cell returns, intact and unaffected, to its normal flaccid state.

There are occasions when remaining limp requires both will and effort. Out of what is the neuron itself composed? what prevents it from melting like a custard? and isn't it true that even dissolution takes time and is a bloody nuisance? The system must be able to store up stimulation as well as simply discharge it. Nor is every source of stimulation of the same kind. We can permit a hot plate to fall from our threatened fingers, but hunger can be only momentarily stilled. It persists and recurs and pursues us however we turn, the way Oedipus was pursued by his fate. With the greatest reluctance we are driven to recognize and act upon the world in order to serve the Minotaur within. In fact, our basic sense of *out* and *in*, even that of *self* and *other*, emerges from these hard conditions.

We can accumulate energy and prevent embarrassing prematurity (the frog's reflexive kick, for instance, or our own knee's jerk) by sharing the incoming flow among a number of neurons so that the initial cell doesn't immediately flood and spend. In this way the barriers between neurons are gently reduced because excited cells direct the flow of energy toward themselves and the paths between cells are facilitated through use.

Freud suggests that there are contact barriers between neurons (a conjecture later found to be correct), and these prevent energy from flowing along without resistance; consequently, the entire neuron fills, then fires, a neighboring neuron fills, then fires, and then another, like Chinese crackers on a string. In time, however, the contact barriers between neurons become, either through sudden trauma or repeated trudge, more permeable and less resistant. The sensory system, with one end lying in the outer layer of the skin and in the skull holes and attentive hair, though the neurons are not numerous there, meets regularly with the greatest stimulation, which it fans through deeper layers and into many other cells.

The stimuli which enter the nervous system from within are far less strong, though more persistent, and these also penetrate continuously into the cortical layers. The three "nervous systems" Freud eventually distinguishes (the physical sensory-motor system, associated with the spinal cord; the memory system, associated with the brain; and the perceptual system, which brings these events into consciousness) differ principally in their distance *in*, though *in* is clearly a neurological image of direction, just as *depth* will be a psychological one.

Readers of the "Project" can now begin to see how trains of thought and habits of association are established in the nerves. A cell which retains some of the initial excitement of its stimulus *remembers*; cells through which energy from some source is regularly distributed are *associated* and light up together; paths down which energy eventually travels without resistance are forgotten for good, as we cannot now recall how we learned to see, and few of us still have any memory of the anger and elation of our earliest toddles. It was Schopenhauer who claimed that to perceive was to experience an effect in the place of its cause, so from these cortical events we distantly infer and sense the nature of their origin in the same way that the feelings in a blind man's palm are lent to what's tapped by his cane.

Energies which are successfully diverted through the system, or converted into action and thus lost, or thinned and unnoticeably spread out the way a large sum is concealed in many banks: such energies are said to be mastered, the system's constancy is thus maintained, and the happy result is felt as pleasure. When the store of stimulation mounts, it is sensed in a particular locale as pain, and in the general tension of the system as unease or anxiety. It is not difficult to see why genital orgasm is such a dramatic and convenient image of the process in question, or why many might hope to reduce their anxieties by drawing and releasing themselves like bows as compulsive masturbators endeavor to; vainly, of course, since it is principally a magical act and thus as futile in direct effect as spilling out buckets of household water in order to lower the level in the reservoir and save the dam.

But in a universe of quantity, why should quality appear? It does not wait on mankind like a maiden eager for her knight or shopper sullen for the bus. In a fundamental way we are one with our awareness, and a certain kind of consciousness, not featherless bipedity or cleverly opposed thumbs, is the most obvious mark of man.

> . . . whereas science has set itself the task of tracing back all the *qualities* of our sensations to external *quantity*, it is to be suspected from the structure of the neuronic system that that system consists in contrivances for changing external *quantity* into *quality*.[15]

Plato imagined that the creator composed the material world as a qualitative expression of quantitative law, but brilliant as this suggestion proved to be, Plato granted sounds, scents, and colors, all the smooths and sours, an eternal home in an otherwise featureless space—*out there*—where the Demiurge, like a croupier at a crooked table, made Change from the relations these qualities entered and left. Instead we might follow Hobbes, who always took the square way round things, and regard consciousness as a kind of discharge of energy out of the system, a gratefully endured entropic loss, but Freud rejects such a solution, even though it has the nice result of making consciousness itself a pleasure.

Since only a part of what happens in the nervous system is ever carried into consciousness (we do not feel our seeing, and recollection is, "speaking generally, devoid of quality"), Freud must assume a third set of neurons whose business it is

---

[15] *The Origins of Psychoanalysis*, p. 370.

to convert not quantity itself but the quantity of quantity, its frequency or period, into sense.

> According to a modern mechanistic theory, consciousness is no more than an appendage added to physiologico-psychical processes, an appendage whose absence would make no difference to the course of psychical events. According to another theory consciousness is the subjective side of all psychical events and is thus inseparable from physiologico-mental processes. The theory which I have here propounded lies between these two. According to it consciousness is the subjective side of a *part* of the physical processes in the neuronic system—namely of the *perceptual processes* . . . and its absence would *not* leave psychical events unchanged . . .[16]

Energy approaching us has two characteristics, then: period and amount. We reject some possible stimuli altogether; we refuse the frequencies of others, and reduce the amount of energy of any we accept. A series of screens and filters protects us from being overwhelmed, and especially keeps our awareness clear for the performance of its basic function: the searching out of objects which will help us master our persistent internal drives. Our primary neurological aim is expressed in the reflex: by an action we remain the same. Our secondary neurological aim is the retention, spread, and maintenance of a minimal energy level throughout the system. The rejection,

---

[16] *Origins*, pp. 372–73. Freud had great difficulty placing this perceptual system among the others, and in deciding what sort of energy operated it. It was a little like trying to string lights on an already decorated tree. He felt compelled to revise the "Project" almost at once in this regard (see Letter 39 in *Origins*), but his revisions were—as he says—in "double-Dutch" and only darkened what he wanted to clarify. It is not the comparatively unsophisticated physiology of the "Project" which causes it to founder, but Freud's inability to find a real place for consciousness inside the machine. Unfortunately, Freud also had a rather innocent conception of "quantity," tending to measure out our life in coffee spoons.

discharge, and storage of quantity does not imply a contradiction since all these activities serve the same end—constancy—as does the appearance of consciousness itself.

Of course in infancy consciousness is able to accomplish very little. Kicking and screaming are more successful than any sort of thoughtful perception. The fetus is automatically cared for by the body of its mother, and the newborn's mewling helplessness speaks for an equally efficient food tube, tub, and swaddle. Cries are its eyes now, yet the baby's awkward motor movements manipulate the world as well as a mechanic, balancing it better than a walker on a wire. They succeed, however, because they are addressed to another consciousness, a bonded and dutiful awareness. It is little wonder our tantrums try to return the immediate environment to this early state of blessed obedience, or that lambastabombulation is the deepest root and secret lure of leadership.

Few infants are born in a wilderness to be suckled by wolves. Far from being locked between the jaws of gentle nature, neither entrusted to the sea nor given up to a hillside, they find themselves in worser sort inside a family, and whether attention, love, or resentment are most called forth by howl-power, the responses which the baby's behavior generally receives ensure that from its first squalling, purple moment forward, most of the connections between the child's neurons will be social, and that social structures will sink into the psyche like stripped autos into river-silt.

So if hunger provokes wailing and wailing brings the breast; if the breast permits sucking and milk suggests its swallow; if swallowing issues in sleep and stomachy comfort, then need, ache, message, object, act, and satisfaction are soon associated like charms on a chain; shortly our wants begin to envision the things which will reduce them, and the organism is finally said to *wish*.

No neuron knows where its energy has been. If the sight of the breast elicits sucking, so may hunger's memory of it, but which is sweet wish and which the sweeter flesh? Up to this point Freud has been able to distinguish instinct from object only in terms of the devices used to discharge their demands (with instinct, as already mentioned, flight fails), and because perceptual stimuli possess a periodicity which some neurons translate into quality, whereas wishes (the mix of memory and desire) do not.

There is in addition an ego, however, which is simply a mechanism for spreading neural excitement evenly throughout the system in order to inhibit neuronasms and retain energy for adaptive use. Actually, it is not so much a mechanism as a habit subject to modification whenever the cells which retain energy alter their relationships and number, just as on a beach the damp sand is rhythmically rewet or dries. Early experience determines how strong an ego is likely to be. Weak egos cannot postpone satisfaction. They suffer an enervating prematurity, while strong egos admit energy from more sources and by cunning dispersion retain greater quantities for later use in satisfying instinct. Therefore an ego can elevate its owner above insect or animal, since instinct ordinarily is unwilling to wait and meets each stimulus with that same pattern of automatic discharge we see in the spider who patiently repairs her torn web through the indifferent bell-ringing wind which rent it and will rend it again.

The ego, in saying "yes" to the id, as Freud eventually thought it did, is not altogether a friend, for its formation is socially inspired, and the so-called reality it recognizes is nothing less than the enduring cultural complex which shaped it in the first place.[17] Relying on the ego to mediate between pleasure and reality is a lot like arbitrating a dispute between factory

---

[17] A point central to the argument of Russell Jacoby's *Social Amnesia* (Boston: Beacon Press, 1975): ". . . psychoanalysis rediscovers society in the individual monad. The critical edge of psychoanalysis is rooted in this dialectic: it pierces the sham of the isolated individual with the secret of its socio-sexual-biological substratum" (p.79).

workers and their firm by calling in to settle the issue a still fat-cheeked former head of the company.

The "Project" was as full of conjectural leaps as a pond of frogs. Patient by patient, Freud's own clinical and couch work was drawing him further from neurophysiology. The language of psychology was richer, looser, more supple and suggestive for him. Increasingly what he found he had to do was "read down" from consciousness rather than try to "read up" from the nerve ends and the brain. This method, moreover, did not seem to push him so persistently toward that pictureless chasm between current and color, impact and scream (so easy to cross and impossible to span) which he was expected to leap.

Therefore it was in every way necessary for Freud to translate neural discharges and energy paths into sensation, thought, and feeling, even if he were forced, as he immediately was, to construct a theory out of neologisms and catachresis, to speak of suppressed wishes and unfelt feeling, of ideas which had never clearly lit so much as a minute's inch of the mind, of psychic conflicts which symptomatically expressed themselves in a war of muscle lengths and inner organs (bowel pitted against belly, blood rising like steam through the skin, the eye an ally of the thigh, the vagina an unviolated victim of the thumb). The appearance of new terminologies and structures, altered models and recharged metaphors, however, did not demand a wholly new design, or mean that Freud had abandoned his neural economics.

The "Project" was repressed only to turn each of Freud's speculative dreams into a jackbox from which the hidden theory then popped with a not-too-startling wheeze. It haunts every line of his metapsychology; in the last chapter of *The Interpretation of Dreams* we hear its heavy tread, throughout *Beyond the Pleasure Principle* its clanking chains, again in the ultimate *Outline of Psychoanalysis* the whistle of its indestructible spirit. The fact is that through the whole of Freud's work the same few ideas are in evasive flight like hares through their images, for beneath differences of poetry (whether of constancy, homeostasis, equilibrium, entropy, inertia ... whether in the meters of hydraulics, geography, thermodynamics, chemistry, or electricity . . . in those verses which describe the body as an engine or a clutch of wires, or those in which the mind is a camera, a stacked set of cities like Troy, or a grayly waxen magical slate), the same sense lies as quiet as a crocodile with shuttered eyes, the doctrine itself a "system of *layers of signs* (*Zeichen*)—waiting to be *trans-lated* (*Umsetzung*: transformed, restructured, communicated at another level of communication) or simply read . . ."[18]

Psychology replaced physiology as early as *The Interpretation of Dreams* (1900), but it was a psychology of signs and ciphers, codes and other kinds of communication, like the raps of a distant prisoner on the pipes of his plumbing. Even if neurons were made up, you could in principle see them; even if their paths were imaginary and their intercourse a fiction, what the "Project" had invented was *perceivable*. The new area of investigation, consciousness itself (that consequence of neuronic light), was private, and more out of reach than if it were covered by layers of bone. Except for his own dreams, his own follies and phobias, Freud could only analyze descriptions: the patient's life in the patient's language.

A difficult and possibly sad situation. Is it not scientifically sounder to deal in visible fictions than invisible facts? The construct, in any case, can always be called to account. Still, the more narrowly the patient's life could be equated with language, the more closely the analyst could come to grasping it. He could listen and read. He could construe. Something inside us is saying something—but what? why? to whom? how? and with what slippery, thick, forked, or tangled tongue?

---

[18] There is a nice rundown of these images, as well as others, in Anthony Wilden's important essay "Marcuse and the Freudian Model," in a double issue of *Salmagundi*, Nos. 10–11 (Fall and Winter, 1969–1970). This quotation is on page 209. An-

It is customary, now, for philosophers to distinguish between sentences and propositions by pointing out that the same propositions can be contained in many sentences, just as the fact that cows give milk can be expressed in various ways. Not only can these propositions be symbolized so that their structure is exposed, but operations of a richly regulative sort can be performed upon them, altering the relationships of terms, making the positives negative, substituting one value for another, switching voices, replacing variables with constants, transforming affirmations into queries, and so on.

The remarkable language model into which, by stages, Freud translated his neurophysiological one imagines that states of consciousness, physical symptoms, and patterns of behavior are sentences; that these sentences contain propositions of a limited and uniform sort, and that, symbolized, they can be expressed in terms of a function (some need like hunger) containing four places: (1) the ego, or owner of the wish, (2) an object (like an item of food) which is expected to satisfy it, (3) an organ or organ path (mouth to stomach in this case), and (4) the resulting disappearance of pain in the reduction of the drive, a reduction which is always a constant (pleasure).

Every complete proposition of the psyche is therefore of the following form: IT (the subject term of the function, and for every want accepted by the unconscious ego, "IT" is replaced by "I") WANTS (the function, which varies in strength, a characteristic we indicate by increasing or decreasing the occurrence of its symbol, W, and which is either actively engaged in taking [$\longrightarrow$] or passively occupied by wishing and waiting for [$\longleftarrow$]) PLEASURE (the positive constant, $+P$, which can of course be some degree of pain, $-P$, as well) from an OBJECT in the world (Ob), by means of an ORGAN of the body (or erogenous zone, Or), thus:

other substantial essay by Robert Jay Lifton, "From Analysis to Form: Towards a Shift in Psychological Paradigm," is in the Winter, 1975, issue of that same journal.

$$WWW(I - +P \longrightarrow Ob, Or),$$

an expression which can be read as: I badly (the strength of
the desire is indicated by the number of Ws) want to take pleasure from the world through my body. The same proposition
in the passive voice looks like this:

$$WWW(I \longleftarrow +P - Ob, Or),$$

and is read: I badly want to receive pleasure from the world
through my body.[19]

The resulting departmental or bureaucratic scheme takes
this form:

The Unsaid & Unsayable	The Sayable	The Said	The Said Aloud
------------- Censor ------------- Censor ------------- Censor ----------			
The Unconscious	The Preconscious	The Conscious	Public Act & Utterance

The unconscious ego revises any proposition offered it until an
acceptable version can be found. The ego may alter itself by
absorbing pleasure-giving things and persons (introjection) or
by projecting upon the world its own pain. It may replace one
term with another in the same formula so that "all cows give
milk" becomes "all chessmen make threats." Finally, it may employ any one or more of four psychological operations which re-
phrase meanings at the same time that they disguise desire.[20]

(1) *Reflexivity* changes the voice of the proposition so that

---

[19] Jacques Lacan takes a different tack in *The Language of the Self* (Johns Hopkins,
1968). See also John C. Marshall's essay, "Freud's Psychology of Language," in Wollheim's collection.

[20] In the 1915 essay "Instincts and Their Vicissitudes." Frequently called "defense
mechanisms," their number varies. Anna Freud, in *The Ego and the Mechanisms of
Defense* (Hogarth, 1937), lists ten, and with a dubious lack of economy, sometimes
many more are added. See Margaret Boden's "Freudian Mechanisms of Defense," in
Wollheim's collection.

if the instinct has been active, it is turned back against the self and the murderer becomes suicidal:

$$(Ref)WWW(I - +P \longrightarrow Ob,Or) \equiv WWW(I \longleftarrow +P - Ob,Or).$$

The reflex of "I badly want to take pleasure from the world through my body" is equivalent to "I badly want to receive pleasure from the world through my body."

(2) *Reversal* not only forces a flip-flop in the voice, it puts pain in the place of pleasure and pleasure in the place of pain. Active love turns into the wish to be disliked:

$$(Rev)WWWWW(I - +P \longrightarrow Ob,Or) \equiv WWWWW(I \longleftarrow -P - Ob,Or).$$

The reverse of "I very badly want to take pleasure from the world through my body" is equivalent to "I very badly want to receive pain from the world through my body."

(3) *Sublimation* is a substitute formation in which a neutral object appears instead of a sexualized one. This often requires a shift in erogenous zone as well. The desire to obtain sexual pleasure from one's mother is disguised as an intellectual interest in nature:

$$(Sub)WW(I - +P \longrightarrow Mo,Or) \equiv WW(I - +P \longrightarrow N,Mi).$$

The sublimate of "I want to take pleasure from mother through my body" is equivalent to "I want to take pleasure from nature through my mind."

(4) *Repression* rejects as ill-formed all sentences which try to express the rejected proposition, leaving the speaker with the urge to speak but not the symbolic means. This urgency may later appear as generalized anxiety, and we can conveniently think of the sigh, moan, and thrash of those gagged and bound by bandits, scruples, or guerrillas. If, however, there are many ways to express the objectionable idea, then the most devious, euphemistic, and remote may reach consciousness. I can't say that I want my father's penis, and I can't say that I want what father has. I can't say that I want to take my father's

place, and I can't say that I wish my father would go away, but I can say (and, indeed, don't I say?) that I want to be big and strong like my father when I grow up.

If I cannot say that I wish to be refused, I can try refusing you, but if I dare not refuse you, I can eventually settle on giving you an inappropriate gift. Sometimes a series of acts is so inept and foolish that we can infer the inward opposite of their publicly painted purpose (Nixon's bumbling coverup, for instance). What we need to know, of course, is how to translate this behavior into its appropriate assertion, and, in addition, what operators ought to be applied to it, and in what order. Generally, only an analysis of the "speaker" will disclose the habitual psychological operators employed, as well as the reasons why these specific ones are chosen rather than some others.

Assuming that we know these things, Freud's scheme allows us to proceed through a series of propositional transformations from an early assertion of infantile desire, for example, to a later, more general, belief about the self, somewhat in the following fashion:

Narcissistic Voyeurism:	I want the pleasure of looking at myself.
	YOU CAN'T SAY THAT!
Introjection ------------	You are a part of me.
Voyeurism:	I want the pleasure of looking at you.
	YOU CAN'T SAY THAT!
Partial Reversal ------------	
Exhibitionism:	I want the pleasure of being looked at by you.
	YOU CAN'T SAY THAT!
Full Reversal ------------	
Masochistic Exhibitionism:	I want the shame of being looked at by you.
	YOU CAN'T SAY THAT!
Repression ------------	
------------	OR THAT!
------------	OR THAT!
	I deserve to be exposed.

If this last statement expresses an extended belief about the self, and therefore represents a set of sentences rather than simply a specific and momentary wish of the id, then we can profitably apply K. M. Colby's programming suggestions to it, transforming at once the whole belief-group in any one (or more) of the following ways: [21]

> I deserve to be exposed.
>
> YOU MUSTN'T BELIEVE THAT!

Projection ------------ I am a part of them.

> Others deserve to be exposed.

Or:

> I deserve to be exposed.
>
> YOU MUSTN'T BELIEVE THAT!

Verbal Deflection ------------ (repression)(try to find a weaker version)

> I deserve to be seen for what I am.

By mid-career Freud was suggesting that there were two instincts, one concerned with the preservation of the person, the other with sexuality. These two instincts were soon so intertwined that they found themselves speaking the same sentences. If I want pleasure from your body, I shall need some power over it, and it is possible that soon my sexual pleasure will stem from the power itself.

The sexual instinct says: I badly want pleasure from your body.

The preservation instinct says: I want power over your body.

The sadistic fusion is: I want the pleasure of power over your body, i.e.,

$$WWW_{sex} (I - +P \longrightarrow Ob,Or) \ \& \ WW_{pres} (I - Pow \longrightarrow Ob,Or) \equiv$$
$$WW_pW_s (I - +P \longrightarrow PowOb,Or).$$

---

[21] Colby's work on the computer representation of Freudian defenses is described and extensively cited by Margaret Boden in the essay just mentioned. Colby concentrates on the programming of beliefs like "I am defective," "Father abandoned me," and

Sexualized power is the root of sadism, and pain has very little to do with its subtler manifestations. Moreover, the sadist is so concerned to be secure he has no time for the blessings of peace, and instead seeks repeated proofs of his safety in the whip.

The economics of sexual pleasure can be worked out on this "marital" square of opposition:

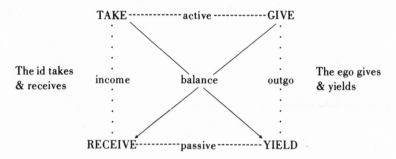

Within the total pleasure of any bonded pair (two people who are serving as introjected objects for each other, food sources, so to speak, as near as each belly, or the ever-present breast, the tender fondle, the happy tweak), the income and outgo for each should be roughly equal over time, otherwise the economy of the country will surely falter, one ego will find itself in debt to the id of another. In such circumstances only power can prevent payment, and soon still another little repressive society will have been added to the world.

Freud's first book was about speech problems (*On Aphasia*, 1891), and it might be argued that his work remained running in that starting place. Even in the silence of the id, there is the beginning of differentiation, of centering, of speech; for the unconscious cannot come forth by day any differently from the way it does by night. There must be fragments of language it can fasten to, images it can distort, concepts to hide under

---

"I descend from royalty." In my sentences the id is speaking to the ego. In his, the ego is considering what it shall say to the world.

as though they were sheep whose woolly backs would soothe the suspicious hands of the Cyclops—come forth! come forth! —and with such sly chicanery, such a clever sleight to the pokered eye of the cyclops, emerge from the cave as a symbol . . . clean as a contest queen from a suburban housewife's womb.

Does the id speak the truth? It always speaks the truth, because the id is a miraculous conjecture. There are no obstacles to myths. The Freud of the "Project" worried about the confirmation of the magnified eye and the knife, as do many of the philosophers in Wollheim's volume, nor did he ever abandon the belief that one day a slide would show the eye a reason; but the Freud who told us the meaning of our slips, jokes, and dreams was a reader and interpreter of texts. How do we know, then, when a code's been cracked? . . . when we are right? . . . when do we know if we have even received a message? Why, naturally, when, upon one set of substitutions, sense emerges like the outline under a rubbing; when a single tentative construal leads to several; when all the sullen letters of the code cry TEAM! after YEA! has been, by several hands, uncovered.

And if the Japanese don't sail their ships where we have said their messages have sent them? . . . then the Japanese have simply not sent their ships where they said they would. Warriors, poets, persons change their minds; but codes are frozen in their formulas of dissimulation like those toothy tigers were in Russian ice.

And so the secret source of the self speaks. What else is soul but a listener? Yet, as Burton has, again perfectly, put it:

The Tower of *Babel* never yielded such confusion of tongues, as this Chaos of Melancholy doth variety of symptoms. There is in all melancholy, like men's faces, a disagreeing likeness still; and as, in a river, we swim in the same place, though not in the same numerical water;

as the same instrument affords several lessons, so the same disease yields diversity of symptoms; which howsoever they be diverse, intricate, and hard to be confined, I will adventure yet, in such a vast confusion and generality, to bring them into some order . . .

	Controversy
	Rivalry
	Envy
What	*Forgetfulness*
It	*Suspicion*
Did	*Idolatry*
	Jealousy
	Obfuscation
	Resistance

The only memorable scene in HD's otherwise muzzy, self-absorbed memoirs of the Professor, mainly taken from two series of meetings she had with him in 1933–1934, when Freud was seventy-seven, occurs during an analytic session. Evidently the deeper fish weren't rising and HD was simply dimpling the surface with her toes. Suddenly Freud begins to beat on the headboard of the horsehair sofa she'd been reclining and reminiscing on till his fist roused her. "The trouble is—I am an old man—*you do not think it worth your while to love me.*"

As Roazen observes,[22] Freud was fifty years old before any of his famous followers came to court. He knew what the lure of maturity was, the accomplishment of a completed self and the magic of a man who has been vouchsafed revelations, not to mention the attraction, too, of someone with livelihoods for sale. But a cancerous old codge—could a libidinous transference be effected for such a precariously pale, jaw-gnawed sage? And can we achieve it today with these spousely familiar texts? how shall they startle our understanding with more than the hammer of an old man's rage?

Paul Roazen's present book on Freud is clearly the result of research he undertook for *Brother Animal*, a fuller and less cautious description of Freud's friendship and falling-out with Victor Tausk than appears in *Freud and His Followers*.[23] The

---

[22] Paul Roazen, *Freud and His Followers* (New York: Knopf, 1974).

[23] In addition to these, and *Freud: Political and Social Thought*, Roazen has edited

earlier study is an extended account of this discipleship, and Tausk's suicide in 1919 forms the dramatic center of a kind of biographical whodunit. Roazen was rightly excited by the material his researchers began to unearth and the "new not so nice" Freud who began to appear out of the dark fog of flattery and reticence which had always shielded him before—hulking a little, I'm afraid, like a menacing figure in another bad Hitchcock film. Freud had warts. Was he the whole toad?

The man defined by these volumes is *said* to be a warm and courageous genius, an inspiring teacher, an amusing storyteller and understanding companion, a source of wisdom and example of pure dedication; but he is *shown* to be aloof, vain, proud, tyrannical, unforgiving and vindictive, suspicious, jealous—in short, a quite unpleasant neurotic. In that difference lies the bias of both books.

Brother Animal is a disturbing work, not because it is critical of Freud while pretending, as *Freud and His Followers* also does, to be "objective," or because it absurdly overvalues Tausk's talent, or even because the conclusion we are asked to come to is that Freud was a seriously responsible factor in Tausk's suicide (a charge, to this reader, more than totally unproved), but because of its very questionable biographical methods. Roazen's use of quotation, the beautiful placement of his omissions, the implicit and often fluctuating judgments, his style (which might be described as a conscious stream of insinuation and unscrupulous contrivance), and his almost total avoidance of substantive issues, were together so outrageous that they provoked K. R. Eissler to a book-length refutation.[24]

a collection of essays on Freud in the Makers of Modern Social Science series for Prentice-Hall, 1973. It consists mainly of essays from psychiatric journals or chapters reprinted from well-known books and contains important pieces by Erikson, Fromm, Marcuse, Adorno, and Sapir, among others.

[24] *Talent and Genius* (New York: Quadrangle, 1971). Although Roazen knows of this book and Eissler's work in general, *Freud and His Followers* is absolutely silent about

Roazen's treatment of Lou Andreas-Salomé is typical, and a few passages can provide a good example of the differences between the two books.

Brother Animal	*Freud and His Followers*
Lou fits the genre of women who have a knack of collecting great men. Madame de Staël in the late eighteenth and early nineteenth centuries, and Alma Mahler in the twentieth illustrate the type. In Lou's case beauty was not her main attraction. Whatever her earlier good looks, she now had to rely on her psychological resources to arouse the attention of any potential conquests. (p. 33)	Lou was of the genre of women who have a knack for collecting great men. Whatever her earlier good looks, she now had to rely on her psychological resources to arouse the attention of any potential conquests. (p. 314)

Eissler points out quite correctly that Alma Mahler and Madame de Staël are not parallel cases; that neither Nietzsche nor Rilke was famous when she was intimate with them; that she in fact preferred Nietzsche's friend Rée; that in Vienna she was most attracted to Richard Beer-Hofmann (relatively unknown to most of us now), and that it was perfectly reasonable for a woman "whose mind was equal to that of the greatest of her times" to find pleasure in the company of the gifted. Victor Tausk, incidentally, is still not famous.

Roazen weaves passages from *Brother Animal* in and out of *Freud and His Followers*, dropping some of his more offensive remarks, but certainly not all of them.

---

it. Eissler himself is *too* angry, *too* strident, *too* concerned to protect the Professor at every point.

Brother Animal	*Freud and His Followers*
Vibrantly responsive to ideas, Lou possessed an extraordinary flair for identifying with men, and especially with that creative part of them most subject to inner uncertainties. (p. 33)	Vibrantly responsive to ideas, she possessed an extraordinary flair for identifying with men, and especially with that creative part of them most subject to inner uncertainties. But

Although Lou was useful to her line of great men precisely because she could identify with that most precious portion of themselves so in need of support, as men fell in love with her they eventually discovered that she had not truly given of herself. She had mirrored them, had helped their creative need, but at bottom Lou withheld herself as a person. Her great men all needed her, but each of her lovers ultimately realized how she had eluded him. (p. 34)

as men fell in love with her they eventually discovered that she had not truly given of herself. She had mirrored them, had helped their creative need, but had withheld herself as a person. They all needed her, but ultimately they realized that she had eluded them. (pp. 314–15)

That she withheld herself is so palpably untrue in the case of Rilke, for example, with whom she remained in long, magnificent, and truly helpful correspondence until his death, that one wonders at the cause of this gratuitous malice.

Brother Animal	*Freud and His Followers*
For the year 1912–13, however, Freud, Lou, and Tausk established a triangle which	For the period 1912–13 Freud, Lou, and Tausk established a triangle which had advantages

had advantages for each. Lou had recurrently had two men in her life simultaneously. She had married Friedrich Carl Andreas after he had threatened to kill himself otherwise; but she slept only with other men. Before Lou was married she had used another man against Nietzsche. (Nietzsche's sister considered her a devil.) Lou, Rilke, and Andreas traveled to Russia as a threesome. And now she had a physical relation with Tausk, alongside her deep involvement with Freud.

For Freud the arrangement had frustrations as well as satisfactions. He was jealous of Tausk's opportunity to have an affair with Lou. Tausk was much younger, more virile, and altogether a larger man physically . . . On the other hand, Lou could give Freud information about Tausk. She could help keep this potentially troublesome student under control . . . For both men she was a buffer. (pp. 45–46)

for each. Lou often had had two men in her life simultaneously. For Freud the arrangement had frustrations as well as satisfactions. He was jealous of Tausk's opportunity to have an affair with Lou. Tausk was younger, more virile, and altogether a larger man physically. On the other hand, Lou could give Freud information about Tausk, to help keep this potentially troublesome student under control. For both men she was a buffer. (p. 315)

That Freud was jealous of Tausk's physical intimacy with Lou is not supported by any evidence; that he used that intimacy to control Tausk (the Machiavellian suggestion) is not supported by any evidence; that Lou used Rée against Nietzsche is a wholly unfair description of that complex affair; the reference to Nietzsche's sister is especially sly, since she was notoriously jealous and unreliable. One may say: small matters, minor details. But they multiply. They comprise a whole forest of whispers in a slanderous wind.[25] In *Brother Animal* Lou is described as fitting perfectly into a passive role, and in both books Roazen writes that

> She could flatter him and still believe everything she said. A woman can more easily dissociate her sense of self from her professional work; so to give Freud what he wanted in no way compromised her integrity. *(FF, p. 315; BA, p. 48)*

In Chapter 9 of the *Followers*, which is entitled "The Women," and devoted to Brunswick, Deutsch, Klein, and Anna Freud, the condescension evident in the passage I've just quoted becomes epidemic.

The characterization of Lou Salomé as passive is, of course, ludicrous. For a while, friends referred to Rilke as the Lou-man; the poet Gerhart Hauptmann wryly remarked that he was too stupid for Lou; she rejected her husband's sexuality, held Rée at arm's length, dispensed wisdom like a Lama, shocked society everywhere with her forwardness. Finally, it is she who kneels in the cart and cracks the whip while Rée and Nietzsche pretend to pull it in that joking Lucerne photograph. What is apparently unforgivable about Lou is that as a

---

[25] Roazen cites Rudolph Binion's *Frau Lou* (Princeton, 1968; paper, 1974), but he selects from it very carefully. H. F. Peters's biography, *My Sister, My Spouse* (Norton, 1963; paper, 1974), is much more appreciative of Lou and certainly more readable than Binion, who is, like Roazen, "correcting the record," but it is also much less secure concerning the facts. For a brief, *fair* account of Lou's relationship with Nietzsche, see Walter Kaufmann's *Nietzsche*, 3rd edition (Princeton, 1969). At least some of Lou's lurid sexual past is overdrawn. It seems that she remained a virgin for many years after her involvement with Rée and Nietzsche.

woman, in all her relationships, she resolutely remained her own man.

Much of the new material which makes *Freud and His Followers* such an interesting book comes from interviews with people who knew Freud personally, either as patient or pupil, and from those others who participated in the movement or were long-standing students of it. Roazen describes in detail his interview techniques, and we learn from this that he did not use a tape recorder but began from prepared questions, took notes, allowed the interview to develop spontaneously when that seemed advisable, and reconstructed the conversation later. Sometimes it was not possible to take any notes at all. While there were obvious and good reasons for adopting the procedures he did, what Roazen was in fact collecting was a mass of material, mostly gossip and reminiscence, colored by personality, dimmed by time, fabricated by weakness and shaped by self-interest, which he then had not only to remember and accurately record himself, but cross-check and evaluate against solider documentation and that less steady but always weighty body of received opinion.

He was fishing, moreover, in a sea of serpents. There were questions of loyalty and disloyalty, rectitude and competence, originality and theft; there were profound jealousies, clever concealments, and human imbroglios like hopeless snags of hair. The truth of a theory is the last thing to matter when ideas become traits of character. Gossip engulfs everything. Did indeed Freud emerge from his consulting room with a visible erection? What did Ferenczi's kisses and cuddles come to? Did James J. Putnam fix the seat on his daughter's bicycle lest she be unduly stimulated? Did Tausk once test a woman's genitals for sensation with a galvanic rod?

Analysts had affairs with patients or with one another. One of Freud's sons took up with a patient of his father's. Confidences were breached. Since every prospective analyst had to be analyzed, too much became known about too many, daisy chains of secrets—of private mouth put to confidential ear, of understanding stimulated to uneasiness, of fear brought on to brotherly betrayal—soon were formed. Out of this even the fairest and most dispassionate mind must come covered with some slime, some self-serving subjectivity, the button of a weakness pressed once too often, perhaps outraged by an attitude or alliance, comforted by a concealment close to home.

Freud was straitlaced, "old-fashioned," insisted on protocol, ran his household by the clock; but it is clear that he had to, *in his position*. He was doubtless too continuously aware of who he was, but he needed that knowledge to hold himself together. In him, career and character happily coincided. He had his weaknesses (chronicled here), but he did not sexually profit from the illnesses of his patients; he had his weaknesses, but he did not borrow his ideas from others—*he did not follow*; he grew old, became ill but never uncreative; he had his weaknesses, but he did not (very often) violate the confidences of the couch; never did his ambition or his pride leave him; he had his weaknesses and among them was an intense dislike of weakness itself, so that his humaneness (and one has only to read him to see it) constituted an extraordinary display of strength.

Although the ideas at stake in Freud's break with Jung or Adler (for example) are referred to, the intellectual pros and cons are never pursued very deeply, and thus the impression is unfortunately given that personal pique, envy, spite, and fear principally widened these divisions; that the ideological differences were merely screens behind which cowered men of small stature and shorter organs. Roazen tends to come down gently on the side of the dissidents by reminding us how frequently present-day analysts would agree with this or that inanity on the part of one of them.

Occasionally the book causes us to forget, too, how little Freud's followers were his equals, gifted as many of them were. That is why one has to compare texts (compare minds,

compare precisions, compare depths), and if Freud sometimes
had the impression that his ideas were in loose hands; that he
had given away a method which was now being used willy-nilly
to draw his image on every blank page and open possibility
about; if he felt that those who had come to him to have their
minds filled, with rebuilt egos and rejuvenated arrogance, then
used the position he had given them to "revise" his ideas in
a way directly counter to the spirit and premises which presumably had drawn them to him in the first place; if this gave
him a feeling of treachery and ingratitude, it is understandable; if he felt that his pupils had purchased their wisdom
cheaply, it was understandable; why should he appreciate
their mucking about ahead of him, planting flags with his maps
and declaring whole countries to be colonies of kings and
queens he couldn't stand? and be pleased as he watched Adler
try to capture Freudianism for the clergy, or Jung drag his doctrines into the realm of mythopeic nonsense?

For Freud did not forget, could not forget, and restated
with classic concision and directness in his final work, the radical nature of his enterprise, the rich real ground of its beginnings, first in the biology of the body, and then in the language
of the instincts, and finally in the early and decisive influence
of the family. So it is not surprising that he grew proprietary
and testy, and wanted orthodoxy, and was grateful for grati-
tude and loyalty, and feared for the future of the movement he
had founded. He was right to worry: the history of psychoanalysis has been the same as the history of scotch whiskey;
there's no more burr beneath that blandness either.

Forgetfulness is the subject of Russell Jacoby's *Social
Amnesia*. It is Freud who has been forgotten. His theories have
been repressed. Whether Freud's views are true or not, it is
evident that most of Freud's followers do not desire them to be.
They are quite friendly. these followers, as the ego is to the id,
but really Freud should not be allowed to say what he says
(they say); surely there is a more acceptable way to phrase

matters than he's found (they insist); there is a brighter prospect to be had (they believe).

It is as if, to the sentences of the inside self which I have previously described, Fromm, Reich, Horney, Sullivan, or Adler operators were applied, one to repress or substitute, another to turn the theory back upon itself, another to reverse both voice and value, so that, first, Freud's scientific materialism is rejected as "old-fashioned" and "a product of the late 19th century"; then his unseemly emphasis on sexuality, always an embarrassment, is said to be "extreme"; the concept of the unconscious, always hard, is avoided; then his stress on instinct and the determinations of the past, so discouraging, is set aside as interfering with our productive adjustment to the present; his notion of the death wish, so unpleasant, is attacked as romantic; the burden of responsibility he places on the person, so grim, so heavy, is transferred to the back of an ass; his obstinate insistence on the importance of theory, so useless to the patient or the purse, for that matter, of the therapist, is simply ignored on the monthly statement.

And in the place of these poor middle-class Viennese views, according to Jacoby (wouldn't the old man have snarled a whole cigar to shreds between the interstices of his teeth?), are put vague pragmatisms, moralizing self-help, and an opportunistic and saccharine liberalism designed to maintain the individual's ability to function in an oppressive social system without coming explosively apart.

So if one were to ask what had happened to analysis in the hands of its followers, the answer would have to be that it had become Rotarized and Chautauqua'd.

So *Social Amnesia* is a polemical attack on what Jacoby calls "conformist psychology." Often witty, and like polemics a pleasure when you generally agree, it sometimes sprawls full length across its similes:

The last preserves of the autonomous individual are under siege. Today human relations are irregulars and seconds at the closing days of the warehouse sale of life. The lines form because everyone knows the rest is junk; all that remains are the remains. (p. 17)

Jacoby characterizes Adler nastily. I laugh and I warmly agree. Good fellow. But he doesn't do enough more than I am doing here. He says so . . . and he says so . . . Like zeroes, say-sos don't sum. He quotes, again Adler for instance—

"All failures . . . neurotics, psychotics, criminals, drunkards, problem children, suicides, perverts and prostitutes . . . [are] failures because they are lacking in fellow feeling and social interest. They approach the problems of occupation, friendship and sex without the confidence that they can be solved by cooperation."

—and assumes that Adler's imbecility will be evident. Alas, it has not been.

Although he follows the lead of Marcuse, whose criticism of neo-Freudians like Fromm in *Eros and Civilization* was among the earliest,[26] he is able to make use of the entire Frankfurt school (Marcuse, of course, and Horkheimer as well as Adorno), and at this later time enlarge the number of his targets to include the so-called post-Freudians—Allport, Maslow, and Rogers—some existentialists, and finally even R. D. Laing and David Cooper.

The Frankfurt thinkers quite overpower the opponents they are pitted against, but the writings of this group, as well as those of many other Marxists, tend too often to travel from label to label and ism to ism, from opponents' error to enemies' mistake, with the noise and ferocity of a barbarian beating his shield with his sword—that is, with more clangor than clarity—

---

[26] Although Paul Goodman's superb critique in *Politics*, II, 1945, "The Political Meaning of Some Recent Revisions of Freud," antedates Marcuse's initial essay in *Dissent* in 1955.

until one feels there might be better results in future if they (and *their* followers) were forced to express themselves only with words like *banana, hausfrau, watchchain,* and *color-guard.*

Jacoby is appropriately critical of traditional Marxism too, as the Frankfurt school has been, and he has been particularly careful to keep his concept of consciousness dialectical. Crucial to his book, and in many ways its best part, is his assessment of the role of therapy in the psychoanalytic movement. Incidentally, this is one of the better features of Roazen's book too. He fully exposes Freud's doubts about (and even disinterest in) therapy, though I suspect this attitude is regarded as still another shortcoming.

In blunt and in brief: for Freud the self is an accumulation of encounters between instinct and society, and from the first encounter on the libido has been bent by power like a hairpin. The world which the ego feels it must accommodate desire to is composed of lies and illusion laid down like law. Society itself is a structured set of individuals who have been socially deformed. Freud is fierce about this: not even the members of a mob will be permitted to escape into a collective anonymity. They simply regress together.

> Think of the colossal brutality, cruelty and mendacity which is now allowed to spread itself over the civilized world [Freud writes concerning the First World War]. Do you really believe that a handful of unprincipled place-hunters and corrupters of men would have succeeded in letting loose all this latent evil, if the millions of their followers were not also guilty? [27]

Illnesses arise when the ego is unable to find allowable ways to reduce tension. Surface therapy is designed to help the ego

---

[27] Marcuse also quotes this passage from *A General Introduction to Psychoanalysis* in *Eros and Civilization* (Boston: Beacon Press, 1955).

do just that. We can compliment ourselves on our cures. Meanwhile, the same mothers lean over the crib the way centers crouch over their ball, and society, as we suffer from it, is preserved.

Of course Freud hoped to help people, but he valued his clinical practice principally because it gave him data. His movement lived upon the therapeutic promises it made, and he remained uneasy about the purity of his intentions. More than the implications of analysis itself, it made him prickly and unsure about the motives of others. Would an understanding as demanding as Spinoza had asked for enable many to rise and walk?

"My discoveries are a basis for a very grave philosophy." Well, Freud knew how necessary it would be for psychoanalysis to free itself from its enemies—religion (even that of his forefathers), many forms of metaphysics, the literature he loved and had a knack for, the medicine he practiced—before his boast could be realized. Not because religion, literature, or medicine were themselves enemies of anything, but because his theories became bent in their service, as altered as Boyle's Law would be as an account of pipelines, sales, or metered service. Inside them, as one of them, his position lost its identity as a profoundly important, though admittedly partial, criticism of society. Open to physiology at one end and to linguistics at the other, everywhere sympathetic with the most rigorous formal programs of natural science, Freudianism is beginning to emerge at last as one of the most complete and vigorous statements of rational materialism philosophy has yet had the pleasure to challenge and ponder.

"But where am I? Into what subject have I rushed? What have I to do with Nuns, Maids, Virgins, Widows? I am a Bachelor myself," Burton writes, "and lead a Monastick life in a College . . . And yet," he says, "I must and will say something more, add a word or two on behalf of Maids and Widows, in favour of all such distressed parties," for did they not begin the whole business? "So," Burton continues in a manner which could not over several hundred years be improved upon,

> . . . must I needs inveigh against them that are in fault . . . and as bitterly tax those tyrannizing pseudo-politicians' superstitious orders, rash vows, hard-hearted parents, guardians, unnatural friends, allies, . . . so to find and enforce men and women to vow virginity, to lead a single life against the laws of nature, opposite to religion, policy, and humanity, so to starve, to offer violence [to], to suppress the vigour of youth! . . . Stupid Politicians! ought these things so to be carried? . . . They will by all means quench their neighbour's house, if it be on fire, but that fire of lust, which breaks out into such lamentable flames, they will not take notice of, their own bowels oftentimes, flesh and blood, shall so rage and burn, and they will not see it . . . For let them but consider what fearful maladies, feral diseases, gross inconveniences, come to both sexes by this enforced temperance. It troubles me to think of, much more to relate, those frequent aborts & murdering of infants in their Nunneries, . . . their notorious fornications, those male-prostitutes, masturbators, strumpets, &c., those rapes, incests, adulteries, . . . sodomies, buggeries, of Monks and Friars . . . I know their ordinary apologies and excuses for these things, but let the Politicians, the Doctors and Theologians look out: I shall more opportunely meet with them elsewhere.

Food and Beast
Language

In *The Colossus of Maroussi*, that cranky and beautiful book about Greece, there are a number of passages which describe Henry Miller's encounters with Katsimbalis, a man once real and now imaginary, who is remade by Miller's inflationary prose into one of the more robust, unmannerly Greek gods. Katsimbalis is a monologist of genius very much like Miller himself, and the style of his talk matches our author's speech stream perfectly. Indeed, why shouldn't it, since the objects of Miller's incessant sentences are sounding boards which echo their origin by responding always "Henree . . . Henree . . ." to every shout.

> He could galvanize the dead with his talk. It was a sort of devouring process: when he described a place he ate into it, like a goat attacking a carpet. If he described a person he ate him alive from head to toe. If it were an event he would devour every detail, like an army of white ants descending upon a forest. He was everywhere at once . . . It wasn't just talk he handed out, but *language*—food and beast language.[1]

And Miller says of Seferis, the Nobel poet, that "when he talked about a thing or a person or an experience he caressed it with his tongue."

[1] *Genius and Lust: A Journey Through the Major Writings of Henry Miller*, by Norman Mailer (New York: Grove Press, 1976), pp. 405–06.

The Henry Miller who prowls the Paris streets, or hires and fires for Western Union, is a hungry man in every sense, and every sense is hungry. It is the secret and the glory of his style. *He drank in her beauty* runs the old cliché, which neglects to mention the emptiness of the result, or the depth of the ensuing belch. He is alert, a little giddy, like one who hasn't eaten, and angry, too, at every bone he can't gnaw, and always on the make, looking out for number one, shrewd, devious, untrustworthy, heartless, selfish as the empty stomach is supposed to be, the parched throat, the blood-puffed penis. And though most of Miller's clinches are clichés, there is no sour aftersmart he fails to mention.

One is reminded, by its difference, of Rilke's Paris, which seemed to the poet then like a hospital for contagious diseases. At last I am learning to see, Rilke's hero wrote, but what did he learn and what did he see? Only horrors: life like spittle on a wall, souls the shape of discarded sacks, fear as general as air—in faces which fell away into the hands which held and hid them, in the urinating nervousness of dogs, in silences which broke the noise of everyday like plates, in the spoonable emptiness of after-midnight streets, and, on the Rue de Seine, in little shops which seemed serene and safe as graves.

The world around Rilke was alive and would devour him. To see, to be, in such a place, to accept and to interiorize experience as his hero felt he must . . . well, it was as though he had taken flies alive into his belly. Henry Miller, on the other hand, like Katsimbalis, is the threat. He is the monster. His are the glances which light like flies. He will sniff the filthy undergarments of the city. He will swallow Paris like a whale: plate scrapings from the restaurants, bookstalls entire, including brittle paper, dog ears and prints of fingers, tarts too, the endless streets and every odor, St. Sulpice, the Trianon, the Dôme. "I could have eaten Lola's hair as a delicacy, if there'd been a piece of flesh attached to it."

The more urgent our needs, the less discriminating we are

about them. Finer points become pointless, because, in the democracy of desire, pies equal potatoes equal stewed meats equal apples equal snails (we'll roast rats, eat our dogs and cats, crunch the bones of our canaries, devour one another the way Saturn swallowed his children); meanwhile every quality is shed but edibility, and what we eventually consume is merely the member of a class, a naked abstraction: Food . . . and what we do is naked too: we Feed.

We have in Miller an ideal instance of the interested eye, one filled with more ego than light, an "I" which lives in a world of utility and blunt satisfactions. Since objects are reduced to their signs (I am edible, I am drinkable, I am beddable), such signs are surreally enlarged and related, so that a woman is simply a collection of hungry concavities which must be approached warily but always with phallus aforethought.

Alas, the penis is such a ridiculous petitioner. It is so unreliable, though everything depends on it—the world is balanced on it like a ball on a seal's nose. It is so easily teased, insulted, betrayed, abandoned; yet it must pretend to be invulnerable, a weapon which confers magical powers upon its possessor; consequently this muscleless inchworm must try to swagger through temples and pull apart thighs like the hairiest Samson, the mightiest ram.

To enter the cave and escape alive—that is the trick. Every boy on the block wants to be brave; every boy on the block knows that a bird in the bush is worth two in the hand; but the difficulty is that one is eaten by what one eats.

> . . . life is merchandise with a bill of lading attached, what I choose to eat being more important than I the eater, each one eating the other and consequently eating, *the verb,* ruler of the roost . . . The plate and what's on it, through the predatory power of the intestinal apparatus, commands attention and unifies the spirit, first hypnotizing it,

then slowly swallowing it, then masticating it, then absorbing it.

So we are safe with women only when what they see when they see us, what they feel when they feel us, above all, what they think of us as they see and feel and contain us, cannot possibly matter, is of no consequence (like servants, their awareness is belowstairs, and like slopeheads and gooks, who cares?); so women are pinioned, subjugated, as food is chewed, coolly, casually, with professional detachment and male disdain; evaluations are made the way we size up cattle, and our comfortable, self-serving theory is that the lamb really bleats to be sacrificed; that we should not treat women as persons because they want to be relieved of conventional decencies in the moment they are relieved of their clothes, which explains why so many of Miller's women pretend not to notice what's happening, they like to feign disinterest, confusion, or sleep; consequently they should be hammered, pounded, slammed, until their sexuality expresses itself in purely masculine terms, until they cry "give it to me" with dreamy frequency; because when any woman's modesties have been driven away, when she has been made as mindless as any man, when mouths appear all over her like hives and she yowls like an animal in heat, she will have made that most satisfactory of all admissions: that she has no high-and-mighty refinement, no superior cultivation or spirituality, tenderness or sophistication; that she is, thank sex, no better than we are—a cow, a sow, a pig; that her "mother morality" is a lie.

Yet that "mother morality" is exactly what we want to believe in—we motherless men—and because mother does indeed belong to the same sex we degrade and despise; because she, who did not do it with dad except out of duty and did not want us to do it even in the line of duty; that same "she" is implicated in each of our proofs so that every success is a failure.

According to pre-Lib wisdom, Mailer observes, there is something in a woman which wishes to be slain, namely, the hypocrisies of her asexual upbringing. He writes that "in every whore is an angel burning her rags," but it seems to me that the social decencies which are outraged and removed in the sexual act are shown to be merely veneers the moment the angel moans, and when the angel moans it's always the whore we hear. In that case, it's not puritan morality Miller is complaining about; rather the fact that that stern dye hasn't evenly colored the whole cloth.

In *The Tropic of Cancer* and *The Colossus of Maroussi*, where Miller is at his best, in spectacular bursts, in similar fits and starts throughout his *oeuvre*, there is an eager vitality and exuberance to the writing which is exhilarating; a rush of spirit into the world as though all the sparkling wines had been uncorked at once; and the language we watchfully hear skip, whoop and wheel across Miller's pages makes an important esthetic point, especially to those of us who are more at home with Joyce or Woolf or James or Proust, and that is that beneath all the quiet ruminations of the mind, the slendered sensibilities, the measured lyricism of finer feelings, even nearby the remotest precincts of being, is a psyche like quicksand, an omnivorous animal, the continually chewing self.

It is a manner—this virility of noun and verb—which is so originally and genuinely male, yet really so deeply human that until women can find an openly lustful, quick, impatient, feral hunger in themselves, they will never be liberated, and their writing, however elegant or well observed or composed of sexual bouts like a fight card, in pallid imitation of the master, will lack that blood-congested genital drive which energizes every great style, whether it's that of a bawdy Elizabethan or a coolly decorous Augustan, of Jane Austen, Colette, or Cardinal Newman.

As Miller's prose extends itself like a weather front over the thousand and more pages of *The Rosy Crucifixion*, this reader at least begins to feel it no longer expresses the hunger of someone who is thin and empty, but the greed of someone who is full and fat, someone who is attempting to remedy an old lack; futilely, too, for today's dinner will not nourish yesterday's body, and the women whom Miller's narrator causes to cry "uncle" with such unreal, therefore pornographic, regularity, are not yielding themselves to the man in him who *is*, but to the boy in him who *was*; so that another feature of Miller's work (noted nicely by Mailer) becomes disfiguringly large like a wart on the rampage.

It is an element in every author's impulse to speech and exposure: the desire to present the worst in oneself in the guise of a gift, as the child feels he has when he's used his pot. Having dined on life, Miller makes us a present of what he cannot stomach, that part of the world which only the front half accepted; and in laying his heart bare (as Baudelaire threatened), he has instead dropped his pants; by shaping this enormous stool of words he expects our parental applause; thus Miller's work in this regard (like Céline's throughout) becomes a splendid example of the excremental style.

Some styles are celebrational, as Miller's often is; some are penitential, like Joyce's, full of self-imposed barriers, hardships, ordeals and penalties; and some are excremental— where the idea is simply to get it out, to write like hell and never look back, as Mailer says, until the words amass and mount in books which resemble the rubble of a prolonged catharsis.

Henry Miller's works are not *written*, and do not belong to the page like Pynchon's; nor are they *spoken* as Gaddis's are; nor do they employ the more formal oral eloquence of Sir Thomas Browne; they are *talked*, yarned like a sailor, endlessly gabbed; and his male readers at last must be reminded of the bluff good-fellow voice of the locker-room brag, the pool-hall cue-fondler's side-mouthed secrets, the man-to-manness of the autumn gunman, or the good ole boy greased on booze: well let me tell you when I saw her huge X, my! it was so Y that I nearly Z'd; and we can hear the Gee-Whiz, Aaaah-Come-Off-It, and Don't-Hand-Me-That-Mulch of a skeptical, envious, invisible audience; and then we can feel the skazlicher

redouble his efforts to astonish, amuse, and above all, *prove*
. . . so that the narrator's consciousness is one of permanently
uneasy anecdotal exaggeration, endeavoring again always to
prove . . . to prove . . . the omnipresence of the lust for power?
corruption in low places? hypocrisy of the church? exploitation
by the monied? perhaps . . . to prove that one's OK? function-
ing? manly? alive? able? maybe; but mainly to prove that one
and all, rich or poor, married or single, cultivated or crude,
humble or hoity-toity, fat or thin, dressed or naked, alone or
together, in knickers or nightie . . . that *they* . . . they are all
alike—they're Ccccczzzs—nothing but Ccccczzzs—and may
they roast for it.

So Miller the author and Miller the fictional figure soon
separate their lives with lies, not only because there is a natural inflation of event in beguiling the boys, but because Miller
has opinions. He has more opinions than his narrator has emis-
sions, and surrounding the action and ennobling the sex are ruminations, conclusions, points.

Miller's omnivorousness extends to print, and print now
and then expresses thought, contains ideas—mind food which
Miller devours with the delightful but unwary eagerness of the
self-taught. Sometimes he actually sounds like a sage. More often, however, the noise is that of a crank. Mailer doesn't think
very highly of Miller's thought or of the metaphysics of the letter F which Miller has spent so much energy and even intelligence elaborating; indeed Mailer's description of his hero's
weak feet and unsound shoes seems to me penetrating, fair
and laudable, because it gives Mailer's admiration greater authority: that of a critic in the form of a very knowing friend,
and not a mindless worshipper or glassy fan.

We've been led through these ruins before, by Lawrence
Durrell, principally, who tried to take a representative sample,
and by Thomas Moore, who was interested only in Miller's
writings on writing. Our present guide is not going to let us see
everything. He will push us past the pornographic paintings a

dozen times; we'll spend hours in the very impressive portrait gallery (and there is something of Goya and Velázquez in Miller's portraits); but he'll not let us near Philosopher's Leap. *The Books in My Life* gets short shrift, as does *The Cosmological Eye*. Not even a wink and a bribe will get us a peek in Critic's Cottage, where something obscenely clean and straight and bourgeois must be going on, so there is nothing from Miller's study of Rimbaud or any of his Lawrence or Balzac stuff, nor is there much from the collections of short pieces or any of the other pasted-up books by Miller which publishers have placed in the world for their profit and our puzzlement. Not all Miller's moods are represented either; for instance, none of his usually embarrassing burlesques are included (though I persist in liking what—in *Plexus*—is done to Goldilocks and the three bears).

Miller has more than one horse in his stable of hobbies, and he tends to ride them yawn and on, so these deletions are by and large a favor to the reader (Mailer is an entertaining, properly garrulous guide), but the picture of Miller and his work which emerges is more than slightly askew. Although there are some good examples of Miller's rant (and he is one of the best ranters in the ranting business), there is absent, everywhere, except in the editor's overview, Miller's reason why, his open-road Whitmanism, his love of books, lists, and the sound of words, his sincere wish to embrace, accept, and live in harmony with nature.

Mailer's commentary is valuable and his judgments generally legitimate if not beyond dispute, though occasionally Miller's style seems to infect and weaken Mailer's, and Mailer will condemn a slack flat passage of Miller's in order to praise a merely flatulent one. Miller anthologizes well because his completed works are usually shapeless, repetitious and shamelessly self-indulgent; but this is a catastrophic condition when it comes, finally, to estimating Miller's position as an artist, for he is simply not a shaper. Overcome by content, he grows repetitive but not recursive, and his work expands without getting deeper. He has great gifts, but his psyche has remained adolescent; and as Mailer himself observes, the mirror-named central female figures (Mona or Mara or Maude or Monica, as well as others of other letters) never succeed in freeing themselves from Miller's obsessions as some of the men do. The narrator, unlike Proust's Marcel, rarely escapes being merely Henry (as Berryman's Henry does), and his ties are not turned into triumphs of vision and form.

Except in those surreal moments when precisely that happens, and Mailer's judgment of Miller, which I find romantically overblown, is sustained by a style which not only carves its object out of words, but modulates our understanding through it seems a thousand keys (reminding us of Rilke's unreal city, unreal rooms), so that we pass from dissonance to harmony, from ouch! to whee! and back again, the way the stomach falls and the breath leaves when we enter the shoot-the-chutes: for example, in this exemplary passage from *The Tropic of Cancer*:

> And down this corridor, swinging his distress like a dingy lantern, Van Norden staggers, staggers in and out as here and there a door opens and a hand yanks him in or a hoof pushes him out. And the further off he wanders the more lugubrious is his distress: he wears it like a lantern which the cyclists hold between their teeth on a night when the pavement is wet and slippery. In and out of the dingy rooms he wanders, and when he sits down the chair collapses, when he opens his valise there is only a toothbrush inside. In every room there is a mirror before which he stands attentively and chews his rage, and from the constant chewing, from the grumbling and mumbling and the muttering and cursing his jaws have gotten unhinged and they sag badly and, when he rubs his beard, pieces of his jaw crumble away and he's so disgusted with himself that he stamps on his own jaw, grinds it to bits with his big heels.

Groping for Trouts

Yonder man is carried to prison.
Well; what has he done?
A woman.
But what's his offense?
Groping for trouts in a peculiar river.

I want to begin with a problem that's also a bit of history. It may at first appear as far from my topic—art and order—as the Andes are from their valleys, or as such remote and glacial mountain slopes must seem to some swimmer whose nose is full of salt. The problem concerns the measurement of nature, and I don't in the least mind saying that on any number of counts it's like groping for trouts in a peculiar river.

We have each seen the motion in bodies. We ourselves live. The newsboy delivers the daily paper. The dime which has slipped from our fist runs in a tightening spiral till, like a bug, we flat it with our foot. Spirits rise, rumors travel, hopes fade. The flesh crawls, felts and satins roughen, and when we lick our ice cream we can even taste the melt. Yes, Heraclitus calls the tune, and like the sound of an accordion is the noisy meeting and passing of trains.

The movements everywhere around us—in us—seem,

well . . . too numerous, too vague, too fragile and transitory to number, and that's terribly unsettling, for we always feel threatened when confronted with something we can't count. Why should we be surprised, then, to find out that creating and defending a connection between what William James called the buzzing, blooming confusion of normal consciousness—of daily life with its unstimulating bumps, its teaseless, enervating grinds—and the clear and orderly silences of mathematics, a connection which will give us meaning, security, and management, in one lump sum, is what our science—is what our art, law, love, and magic—is principally about?

That newspaper—we might mistake it for the white wings of a passing pigeon. Do we see the line it draws? Think how Galileo would have rendered it. He'd notice neither newspaper nor pigeon. He discovered that the distance which the paper might be tossed could be expressed—how wonderful his image —as the area of a rectangle. The match-up was astonishing: Velocity could be laid out on one side, time on another, and since he knew so much more about rectangles than he did about motion, his little Euclidean model (for that's what he'd managed), to the degree it held firm, would immediately make a science of physical movement possible . . . in terms of dots and dashes, points and paths . . . and he went on to describe all evenly accelerating motion in the cool and classic language of the triangle. Had Dante been more daring? I think not.

Now imagine that Alice (the girl conceived by Carroll— minister, poet, and logician), having eaten what she's been told to and drunk according to instructions, is swelling as she tiptoes through her tunnel, and imagine in addition that there is a light like those which warn low planes of towers, chimneys, or intrusive steeples, attached to the top of her head. Can't we see her as an elongating wand whose end is then a point upon a curve? A most monstrous metaphor, yet inspired. Any curve, Descartes decided, could be considered to enclose a set of lines whose ends like trimmed logs lay against it. Only moments later, so it seemed, so swift is thought translated into history, Descartes had devised a language to describe these points and lines, these curves and squares, in numbers. Every place upon a line had its address, and with that went directions: you went along Rue X a while, and then up Y till you were there. As simple as children, but all quite absurd, for motion only alters the overlaps of colors—we know that; there is nothing rectangular about passage; and surely squares and curves are never numbers—abstract, inert, and purely relational; they stretch their legs like cats. Yet in a generation (we speak now like the critics), Galileo, Fermat, and Descartes had first created, then speeded up, mechanics. Beyond the Pythagoreans' wildest dreams, motion had become number.

Again: how was it managed? The paperboy's paper is dispensed with. It becomes a point; its flight, a line. That curve itself is seen to be a row of dots, or so we might conceive a string of pearls if we were mathematically inclined. Next, each dot is said to represent the top of a slat, a vertical fixed like a post in the plane of the paperboy's feet. A picket fence, in short, has unfolded from his throw. If you prefer: it's a Venetian blind on its side, on edge. But no, the tip of each post is the elbow of an angle, the corner of that old friend, area, again, and thus this simple little daily act is actually, in our new poetry and picture book, exactly like a perfect fan of cards. Plato's intuition has been confirmed: the world we know and swim in is everywhere it flows a qualitative expression of serene, unchanging quantitative laws. The ambiguity of "point" makes many of these verses possible. Who knows? it may be the peak of a witch's cap, the climax of the geometer's cone. *Point*: it is truly a word to wonder at, this minute mark like a prick, this place in space less large than a hair's end or the sound of a silent clock, this piercing part and particular of discourse, this dimensionless speck which has been spelled, alone in English, sixteen different ways already—should we not salute it?

So yonder man is carried to prison. Shakespeare measures matters in quite another way. This sort of sexuality is seen as poaching . . . poaching in a peculiar river. The term is technical, and requires that we feel for the fish with our hands beneath an overhanging bank. "Fish must be grop't for, and be tickled too," Bunyan writes. When Hamlet tells Horatio how

> *Up from my cabin,*
> *My sea-gown scarf'd about me, in the dark*
> *Groped I to find them . . .*

he is using "groped" less precisely, more generally, than in this passage from *Measure for Measure*. Tickling is apparently essential to it, for Maria awaits Malvolio, whom she plans to dupe, with the words: ". . . here comes the trout that must be caught with tickling." And what was thought as *peculiar* then was, in particular, private property.

For instance.

We hate to think that through much of our life we window-shop and rarely purchase. Therefore, I suppose, it does dismay us to discover that of all the time we spend on sex—in thought, dreams, deed, in word, desire, or feeling—there is so little spending done to show for it that nothing's bought. Yet notice how predictably I've put it. I should be ashamed. First I spoke of spending time, and then I spoke of sperm—our sacred future—in the same way. Well, time is money, don't we say? and maybe our seeds are simply many pennies. Both, at least, are quantities—methods of accounting, blueprints, masterplots—and perhaps Protagoras really meant to tell us that man is the measurer of all things, not merely the measure, for I honestly believe it is his principal concern.

Certainly man will seem, in impoverished circumstances, to be interested only in getting himself fed, and of course if he feeds he will belch and break wind, he will wipe his behind with leaves, he will stopper his heart, allow his belly to rust, his skin to scale, and eventually he will inflate his bladder to embarrassment; but we cannot accurately measure man's nature in terms of what he *must* do (he must breathe, for example —all of us manage—yet few of us take much pleasure or even an interest in it); no, we have to observe him in the latitudes; in just those moments when the world unpins his shoulders from the mat; moments in which, if we were speaking of clocks, we would sense a wobble in the works. And if we think it's satisfaction that man wants, a simple easing of his needs like the release of stool or the fall of pants, remark how he collects in order to arrange (shells, coins, stamps); overeats to set a standard (ice cream, clams, corn, pie, cake, melons for a prize); makes rules as rapidly as clubs; commits to memory even fractional statistics, decimal notations (how fast six furlongs has been run, what Willie Mays is batting, what the market's done); turns the simplest "good day" into a social rite as empty, bored, and automatic as prayer or genuflection, any sign of the cross; passes laws and calls them measures; lays out all the acres of his days in stingy tracts with the ruthless greed of a plot developer. He arranges everything he hears, feels, sees, in decorous ranks like pallbearers beside him, and says he's "informing" his visual field. He lives a lot like a pin in a map—he calls it "growing up"—and there he indicates the drains. No, he does not copulate, he counts; he does not simply laugh or sneer or shout, he patiently explains. Regardless of the man or woman whom he mounts, throughout his wildest daydreams and even in the most persistent myths of his pornography, he will imagine in amounts. As our poet warns us, in the following boast:

> *Some glory in their birth, some in their skill,*
> *Some in their wealth, some in their body's force;*
> *Some in their garments, though new-fangled ill;*
> *Some in their hawks and hounds, some in their horse;*
> *And every humour hath his adjunct pleasure,*

Wherein it finds a joy above the rest:
But these particulars are not my measure . . .

Some writers are worthwhile, even if the other virtues they possess are invisible, because, like cooling soup, all the scum is on the surface.

What does De Sade do, for example? He measures his thing; he organizes orgies; he makes change; he not only contrives novel entanglements, he classifies them, tagging participants, numbering the blasphemies, designing relationships, keeping count of screams. In short, he commands; he orders— on paper nowhere better—for no one slips from *his* pyramid of bodies with an "oops!"—not in *his* books—no one misses the mark or fails to come up to it or interrupts the action, that is to say, the argument; because there was nothing De Sade disliked more than the sense that matters were getting out of hand (do not be surprised to find a revolutionary loving order, they can't wait to issue edicts and pass laws), and where were they more likely to but during fornication? It's an unprotected time. Both soul and body are in danger, and Plato was neither the first nor last philosopher to suggest that lust was another name for chaos. Take off your clothing—did not the Dukhobors?— and you attack the state.

We have strict statutes and most biting laws,
The needful bits and curbs, to headstrong weeds,
Which for this fourteen years we have let slip;

. . . .

[Now] liberty plucks justice by the nose;
The baby beats the nurse, and quite athwart
Goes all decorum.

This is the judgment of the duke in *Measure for Measure*, and this judgment motivates the plot. Take off your clothes. Be gymnastic. Public. Be perverse. Attack the deepest laws. De Sade, however, was no Galileo, even though his record as a prisoner was longer. The scientist represented motion geometrically because he wished to understand it. He did not so dangerously confuse his model with the world. But De Sade saw persons as pieces of earth in order to treat human beings like dirt. Sodomy was still a revolutionary act, but lust was some exasperation of the nerves, nevertheless, like a humming in tightly strung wires.

That light travels in straight lines; that a body set in motion will continue unchanged unless something else hinders it; that all things seek equilibrium or act to maintain themselves in any given state; that men seek only their own pleasure or act always to preserve their own lives; that we perceive only sense data; that we are machines: all of these are opinions so plainly desirable for the translation of data into abstract systems, as are both atoms and the void, that it seems unlikely they are more than rules of representation like the principles of perspective in painting.

It was Hobbes who understood clearly the consequences of Galileo's model as a universal measure. The advantage of thinking of matter in atomic terms was ultimately the resemblance of atoms to points, and as points stood for intersections, the corners of shapes, so atoms could be augmented by others and shrewdly arranged until the assemblage appeared as a visible object. If there were laws for the behavior of these, then might not men, considered as a house built of atomic bricks, be treated as moving bodies too; and finally, could not groups of them be regarded just like even larger bodies also on the move? In this way impressive sovereignties, in the drama Hobbes composed for them, became solarized systems, like vast constellations, crashing through space, and the erratic rattle of humans against one another and the side of the State was no more confused in fact than the dance of shot in a metal bowl. Chaos, like darkness, had been snuffed out.

Chaos, of course, is an enemy of art, an inversion of one of its essential qualities; but chaos, as George Santayana has pointed out, is simply any order incompatible with a chosen good, like a set of files that's indexed alphabetically by middle name: and a world in which events leaf out at random—the honest card or crap game, for example—is still one where the odds can be stated with precision. The disorders of the streets, the fickleness of crowds, gangs, or mobs, like the heavy rushes of a bull, are often more predictable than the moves of a chess master, and we usually feel that even the quirks of great winds would be perfectly understandable if we knew their backgrounds better—who their parents were and how they were raised. The straw which a mighty storm has driven through a post, the house which has been moved a mile and set down like a tray, seem whimsical acts because, like putting the shot, so much energy has been expressed in them they ought to have been meant, and we believe, in our less faithful moments, they were not.

No, we can put order anywhere we like; there's not a trout we can't tickle, a fish for which we can't contrive a net; we can find forms in ink blots, clouds, the tubercular painter's spit; and to the ants we can impute designs which Alexander would have thought himself vainglorious to dream of. But to think of order and chaos in this relative way is not to confuse them, or put conditions out of the reach of judgment. There are clashes between orders, confusions of realms. Not every arrangement is equally effective. And we must keep in mind the relation of any order to the chosen good.

Descartes said that Euclid was too abstract and too dependent on figures: "It can exercise the understanding only on condition of greatly fatiguing the imagination." I know many books of that kind. Algebra, on the other hand, was overly rule-bound: "there results an art," he said, "full of confusion and obscurity calculated to embarrass, instead of a science fitted to cultivate the mind." Orders vary in both their vices and their virtues, in kind as well as in degree. Some are futile, others cheap. Among the worst are the illusory: politics and witchcraft, astrology and diets. Among the noblest are a few measurements of measure like Valéry's *Eupalinos*. It does not matter whether we are "arranging" things to fall into an order, the ordering is an act of mind which brings together like two hands that buzzing blooming confusion of which James spoke, and some sublimely empty abstract system like that which Euclid once devised, or the inventors of the diatonic scale . . . brings them together till they clap. The result is a quantity qualified—that's Plato's recipe for the world—and in the past the most successful systems have had their source in music and in mathematics, while we have found our models, as often as not, to be examples of physics and astronomy, religious books, long poetical plays or lengthy epical poetry.

Let us count.

One. We find, perhaps, on a lottery ticket, the most primitive use of number, inasmuch as the number is not even a name there, not even an elementary designation like "Peewee," "Nitwit," or "Gramps." The paper provides a place for their printing; it carries the figures, and these, by themselves, are mere grunts. Why do we number them at all? Why not print "Dimple" on one, "Nymphet" and "Spider" . . . then "Zealously," "Viper," and "Young"? We don't care for sequence here, only for difference. In manufacturing such tickets, however, we want signs which can be simply produced, and a scheme for their production which will ensure there is no duplication. The ordinary number system pays that bill promptly. It can generate new and unique names indefinitely (no other is so efficient). Not even a language like Latin or English, each capable of a multitude of novel arrangements, can match its easy-going power.

Two. There are dog tags, Social Security, insurance, draft, or other numbers which name documents or people marking them uniquely. These numbers are true names. They are almost too pure, for they tell us nothing else, and the figures themselves simply come from a convenient pool of signs.

Three. The next level is the ordinal use. The sequence of numbers has a little meaning now. The numbering of the pages of a book is not quite an example, because it will tell me that some leaves are missing, or that, in my copy of *Under the Volcano*, a whole gathering has been repeated. For the first time, nevertheless, it makes sense to speak of measure. Take the scratch test for hardness: suppose I have five rocks. I scratch them turn and turn about as Beckett's Molloy sucked stones, and then I arrange them serially in terms of who scratches whom and who is scratched by whom, assigning any figures I like so long as they reflect that scratching order: 1 through 5, perhaps, or 0, 4, 25, 92.3, and 112. Either list will do. Of course I could have called one Ruth, another Lou, and so on, but the names wouldn't tell me whether Ruth scratched Lou or Lou, Ruth, and that won't do. Even so, the stone labeled 5 in its sequence is not thereby that many times harder than 2, although this is a mistake which is frequently made.

Four. Counting is the cardinal use. What is the number of shoes in the store? Order alone is not enough here, and I must always proceed in whole units—that is assumed. The consequence of my counting, of course, is a sum, but the figure any particular shoe happens to receive is without significance. In the case of labeling hardness, I might have gone 0, 10, 25, instead of the 0, 4, 25, I used, but I could never have run 4, 0, 10, or 9, 6, 21. This floating or fastening of names is important in some metaphors.

Five. If you are number six in a simple count, it does not mean that you are in some way twice the fellow who was three. Addition is an additional property which we reach with luck and often genius only at this stage. Time and space are additive, hardness and heat are not. It is clear, by this time, isn't it? that my knowledge of the relations between numbered *things* depends wholly upon my knowledge of the relations between numbers. The Pythagoreans said grandly of justice that it was "4." Presumably this told us something of justice (actually it told us everything about justice, for the number was not only the *logos* [word] for justice, it was also the *logos* [or theory] of justice), but not even the zealots imagined that justice informed us about the number. Mathematical models (and this is important) are designed to tell us things about the data they shape, but the data are not expected or even allowed to snitch in the least on the system.

Rules of representation, I repeat, establish a link between the thing to be ordered and the order to be imposed. Let the face of this paper be the face of the earth. That is a rule of representation. The face of this paper is not the face of the earth, but neither is distance rectangular. Nevertheless, assuming one may enable me to find my way, assuming another may enable me to measure it.

Not all measurement, we have to notice, is direct. The scratch test is, but temperature taken with a thermometer is not. We measure the dance of the mercury because it undulates with the heat. My uncle's sweat, collected in a cup, would serve as well if only he were as reliable in his response as the metal.

Suppose I were to say, of a married couple, that in their life together the wife played left tackle. Have I made a good model? Where are the other twenty players? who are the coaches, trainers, where are the stands? Tennis would serve a loving couple better. Then I might be able to observe how the wife stayed on the baseline, seldom coming to the net; how she characteristically lobbed her return to his drives; what sort of spin she put on her serves, and so forth—*if that's what she did*. Or if I were to compare a football match to a chess game, I might carelessly see the two quarterbacks as the opponents—a mistake. The opponents have to be the coaches, since in chess the players are never pieces. And unless my measurements are meant to be skimpy, I have to assume that the moves of the athletes are fixed; that they act only as ordered. Well, my measurements *are* skimpy, my suit a poor fit, for when is that ever true?

Facts are not so stubborn as we sometimes like to think.

The world may be a plenum, but it's also hollow as bamboo, both stiff as straw and limply flexible as string. We can often talk things into being only what we want to say about them.

Perhaps you know the game in which two players suddenly and simultaneously show one another either an open hand, two fingers, or a fist. The open hand is paper, and it is said to be superior to stone, which the fist represents, because paper covers stone, although the stone can blunt the scissor-shaped fingers, and they, in turn, can cut the paper when they meet. This unusual arrangement comprises a viciously circular pecking order. Imagine that only untouchables gave orders to kings. The superiority of each symbol to the other is inferred from the presumed properties of its name. Scissors cut paper, paper covers stone, stone blunts scissors. Totem names are like our numbers: metaphors seriously meant and socially applied, as instanced in this passage from Lévi-Strauss's essay on social poetry and measurement, *The Savage Mind*:

> The following clans stand in a joking relationship to each other among the Luapula: the Leopard and Goat clans because the leopards eat goats, the Mushroom and Anthill clans because mushrooms grow on anthills, the Mush and Goat clans because men like meat in their mush, the Elephant and Clay clans because women in the old days used to carve out elephant's footprints from the ground and use these natural shapes as receptacles instead of fashioning pots. The Anthill clan is linked with the Snake clan and also with the Grass clan because grass grows tall on anthills and snakes hide there. The Iron clan jokes with all clans with animal names because animals are killed by metal spears and bullets. Reasoning of this kind allows the definition of a hierarchy of clans: the Leopard clan is superior to the Goat clan, the Iron clan to the animal clans and the Rain clan to the Iron clan because rain rusts iron. Moreover the Rain clan is superior to all the other clans

because animals would die without it, one cannot make mush (a clan name) without it, clay (a clan name) cannot be worked without it, and so on.

When we number objects, animals, places, schemes, the things numbered remain unaware of their names (the Skunk Cabbage does not know that it is one), but when we label ourselves, we try to live up or down to our titles: I know I rust iron, and you know it too. Eventually we prove the matter to ourselves, and I rain down on you.

I've been groping for trout in a peculiar river, and perhaps I deserve to go to prison for it. Certainly the mathematician may feel that I'm poaching; but in all of my remarks I have merely been developing a metaphor for measure which will fit fiction, though I should like, like a sock, to see it stretched.

I ask you finally, then, to think of every English word as Euclid for the poet, a wildly ordered set of meanings and relations, maybe, but settled down there, right at home there, nevertheless; to see that each one is, like a piece in chess, the center of a network of astonishing relations. A poem or a work of fiction is a system of such systems, and perhaps the novel, in particular, is an indirect measure of life. To do this it need not resemble, nor does it need to make, for the sake of a certain precision, the sacrifice which Galileo had to when he took all the color from mass or all grace from precision. We are sometimes inclined to think that measuring must thin its object—a line, in fact, has but one dimension—for where are the white wings of the pigeon when the paperboy's paper is transcribing its stringy trajectory? and if De Sade thinks of sex like a cook who opens cans, if many of us live like pins in maps, our hearts a red head, what can recommend measuring? It's true we should watch out for images which are merely telephonic sums, for explanations which aren't really meant but are, like plastic bosoms and paste gems, only designed to dazzle. We confine ourselves to too few models, and sometimes live in them as if they were, themselves, the world.

Remember that as we moved from lotteries to temperatures, and from temperatures to the interplay of gravities, our
models were able to take on more and more of the properties
of the numbers which were being used to construct them, and
that as we went along, our knowledge did not dwindle but it
grew. However, numbers are morally and metaphysically neutral. They are nothing but relations, and quite orderly relations, too, while words are deposits of meaning made almost
glacially, over ages. It the systems, in mathematics, exist
mainly, like glasses, to be filled, they are also clear as crystal,
and are not expected to stain anyone's white radiance; while
words, again, are already names for thoughts and things, acts
and other energies which only passion has command of; they
are not blank, Barkis-willing, jelly labels. Prufrock did not
measure out his life, One/Two, One/Two, but carefully, in coffee spoons, from which the sugar slid, no doubt, like snow, and
the beverage circled to their stir as soundlessly as a rolled eye.
Mornings, evenings, afternoons: there was the polite chink as
they came to rest in their saucers—chink chink chink . . . A
complete world unfolds from the phrase like an auto map reveals its roads. In metaphor, meanings model one another,
wear their clothes. What the poet tries to measure is the whole.

"Tell me, Apollo," Troilus cries, "what Cressid is, what
Pandar, and what we. Her bed is India; there she lies, a
pearl." Don't we know, then, where *we* stand? It is a distant and
exotic place, the object of voyages by many men, rich in silks
and spices, more guessed at and conjectured of than known.
Our proper attitude should be one of wonderment and longing,
curiosity, more than a little desire, more than a little greed.

But we must not suppose that "India" is merely a lens
through which we peer at Cressida's bed as through some
shard of colored glass we've found randomly at hand, since the
syntax of our sentence is also odd, and thus the angle at which
the lens is held is strange. It would be normal to say: her bed
is big, or, her bed is walnut, her bed is unmade. It would be
normal to say: her native land is India, or, her name is Cres-

sida. And if we said that her bed was a boat, our grammar, at least, would be unexceptional. There would be no syntactical collision. But her bed *is* India.

When we measure nature with a yardstick or another sort of rule, the qualitative world does not seem to shadow us so obviously as normal sentences surround abnormal ones, because we are satisfied to say that we are measuring the heights of the tree, not the tree, the frequency of light, not light, the temperature of the air—in short, an abstract property—but Shakespeare is not measuring some exotic quality of Cressida's bed. Her entire sexual life becomes a matter of geography, history, danger, travel.

Each metaphor establishes between its terms a quite specific *angle of interaction*, and the movement of the mind which reaches, exploits, and dwells on this, so swiftly as to seem quite effortless, is nevertheless a momentous factor. Because of the comparative emptiness of numbers (something which I have now insisted upon so often I am ashamed to mention it again), when we raise our hand to the teacher, requesting to be excused to do, or otherwise perform, No. 1, we don't feel that our expression is metaphorical. The number is merely an evasive name; whereas if we had, instead, to say that we wished to leave the room to wash our car ("Excuse me, teach, but I got to go to wash my car"), then think what light (to seize a passing word) would eventually be shed on the relief of the bladder . . . or, for that matter, on actually washing one's automobile. The mind is a persistent logician. If doing No. 1 is: wash the car, then what is No. 2?

Let's go back to "bed" for a moment. In this Brobdingnagian image, if Cressida's bed is India, what must her dressing table be? Think of the size of Cressida herself. Truly, she must be a divinity. Some of these consequences occur to Shakespeare:

> *Tell me, Apollo, for thy Daphne's love,*
> *What Cressida is, what Pandar, and what we.*

> *Her bed is India; there she lies, a pearl;*
> *Between our Ilium and where she resides,*
> *Let it be call'd the wild and wandering flood,*
> *Ourself the merchant, and this sailing Pandar*
> *Our doubtful hope, our convoy and our bark.*

If "Her bed is India" enlarges her, the image which closes on it like the other half of a walnut is Lilliputian in its effect, since Cressida's bed becomes that of the oyster, and what once floated on the surface of the ocean, so to speak, has suddenly sunk in restful sleep beneath it. The conclusion is a proportion: that Cressida is to her bed as a pearl to its oyster, but this is reached by means of an intermediate step which is best forgotten, because initially we'd have to assume that Cressida lies in her bed the way oysters lie together in theirs. In that case there would have to be as many Cressidas quietly snuggled up beneath the sheets as anchovies in tins. The entire expression endeavors to play Descartes to Galileo: to translate one model immediately into another, just as the offense of "doing" a woman is re-seen as poaching—the theft of private property.

So what the poet tries to measure is the whole *with* the whole—the paper as bird, the bird perhaps as paper—but he does not always succeed.

The Duke is in a sweat of explanation:

> *We have strict statutes and most biting laws,*
> *The needful bits and curbs to headstrong weeds,*
> *Which for this fourteen years we have let slip;*
> *Even like an o'ergrown lion in a cave,*
> *That goes not out to prey. Now, as fond fathers,*
> *Having bound up the threatening twigs of birch,*
> *Only to stick it in their children's sight*
> *For terror, not to use, in time the rod*
> *Becomes more mock'd than fear'd; so our decrees,*
> *Dead to infliction, to themselves are dead;*
> *And liberty plucks justice by the nose;*

> *The baby beats the nurse, and quite athwart*
> *Goes all decorum.*

What he wants to describe is a condition that eventually occurs in any state which sets aside its laws like a dirty fork in a fine café. He does not pile one image on another as if he were translating each to a higher sphere; rather, he looks rapidly through many eyes as though he were an insect, instantly, antennaed every eighth of every quarter inch. First, the laws are like the bit and bridle of a horse which, once let slip, will cause the horse (and heroine) to bolt; they are like the tools of cultivation left in idleness to rust their garden into weed; they are like the spared rod which spoils the child; and the king, himself, who will not keep the birches at their stinging, as though the smart burned both skins like a slap, is finally a lion who will not even leave his fattened sleep to hunt.

Most of these images have an equal weight, and consequently his description draws upon what otherwise would be conflicting areas of meaning without the least hesitation: the phrase, "biting laws," suggests "bits and curbs," which suggests "headstrong," something which horses sometimes are. But what are we to do with the word, 'weeds,' which has suddenly sprung up in the cultivated midst of our account? the bits and curbs of headstrong weeds?[1] though not so accidentally after all because headstrong horses do bolt, and that word suggests an undesirable going-to-seed. The poet slips from one role to another like an improvisor, each easily to each, because the passage does not merely say that the king and his decrees, the people and their condition, are as a farmer to his crops and fields, father to his children; it maintains that farmer, rider, lion, father, king, are *one*. This is the multiple metaphor which

---

[1] Although the First Folio has 'weeds,' most editors conjecture that 'steeds' is the correct word. I suggest some reasons for defending the First Folio (note the "o'ergrown lion" later), and the dizzy shift of kinds is characteristic of Shakespeare's style; nevertheless, 'steeds' seems clearly the most rational choice.

moves these lines to their conclusion: that "liberty plucks justice by the nose, the baby beats the nurse, and quite athwart goes all decorum."

"The baby beats the nurse" is a phrase which has certainly been singled out for popular acclaim, yet the form of the flip-flop intended is not quite right, because otherwise we'd have to think that nurses beat babies as a normal and happily ordered part of their duties, a practice encouraged in well-run states. Headstrong youths may be birched, possibly, but not babes. In the proper turnabout, the baby would give suck to its nurse; but Shakespeare didn't want us to imagine the world turned simply topsy-turvy. Laws upside-down would still be upside-down laws. The Duke fears an absence of orders, a lapsing of powers, the disappearance of value.

Shakespeare was greedy. He wanted everything. He generally does. He wanted Cressida shining in her bed, but he also wanted Troilus's eye there, and his straining loins. He was greedy, but that is what this bloody breathtaking business is all about. Paper covers stone. There are too many books in which the baby beats the nurse, in which form has been forgotten for the sake of some momentary fun.

Yonder man is carried to prison. But what's his offense? Violation. "What," Mistress Overdone exclaims, "is there a maid with child by him?" "No," her servant Pompey says, "but there's a woman with maid by him." No money to marry. The poor are always with us. Groping for trouts in a peculiar river.

Yet what is measured with these terms? To what shall we assign the number "grope"? and where do these trouts lie concealed? what is the name of the river? Yonder man . . . perhaps it's I? Then what's my crime? Between what banks did I reach down to touch, in darkness, and to tickle . . . My crime: where are its straight lines and equilateral dimensions?

But perhaps it would be best not to think about it.

Carrots, Noses,
Snow, Rose, Roses

Marcel Proust has once again taken his vacation at Trouville. While there he contemplates adding to his monumental work a section on sea urchins and salt spray, having seen several handsome urchins worthy of his merciless and immortal memory. Meantime, in inclement weather, fogbound in the hotel lobby or by the sniffles kerchiefed to his chamber, he undertakes a novel by M. André Gide and considers composing, in his best Ruskinese, a critical note on its author's use of the hyperbolic past. This he will place, naturally, in one of the more elegant reviews. And he must pen some flattery to his friends, some bitter gossip too, some biting wit. There is always so much to do. Lady Transome, a tiny but petiteless grand dame of comical Englishness, has provided a few phrases of superlative stupidity which Proust has overheard in the garden despite the dense muffling fog but thanks to a penetrating French which is like that horn that's always staring at the dog. But in whose mouth shall he put them, these squalid epiphanies? Mme. Verdurin?

For anything you like, Proust is always a good case. For instance, he often did not appear to know the difference between his many occupations: his writing, his social climbing, his frequently sordid sexual career. Indeed, was there one?

Writing A, B, C—all the same. Words, words, words, as Hamlet sneered. No—no difference between life and language, itch and urchin; no difference between conversation and news, a letter or an anecdote, history or advice, psychology or travel; no difference between A (writing fiction), B (composing criticism), or C (constructing a theory). Let us read at random in *Le Temps retrouvé:*

(1) a little pimpish conversation—

"Ah! that is extremely interesting," said the Baron with a smile. "But I'll tell you whom I have here: the killer of oxen, the man of the slaughter-houses, who is so like this boy; he happened to be passing. Would you care to try him?"

(2) some summary narrative, occasionally called history—

Saint-Loup's death was received by Françoise with more compassion than that of Albertine.

(3) a piece of psychological analysis—

. . . the lover, too impatient from the very excess of his love, does not know how to wait with a sufficient show of indifference for the moment when he will obtain what he desires.

(4) a letter inserted through a slot in the story—

My dear friend, the ways of Providence are inscrutable. Sometimes a fault in a very ordinary man is made to serve its purposes by helping one of the just not to slip from his lofty eminence . . . and so on.

(5) critical theory—

. . . the kind of literature which contents itself with "describing things," with giving of them merely a miserable abstract of lines and surfaces, is in fact, though it calls it-

self realist, the furthest removed from reality and has
more than any other the effect of saddening and impover-
ishing us . . .

Etcetera. To serve as (6), let me cite without quotation the extensive pastiche of the Goncourts' *Journals* which Proust
places beside the sand urn and the ficus in the foyer of the volume, in a manner later to be that of Borges, in which the Goncourts comment on characters in *A la recherche du temps
perdu* as if they were in Paris and not in Proust.

Nor was the master without company in these confusions,
nor is he now alone. Half of the novels we encounter are made
from diaries and journals, left-over lifetimes and stale aperçus.
A theory of fiction looms large in the *Counterfeiters;* every
third hop in *Hopscotch* finds your shoe coming down in a pile
of it; Orlando lives through three centuries of English literature
and one sex shift like a careless change of clothes; Mann
packed his works with ratiocination of every description; Rilke
threw into *Malte* huge hunks of his Paris letters—what the hell
—and *Finnegans Wake* contains all its explanations. Let nothing be lost. Waste not even waste. Thus collage is the blessed
method: never cut when you can paste. No question it works.
It works wonders, because in collage logical levels rise and fall
like waves. Only an occasional philosopher is stricken with
mal du métalangue. In the example I just mentioned, the
imaginary pages of a counterfeited work are said to describe
Swann, Brichot, Cottard, and others, so much more vividly
than Proust's narrator has that he despairs of having any real
vocation as a writer; yet ironically the details of dress and jewelry, cough and stutter, so characteristic of the Goncourts,
do not reveal the luminous essences behind their eyes, regardless of iris and color. This redounding of reference, which
I have incompletely rendered, like a Klein worm turning to re-
enter itself, is positively vertiginous. Such sea journeys, however, are otherwise soothing and strengthen the constitution.
It's the salt in the salt spray, the wind up your nose.

If Proust had kept to his room to write in a letter to a friend, let's say, a scathing criticism of a performance of the *1812 Overture* by the town band, there would be no possibility of confusing the artillery which went off too loudly and too late, flackering the pigeons into a shower of poop, with Marcel's amused description of the cannons' thunderously tardy entrance. It's the fog again, which has dampened the fuses. Hector Berlioz, likewise, would never have been tempted to dump a few chapters of his *Evenings with the Orchestra* into the score of *Les Troyens*.

Despite appearances—always scribble, scribble, scribble, eh, Mr. Gibbon?—the words on checks and bills of lading, in guides and invoices, the words which magnify themselves on billboards, broadsides, walls and hoardings, which nuzzle together in *billets-doux* and heart-to-hearts, words which smell a lot like stools in presidential proclamations, army orders and political orations, whose heaps create each of our encyclopedias of information, our textbooks, articles of confederation, rules and regulations, charts and tables, catalogues and lists; the words whose ranks form our photo captions, chronicles, and soberest memorials, fill cartoon balloons with lies as bold as produce labels, comprise the warnings uttered by black skulls and red-crossed bones, make up harangues and exhortations, news, recipes and menus, computations, criticism, columns, obituaries, living bios, book reviews—so many signs from every culture and accreditation—legal briefs, subtitles, shopping lists and memos, minutes, notes, reports, summations, lectures, theories, general laws, universal truths—every other mark whatever, whether sky-writ, in the sand or on a wall or water—these words are not in any central or essential sense the same as the passionately useless rigamarole that makes up literary language, because the words in poems, to cite the signal instance, have undergone a radical, though scarcely surprising, ontological transformation.

Gautier cried the truth out well enough to make it once for all, although for most of us an excellent outcry isn't economi-

cally a sound, therefore is actually *sotto voce*, not impressive
to the market or the masses, thus not well, not true . . . still,
well enough or not, he said:

> No, fools, no, goitrous cretins that you are, a book does
> not make gelatine soup; a novel is not a pair of seamless
> boots; a sonnet, a syringe with a continuous jet; or a
> drama, a railway . . . etc.
> By the guts of all the popes past, present, and future, no,
> and two hundred thousand times no! u.s.w.
> We cannot make a cotton cap out of a metonymy, or put
> on a comparison like a slipper; we cannot use an antithesis
> as an umbrella, and we cannot, unfortunately, lay a med-
> ley of rhymes on our body after the fashion of a waist-
> coat . . . and so on.

It may be scribble, scribble, scribble, Mr. Gibbon, but scribbles differ, not only in their several aims, the nature and value
of the objects these activities make or their appropriate effects, but also in the character and quality of the mind and
hand that makes them, and most importantly in the medium
that hand shapes or mind employs: once more merely words,
words, words.

The scribbles of the poet and the clerk, the novelist or biographer: they are not different the way eating soup and steak
are, or even as two activities necessary to life like moving one's
bowels or fucking one's spouse. It isn't simply that they can't
be done at the same time like swallowing and sneezing, nor are
they in conflict the way two wishes can be, such as eating cake
and having it. Rather they are opposed like people playing
chess and checkers on the same board.

My concern at the moment is with the medium—sounds,
shapes, concepts, designations and connections—and I began
by mentioning the novel because the novel, like a city with its
apparently heterogeneous residents, has done more than any

art form to mess up our understanding of the vast difference between the literary use of language and any other. A rose is a rose, Miss Stein, isn't it? we are likely to say; and a word is a word.

Paul Valéry understood the issue as few have, yet the concern of Valéry and Mallarmé for the purity of their medium, and their ardent measure of the problem as it touched poetry, led them to set the differences between poetry and fiction on the wrong stove; for they did indeed see the poet as the master of the *haute cuisine,* and the novelist at best as a bonne femme, a fabricator of *bouillabaisse* and *cassoulet,* of immense, rich though economical, coarse but nourishing, peasant fare, a kind of kitsch and kitchen *bricoleur,* one who skillfully made-do with *pot au feu, marmites,* chowders, stews: fat books, fat bellies, and heavy beer. In a way they were right, of course, but the peculiar literary function of fiction, from at least Boccaccio, and certainly to the present, has been first of all the transformation of life into language, and then the further metamorphosis of that language into literature . . . still another, much remoter, squarer sphere.

And of course now fiction is the advanced, the hard and formal form, since poets have embraced carelessness like a cocotte.

Although I've given it a name as distinguished as any duke's, ontological transformation is such an unassuming process it often passes unnoticed, as indeed does osmosis, and much of the time, digestion. Its action is often abrupt, simple, miraculous. A succulent center-cut porkchop, for instance, which has slid from its plate into a sack of garbage, becomes swill in a twinkling. I don't know how we should describe a toilet bowl impastoed with raw ground beef (if not an old Oppenheim or a new Duchamp), but the hamburger has, in this case, been digested without the trouble of taking the usual tubes. And what about the transformation of the bowl? Conversely, anything thrown into Proust becomes Proustian, because this

great novel, like so many others, is a veritable engine of alteration, a vast vat of cleansing acid—rendering, refining, purify-
ing—polishing its particular mode of Being to the point of total
wordshine the way a Bugatti body spells out speed.

Yet what is this purity which Mallarmé strove so prodi-
giously to achieve and sustain if it is not simply snobbery, a
kind of paper aristocracy set up for the word, a misplaced fastid-
iousness, an excuse for weak, even unmanly, hyper-atten-
uated poetic effects? I believe, quite to the contrary, however,
that Mallarmé's aim is so central to the artist's enterprise that
our definition of the medium, our understanding of the activity,
and our appreciation of the results, is conditioned by it; for the
fact is that the language of the poet or novelist is not the language of everyday, nor is the grammar of his sentences, if he
chooses to write such things, nor are the general forms of his
compositions, even if the words of gutter and grade school appear in them, or they seem to mimic the flattened formats of
history, or to be tainted by psychology, or to wear ennobling
morals on the ends of their sleeves like paper cuffs.

Sometimes we sense the dissimilarities at once. What
happens when we stray into Kafka, *Three Trapped Tigers*, *Pale
Fire*, Hermann Broch, Beckett, Barth, or Borges? It's as if
we'd stepped into a two-pound puddle of mirror glass and come
out as wet as Alice.

So one says, but simple saying, unlike simple syrup, will
not soothe. Poetry, I shall nevertheless insist, is concerned
with a certain purity, fiction with purification, while prose, in
essays such as this one, experiments with the interplay of
genres, attempting both demonstration and display, skids of
tone and decorum associated formerly with silent films, jazz
bands, and the slide-trombone.

Ontological transformation, purity, and form: these three
notions must now be knotted together—tangled too—for what
is a knot but a tangle made on purpose? Suppose we take up
transformation first.

2

Let me make a snowman and see what comes of it.

I begin by gathering snow around a tightly fisted core the way a leaper on a ledge collects a crowd, pressing it together from above, enlarging it with repeated rolls until it can't be budged. For this work I certainly don't want leaves, bare earth, or bumpy ground.

The roll appears to stand well where it is. Good.

As it happens, I can barely lift the next lump above my knees, which leads me to consider whether God was ever stupid or clever enough to grow a lemon so sour He couldn't suck it, as I seem nearly to have done. Gertrude Stein, I remember, wondered whether God could make a two-year-old mule in a minute. Impossibilities of every kind confront us. Anyway, the last hunk is the size of a soccer ball and elevates easily. I don't care at all for that hole in my mitten. Curse the cold.

Now that I've stacked these three chunks like cups, into the head I'm prepared to press two pieces of coal, a carrot, and a long mop string. A pipe helps hold the string, which is rather limp, to this freshly Adam'd face. There is a semblance of a smile somewhere on this cold waste, but I wanted something enigmatic . . . a fierce expression . . . or a sad one . . . anyhow holy . . . at least wise . . . Curse chance. Curse fate.

Large coals button down the belly. Three of them like sweet dark cherries. I decide against a belt. Around what is now the throat I wrap my muffler with the filthy fringe. Then through what might be arms I thrust the handle of a broken broom and at the snowman's shapeless feet I place a pair of sullen overshoes whose buckles will no longer snap. It's been rather messy, making this metaphysical miracle, but great fun, and certainly simple enough if you don't mind chapped hands. So. Voilà! It's done, and it will do.

No. Not quite. The head wants a hat.

Now I have not made this snowman to amuse my children.

Did God create the world to amuse His? The snowman stands there, smiling into the wind, a lesson in ontology, an incredible confluence of contexts, a paradigm for poetry and the pure world of the word.

I am able to make the snowman because the snow on the ground is of the right wetness and because I have learned how such snow packs. Futhermore, I am able to make the snowman, not because I know how to reproduce the shape of a man in snow (I don't), but because I know how to reproduce the traditional form: three heaps, five coals, one carrot, and assorted props as they prove available and are desired: muffler, broom, shoes, pipe, and hat. The mop string is my own improvement. The creative impulse tires but never sleeps.

Now if some discornered dunce were persistently to wonder what a carrot was doing in this mound of snow: pointing at it, laughing, and then growing suspicious when we told him he was looking at a nose (not a snownose, naturally, yet the nose of a snowman); we should have to conclude that he hadn't grasped the set of crossed contexts which establishes the figure, and therefore that he couldn't understand the carrot's ontological transformation; just as we wouldn't be able to grasp it either, if the carrot were simply stuck in a small ball of snow or left lying on a drift, for we would surely ask, what is that carrot doing there? and imagine that somewhere nearby a snowman had been both created and destroyed, and that this was the root that was his nose, and these were the coals that were his eyes.

The snow that makes up the snowman remains snow, though it has also become body—snowbody, one must hesitate to say—but the coals alter absolutely. They are buttons or eyes. Because of its natural shape and the new relations it has entered, the carrot does not simply stand for or resemble a nose, *it literally is a nose now*—the nose of a specific snowman. Several characteristics, which were central to its definition as a carrot, carry on. Its slim funnular form is certainly suitable, and we can pretend that orange is red in order to imagine that the nose is cold . . . uncomfortable and runny. Coals are excellent eyes because, although they cannot see themselves, they are easily seen, whereas a gray mop string may only faintly make its smirk.

Already it's plain that there are degrees and distances of ontological transformation. We can also begin to formulate some canons of correctness or competency or completeness, since a carrot will clearly work better as a nose than a jelly spoon or toilet tube; coals are better eyes than gravel, and better buttons than buttons, if the buttons are small or pale or pearl or gold. If an expensive meerschaum were placed in the snowman's mouth, a silk Parisian scarf wrapped around his neck, a fine shiny top hat pushed down on his head, and winter shoes by Gucci fitted to his feet, we should still know what these things were supposed to be: the snowman's scarf, hat, shoes; but they would be Guccis still, a hat, a pipe, to be rescued, wiped, restored to a context more protective of it. My god, the cry would quickly come, that's my Yves St. Laurent you've wrapped round the neck of that frozen spook. So again, if emeralds were his eyes, we should wonder, and resist the intended transformation; but if a Buddha or a great statue of Zeus were bejeweled, if the rings on the fingers of Siva were rich beyond estimate, we should not be in the least surprised. We know that the halo of the Madonna may quite properly be gold. Expense is appropriate to the priceless.

To be sure we understand what's going on, let's run down the figure of the snowman like a melt of ice and evaluate what's happened.

Hat: it is clearly still a hat, and it is exactly where a hat should be (on a head or on a rack), but since the head's a snow head, the hat can't function in a hatty manner, hiding the hair. The transformation has scarcely taken a quarter turn, since the relation of brim to crown remains the same, as does that of hat to head. It's not, however, the head of a walrus or an

ape. It's not, in short, a simple shift of species. Rather, the
move is mimetic, because if we had sculpted an ape in the
snow we might well have hatted him.

Head of small snow: snow in the head and body of the
snowman has gained definition. Snow has been removed from
snow and fastened to other snows so that the ordinary idle relation of flake to flake has been irremediably altered. There are
no longer any bits to the ball (the crystalline stars have been
mashed like boiled potatoes), but the relation of snow to snow
is now significant, not haphazard as before. Of course we know
that nowadays a snowman needn't be made of snow. It can be
made of Styrofoam, for instance. Pink snowmen are possible,
and I once saw a snowwoman in the front yard of a frat house,
with big boobs, naturally, and a crowd of soapless Brillo pads
for pubic hair. Incidentally, this illustrates another kind of resistance: the drag of commentary and the tow of wit, since we
are forced to smile, albeit wanly, at the symbolic appropriate-
ness of the rough mesh, and return again and again to Brillo's
humble abrasive function in the world.

One might argue, of course, that a Styrofoam snowman is
an imitation of a snowman the way the snowman is an imitation; but is a man with a wooden leg a man, and would we continue to say yes, if his eyes, nose, brain, and tongue were too,
so long as he saw and smelled and spoke, even in wooden
tones? and reasoned, and paid his bills, begot with a clothespin
and died of gunshot wounds? One might as well deny that soy-
bean steak is steak. But I shall leave such gentle questions to
the metaphysicians, who in future may be formed of Styrofoam
too, that splendid insulation against opposites: the wet and
dry, the heat and cold, the love and strife of Reality.

Eyes of coal: changes of the kind we've been considering
consist of the rearrangement of defining characteristics. Deepest darkness is quite ho-hum and by-the-way to carbon, but to
the snowman, sooty eyes are traditional and basic. Coal could
be pink or green (who would care?), but snowmen are composi-

tions in black and white. Obviously, we are dealing in valueless chips, because pieces of coal a snowman's eye-size are but fallen crumbs to a hungry flame. Some substitutes can be tolerated: licorice drops for instance.

Nose of carrot: one might use a white radish or a turnip or a beet for variety, but the nose must be a winter root and like the coal a customary winter object. Eatability is not a virtue.

Smile of limp mop string: here is something out of character. Originality's sole opportunity, the string is, by itself, the most expressive element, not merely because it forms a mouth, but for the same reason that a fifteenth line in a sonnet, or a triple rhyme, becomes the verbal focus of the whole.

Pipe: a cheap corncob, of course, not only to cut down our resistance to these rearrangements, but also because the fellow we are creating is invariably a tramp like the scarecrow, or, as the hat has already suggested (and the broom will reiterate), a chimney sweep composed ironically from a contrapositive print.

Muffler: hat, pipe, and muffler are all giveaways (the Good Will will get them otherwise), and their insertion into this reality will only modify them somewhat. Any man made of snow is a kind of icon, but the letters of a word are not signs in the same sense that the word is. Similarly, the parts of a snowman are not normally themselves signs. They are simply parts. Replacing a part with a sign for that part is a little like having run out of *A*s during anagrams or scrabble, and pressing a few spare *Z*s into service to stand for them.

Torso of middle-sized snow: the human body has been divided into three pieces, but the section that is most massive in the human being is reduced in his imitation, because the stability of the snowman requires the larger roll at the bottom. Part of the art of any art consists in persuading reality to give up its mimetic demands. Did not Plato tell us, in the *Timaeus,* that Reason had, often, to persuade Necessity? Soon enough, indeed, genres become themselves tyrannical. Snowballs hurled with force into the chest may change the sex of the statue without appreciably enlarging its center, but a snowman with sculptured scarf and hat and pair of boots would be more purely *snow*, but less traditionally *man*.

Buttons of coal: notice how easily the same piece may be a button or an eye, and the same mark may be a rose·rose or an arise·rose depending upon its placement. So a coat-button may suggest the button of the belly, *Tender Buttons*, other buttons. Sly.

Broom: we have already spoken of the sweep. Unaccountably, as though covered by a cold unconsciousness which protects it from a deeper, harder freeze, the distant origins of the image remain alive to push through the slush like a crocus.

Legs of large and pedimental snow: in its role as the bottom of the body, our initial lump lies largely neglected unless some effort is made to tent the base or force the footless trunk into leaky boots or a floppy galosh. Otherwise, this primal mass mainly elevates the buttons and the eyes, the hat, the secret smile, above the vast layer of impersonal snow which surrounds and blankets everything, till each of them reaches an area of visual prominence. It had better be the first thing we shape, because it not only is an Atlas to the rest, its diameter determines the dimensions of the torso and the head, and its place becomes our snowman's station in the world. As a matter of simple priorities, even a dog knows to get a leg up before he wets the post. Snowmen are not meant to locomote, but to stand stiffly where the first roll rests, and later to decay in the advancing sun, *memento mori* for the winter, waterclocks to count the coming of the spring.

So the snowman is a poet after all. May he melt languidly down the fair cheeks of our subject. When H and O make water, we can turn our heads away, but it won't matter, because the transformation takes place quite invisibly and without any noticeable fuss. The ingredients in cooking do the same. Seurat's dotty color mixes, likewise all of Mondrian's jittery squares, do their work without our conscious aid. Op Art counts, like rhetoric, on this underhanded handling. There is also a large class of ontological transformations based upon the mysteries of term change: the mash of crystals in the pack of snow, for instance. There is another in which one term is permitted to retreat in the direction of the sign (or to advance, as your prejudice requires), which is what the broom, pipe, boots, and muffler did. Hat too. Language slips from mode to mode with scarcely a hiss, as in "Johns love Mary," where the *s* has simply slid back a syllable in a standard demonstrational sentence. Or the relation itself may change, as the carrot's did, the string's, the coals', or as in "John is transplanting Mary." What we are looking for is a fundamental alteration in the way a thing is, and that's why I played a little game with oxymoronic combinations earlier. String beans big as bombs are just big beans. "Robert robs Phyllis" clearly doesn't do it either. The difference doesn't have to be dramatic, though the consequences often are. John can believe Mary, but what happens if he asserts her? He gets slapped.

Stendhal put it perfectly:

The young woman leaned over the counter, which gave her an opportunity to display a superb figure. Julien observed this; all his ideas altered.

If we travel the axis from raw to cooked, in the phrase of Lévi-Strauss, we carry our carrot out of nature into culture, out of the cave and into the sun, which, like becoming a lawyer in order to be a judge, a candidate and then a mayor, requires a change of status which can be expressed only in big bills. We have appropriated the wild plant, selected the seed, cultivated the root, pulled it from the earth in a moist moment, scraped it clean, chopped it into rounds like the rings of trees, and cooked it slowly with thick chunks of beef; but the carrots we find flavoring our stew are still carrots, however educated the chef has made them. We eat the raw carrot as readily as any other kind, and call both by the same name even when there has been a considerable alteration in appearance. The cold unscraped carrot we planted above the snowman's mouth, on the other hand, resembles its former self perfectly, rooty all the way, just as the words of poems do; for poetry is not a process of acculturation, but a process of ontological transformation, and essences, not appearances, mere accidents and qualities, are involved. For the cooked carrot there's a different taste; we can see what's happened to it; while the bland face of the word remains unruffled regardless of what it's been forced to say; thus the change (so secret, so internal) needs another signal.

Fiction has never enjoyed the grand proscenium or gilded frame or pneumatic breasts which plays, painting, women, and poetry possess to announce their nature—poems scattering their words on the page like a burst packet of seed. Fiction has no undermound to raise its sentences into the wind or to shadow the page with a written shout, and this has meant that the number of dunderheads reading Balzac the way they would skim *Business Week* is considerably larger. Language needs these signals. In most cases, the writer doesn't respell his words, though Joyce does, and the flavor of Locke and Hobbes depends in part on punctuation. Significantly, the major changes take place through the intervention of that rare reader who perceives the shift, as we do when we contemplate the carrot's nosey, phallic, icicular shape, and that shift is, again, primarily relational.

Meanwhile, imagine that John is translating Mary into Japanese.

And all the elements that make up the figure leave at least some of the relationships that previously defined them, abandon at least some of the functions they formerly had, to create together a novel context from scraps and shards of old ones, to face one another like the coal or carrot in the snowman's face. As eyes and nose, they need each other; as carrot or coal, they couldn't care. And this figure we heaved up and patted

round and tricked out—it will do nothing from now on but suffer; and we shall photograph our children standing beside it to
show how large or small it is/they were.

Picasso's snowman we encase in a glass-faced freezer. Why
couldn't he have molded his of Styrofoam like a good fellow?
The flux is such a pain.

3

We could try to start clean. Suppose, as composers, we had
to work with hydraulic sighs and door squeaks, warning whis-
tles, temple bells, and warwhoops. We should have, first of all,
to snip these unruly noises from their sources (we hear a steal-
thy footfall in the floor's creak), and then remove them from
any meanings they might have been assigned (fire, four
o'clock, beep beep, watch out!), otherwise we wouldn't be
composing music but creating sound effects. Instead of the
Bolero, we'd hear a chorus of heavy breathing. There would
be, inevitably, *plot*.

There are notes, and there are noises. Notes never occur
naturally. God, during His half-dozen days in the sun, did not
command a single violin to sing. He made light, land, growing
things, fish, animals, man; but nary a painting or a playlet. Let
there be tympani. He never ordered it . . . the insufferable
bourgeois.

When he considers the composer, envy covers Valéry like
the skin of a drum. The ultimate in craftsmanship is devoted
to fashioning the instruments that resonate the strings; endless
hours of practice perfect their playing, and skills are discovered which Nature for centuries let go to waste (the Greeks
produced not a single gifted pianist, and for want of a Wurlitzer
who knows what Bach lost or we were spared?). In contrast,
what must the poem suffer? Everything. Shakespeare, that fortunate man, did not live to hear Hamlet say "words, words,
words" with a Southern slur, and what of all those pupils in the

Bronx reciting "O my Luv's like a red, red rose"? or the bac-
chantes who have lately torn Rimbaud limb from lovely limb?

Then, too, like that signal I asked for, ceremony surrounds every musical performance. The conductor lifts his ba-
ton. A hush falls. Our ears are finely tuned. We are ready to
listen . . . and it isn't for burglars in the basement. But a book
falls open to "An Ordinary Evening in New Haven," and it is:
it is quite ordinary; there is the bustle of the bus station, perhaps, the raucous rattle-tattle of children, the slam of pans—
we're here, we're there, at home or out of doors—and when the
book falls open there is no trumpet blast, no one flashes a
painting in front of the startled air, nothing whatever happens.
We see the words of Wallace Stevens as the poem begins:

> The eye's plain version is a thing apart,
> the vulgate of experience . . .

but we do not begin. We see the words but do we dare perform
them? Let them lie there, pepper on the page. Besides, the bus
is late.

> Words, lines, not meanings, not communications,
> Dark things without a double, after all . . .

and we stumble down the stanzas like unlit stairs—was that
our call? why are the people queuing? where's our case?—until
we topple into the blankness of the ended page:

> A great bosom, beard and being, alive with age.

A word is a wanderer. Except in the most general syntactical sense, it has no home. 'Rose' is a name, a noun, an action:
where does that put us? somewhere between Utah and the invention of the Ferris wheel. Sounds, however—the notes of
music—they are as relational as numbers; they appear in a
thoroughly organized auditory space. Even when nothing is
playing, even during the dead of night when the clock ticks

with trepidation, the great grid is there, measure after measure marked with rests.

Such is the purity of music, not the purity of poetry, and certainly not the purity of prose (there, where the rose is, blooming beautifully behind its protective, nitrogenic consonant), because fiction is in ever worse shape, contaminated beyond redemption by anyone but a god. The poet struggles to keep his words from saying something, although, like the carrot, they want to go to seed.

If the composer's material has already been transformed for the purposes of his art, so that if we woke up to the oboe, it would be *that* (A on the oboe) we'd wake up to, think what the maker of our snowman (I believe, indeed, that it was I) must do to achieve the same results. So if I succeeded in impressing my work with inner worth the way Yeats did his symbol system, you would have to be reminded that it was not snownoses that were being served for dinner alongside the roast; while Picasso, or while Joyce or Proust, to continue the parallel, if they shaped that frat-house joke, would cause us all to wonder why we were scouring our pots with pubic hair. Meaning depends upon what context is the master, Humpty Dumpty sort of said, and Humpty Dumpty was, as usual, right when revised.

Here is a summary of the kinds of changes which progressively take place as language is ontologically transformed in the direction of poetry. Everybody knows about them already. It is the consequences that are ignored or denied.

(1) Adventitious, accidental, and arbitrary properties of words, such as their sound, spelling, visual configuration, length, dentition, social status, etc., become essential; other properties, normally even more problematic and tangential (whether the word is of Anglo-Saxon origin or has Romance roots, and so on; or even whether "sore" is an anagram or that "rose" rhymes with "squoze"), make themselves available. I furnish the following example of an anagrammatic rhyme:

> *I once went to bed with a Rose*
> *whose petals I hardly let close.*
> *Then I said to my florist:*
> *never mind what the cost is,*
> *send me a dozen of those.*

The way ordinary ink becomes a sign by coiling about correctly until the insensible suddenly says, "Salamander!" and enters the spirit the way that lizard is alleged to do—safely as moist fingers through flame—that way, the way of the ink, is almost the best example of ontological transformation we have; and it is ironic that poetry works to retransform the word into its ink again, make it neither pure meaning nor matter, but that fabled "third thing" of which poets, alchemists, and Hegel speak.

(2) Logically necessary connections between concepts are loosened or untied altogether, and meanings which are characteristically associational become strictly implied. In Blake's poem

> *O Rose thou art sick.*
> *The invisible worm,*
> *That flies in the night*
> *In the howling storm:*
>
> *Has found out thy bed*
> *Of crimson joy:*
> *And his dark secret love*
> *Does thy life destroy.*

it is still true that the rose is a flower, but we cannot go much further in that direction, the genus is scarcely implicated. *In this poem*, the rose is a maidenhead (by no means accidentally), and its enemy, the worm that flies in the night, is invoked as much by the implicit rhyme with 'sperm' as by the idea of the phallus. The maiden, the flower, and the maiden's flower, are being addressed simultaneously, and they're being told that time flies, beauty and youth are fragile, life feeds on life, good attracts evil, and so on . . . clichés of an unconquerable dullness.

(3) Grammatical categories are no longer secure. Here is Joyce's gloss on the inheritance of the meek, the emancipation of the slaves, the freeing of the serfs, and the liberation of women—a passage which like Proust, illustrates everything . . . almost *proves*.

> Hightimes is ups be it down into outs according! When there shall be foods for vermin as full as feeds for the fett, eat on earth as there's hot in oven. When every Klitty of a scolderymeid shall hold every yard-scullion's right to stimm her uprecht for whimsoever, whether on privates, whather in publics. And when all us romance catholeens shall have ones for all amanseprated. And the world is maidfree. Methanks.

In some contexts not only are the words put out of their customary place like cats out of doors, the standard syntax of the language is scarcely operating even as an implicit grid. Mallarmé's famous *Un coup de dés* is an example.

(4) The language no longer denotes or names, in the ordinary sense. The carrot does not name a nose. It is one. The word 'Rose,' in the following little jingle of Gertrude Stein's, does not name a girl, it is the girl . . . a verbal girl to be sure, the best kind.

> *My name is Rose.*
> *My eyes are blue.*
> *My name is Rose,*
> *and who are you?*
> *My name is Rose,*
> *and when I sing,*
> *I am Rose*
> *like anything.*

When a rose has been picked, popped in a vase, peered at, rearranged and watched, the flower has left its function, family, future, far behind; but language, conceived as the servant of our needs, is denied that possiblity. I can hold a stone to the light, set it in silver, let it decorate my finger, even permit it to reveal my marital intentions, but I'm not supposed to walk through Kant as through a cathedral, admiring the beauties of the nave, transept, and choir, curious about the catacombs, dubious about the dome, and positively frightened by the spire. What an affront to the serious purposes of the great man! Isn't that the conventional opinion? Only the writer who writes to provide such careless strolls is worse, they say. This villain, who puts words together with no intention of stating, hoping, praying, or persuading . . . only imagining, only creating . . . is to many immoral, certainly frivolous, a trivial person in a time of trouble (and what time is not?), a parasite upon whatever scrofulous body the body politic possesses at that moment. And roses are intolerably frivolous too, and those who grow them, snowmen and those who raise them up, and drinking songs and drinking, and every activity performed for its own inherent worth.

(5) Verse forms, rhyme schemes, metrical devices, and so on, are as peculiar to poetry as the scale is to music. No doubt, in early oral cultures, they had an important mnemonic function. Now, though of course they do help to make poetry memorable, they have become almost as arbitrary and remote from life, meaning, and any useful exercise of mind as the sounds of words themselves. I cannot see any significant connection between the sonnet and its favorite subject, love (have you noticed anything fourteen-line-ish about it?), whereas the tabular structure of a tide table immediately furnishes its sufficient reason. These poem patterns are like hurdles. Low or high, they do define the race; but there might easily be others: a leapfrog relay, or the hundred-meter cartwheel. In any case, the limerick, the villanelle, respetto, do not suffer transforma-

tion. They are already where they need to be, but the patterns they insist on require many of the changes I've suggested occur.

(6) The language of literature does not disappear like steaming breath or memos in the shredder, nor is it preserved for patriotic purposes ("Give me liberty, or give me death!"), out of religious awe, like Deuteronomy, or historical reverence, like Washington's Farewell Address. "Come live with me and be my love" is not an invitation. Nor is Raleigh's reply a real one. The text is surely not sacred, and, though utopian, unpolitical. Its mode is that of blandishment and seduction, but it is addressed to no one, all sexes are equally charmed. The poem is not bent on getting anyone to bed. It certainly contains no truths, pretends to none, and will in no way ennoble its reader. And how much wisdom you expect to find as you move along from Marlowe to Shakespeare ("Where the bee sucks, there suck I"), and thence to Donne and Milton, will depend on how foolish, unreflective, or unread you are.

It was this quality of maintaining itself in consciousness, of requiring continued repetition, of returning attention over and over again to itself like a mirror that will not allow reflections to escape its surface, that Valéry found most significant and valued most in every art. All the transformations I've talked about have this ultimate integrity in mind; for against what do the great lines of poetry reverberate, if not the resoundings of other lines?

(7) I said that the poet struggles to keep his words from saying something, and as artists we all struggle to be poets. Yet what does this come to? Does it really mean that poems can't speak? that they are gagged or threatened? Both the snowman and the daffodil can measure spring; my ring says I'm engaged or a graduate of the class of '43, and we all know about the last rose of summer. The true muteness of any expression can be measured by the degree to which the justification of the symbol combinations comes to rest within the expression itself, just as

the reason for putting a coffin in the ground is that there's a body in it. If I cry "Fire!" we look around and sniff for smoke. If I make a promise or hold a belief or adopt a faith, where is the profit? If I make an assertion, what is the truth? If I draw a conclusion, where are the premises, what is their ordering, how goes the proof? One could continue this catechism for all the conditions that bring any speech or piece of writing into existence, graffiti included, common prayers a specialty of the house. So what justifies the snowman? symbolism? photos of the children? its service as a slushclock? . . . fun. Building a bigger snowman than my neighbor might explain my exertions, but it wouldn't vindicate them, and of course most of our actions have little clearance from the gods. Like light under a door, we do them for the thickest of causes and the thinnest of reasons.

We must not be misled by the ubiquitous presence of causes like bugs at a picnic. A hundred thousand factors, including evidence, may lead a man to his beliefs; however, for their scientific adequacy, only the evidence matters. Similarly, the causes of the composition of *Finnegans Wake* might mount into the millions, matching the misprints, but only its own inner constitution (its radiance, wholeness, clarity) will guarantee its right to be read, to be repeated, praised, and pondered; without further service or apology to confront our consciousness with an overwhelming completeness, an *utterness* a god would bite its lip to see, and which, as those same gods once were, totally entitles it to be.

The responsibility of any science, any pure pursuit, is ultimately to itself, and on this point physics, philosophy, and poetry unite with Satan in their determination not to serve. Any end is higher than utility, when ends are up.

We can approach the problem from yet another direction. We are tiresomely familiar in philosophy with the distinction between analytic and synthetic propositions, and one way of describing the difference between them depends upon the kind of things one would do to justify forming the propositions in the first place. The presence of the predicate, in an analytic proposition, is justified (1) by grammatical form, and (2) by the appearance of that predicate in the definition of the subject term. Such expressions ("A bird is an English chick"; "A chick is an American doll"; "A doll is a man-made plaything") can be said to be equivalences or exfoliations of meaning rather than statements of fact (as "The price of a proper plaything is a hundred bucks a night"). In the latter case we justify the presence of the money in the predicate by going to the unseemly world outside the judgment and finding the corresponding relation. Actually, as Plato argued, analytic judgments refer to an organized system of concepts, and analytic judgments are true when they reflect that system correctly.

In any case, literary language, rather than empty as analytic formulations are sometimes said to be, is so full, so overdetermined, so inevitable in its order, that to look elsewhere for reasons why Hopkins's physically and contextually responsive lines run on as they do:

> *Summer ends now; now, barbarous in beauty, the stooks arise*
> *Around; up above, what wind-walks! what lovely behaviour*
> *Of silk-sack clouds! has wilder, wilful-wavier*
> *Meal-drift moulded ever and melted across skies?*

is to want reductive causes, as if to explain Homer, Milton, Joyce, or Euler, by their blindness.

To sum up, before saying a final word about the function of fiction: as language moves toward poetry, it becomes increasingly concrete, denying the distinction between type and token, the sign and its significance, name and thing. It does not escape conventional syntax altogether, but the words may shift grammatical functions, some structures may be jettisoned, others employed in uncustomary ways, or wrenched out of their usual alignment. Terms redefine themselves, relegating what was once central to the periphery, making fresh es-

sence out of ancient accidents, apples out of pies. Language
furthermore abandons its traditional semantic capacities in favor of increasingly contextual interaction. The words respond
to one another as actors, dancers, do, and thus their so-called
object is not rendered or described but constructed. Consequently, such language refuses all translation, becomes frozen
in its formulas, and invites, not use, not action, not consump-
tion, but appreciation, contemplation, conservation, repetition, praise. If we are prepared to grant that a class is different
than a thing, a hymen other than a flower; that an adverb never
was a noun, validity a various aim than truth, snowmen not
mere assemblages of old clothes, coals and carrots, yesterday's leftover snows; then it becomes impossible to imagine
that the language of literature is not ontologically of another order than that of ordinary life, its chronology, concerns, and
accounts.

In terms of the ordinary meanings of meaning, poems,
made of words, contain none.

Yet I hear, undaunted, undisturbed, the voice of Tolstoy
chiding me: why are you wasting your time with snowmen
when the basement needs cleaning? some starving ghetto baby
would appreciate that carrot; that muffler might keep many a
cold neck warm and these boots, despite their holes, would do
wonders for a wino.

True . . . true . . . all true—these echoes from *What Is
Art?* that masterpiece of the missed point.

When fiction turns its back on the world and walks into
wonderland, it seems an even greater betrayal, because fiction
has been such a repository of data, dense as the population of
Calcutta and long as the Eastern Seaboard, and because fiction has so plainly explored social, economic, and political issues, manners and masturbation, rabble and rouser, religion
and race. Furthermore, fiction has always followed prose
forms developed for other than artistic reasons, composing
imaginary letters, newsy lying gossip, and made-up lives; but

the history of the novel tells another story too. Except for those original, narrowly mnemonic patterns which prose eschews, and the tight rhymes and regular rhythms these sometimes require, fiction now unabashedly employs every other resource of poetry, inventing new modes and methods, but at the same time reaching back for the rhetorical schemes of the great stylists like Sir Thomas Browne, Hobbes, Burton, and Taylor, straight through Schopenhauer, De Quincey, and Cardinal Newman to Nietzsche, Santayana, and the limpid yet palpable intelligence of Valéry himself. There are few poets today who can equal, in their esthetic exploitation of language, in their depth of commitment to their medium, in their range of conceptual understanding, in the purity of their closed forms, the work of Nabokov, Borges, Beckett, Barth, Broch, Gaddis, or Calvino, or any of half-a-dozen extraordinarily gifted South Americans.

Joyce did data in, Mann ideas, Proust all the rest. With language still guidebook-right about the region, and thus with language which is reluctant, like the Brillo pads or Gucci boots, to leave its world of fruitful description and honest use, Joyce transforms an actual Dublin—even Dublin, think of that —into an idle centerpiece of gleaming conception, yet for all its idleness and gleaming, an object with more realized human value, and a greater chance for immortality, than the city itself; because when, like Bloom, we enter a bar, what do we see there, what do we hear? words humming like a craftsman deep in his work; words folding in on one another like beaten eggs, like lovers mingling in the middle of their sleep; words sliding away into sentences never before imagined or discovered . . . words.

An illgirt server gathered sticky clattering plates. Rock, the bailiff, standing at the bar blew the foamy crown from his tankard. Well up: it splashed yellow near his boot. A diner, knife and fork upright, elbows on table, ready for a second helping stared towards the foodlift across his stained square of newspaper. Other chap telling him something with his mouth full. Sympathetic listener. Table talk. I munched hum un thu Unchster Bunk un Munchday. Ha? Did you, faith?

When Joyce describes Dublin his lines literally rub it out, the city disappears beneath them, as Plato says Atlantis did, on account of ambition, to leave no word in writing.

Think of a whole world rubbed out and rearranged in music, voice, and meaning. A dangerous game. Can the novelist find a form which will accept it all—a Moloch—a way to the underworld, through the mouth of a demon, for the world? The novel, we used to think, was an instrument of secular love; it brooded upon the universe of people's passions and their things; both landscape and social scene were happily alike to it, and the brooding too was brought in democratically like the nurse with the child. Now with some alarm we notice that right along the love was sacred, for the saint who shows his saintliness by kissing lepers loves not lepers but saintliness, and life has once again been betrayed by form.

In the slag of time, numbers were forced to shed like snakes their dizzy altitudes and deeps, their splendid curvatures, their shapes which were like snowy fields dotted with stones; or if the triangle of four, like a flying wedge, or if nine, like the disposition of a marching band, although Pythagoras would have seen a different image. And rectangles, circles, hollow squares, the blessed spheres themselves, were eventually compelled to deflate like the lake's last inner tube, one dimension collapsing upon another until even points disappeared like midges in a wind, and the vast empty regions of space were left to the merely regionous, not even round dwelled there; and physical bodies, which formerly had slid down inclined planes with all the dignity of elephants, crossed the street like fickle customers to become the cash concern of massage parlors and sun lamps, not physicists as before, who suddenly ceased stitching cannonballs across the countryside and took up equations like drink, so that the substance of their studies became far too subtle and refined by our time to sweat.

Why should we be surprised to see the same development in literature? Connections in the world, the rule of thumb, the sun, the lever in the leg and arm, the yearly thaw, as we begin to understand them, are ultimately replaced by those ambitious understudies, the ideas themselves, and once where hinges were, and without oil, were squeaks, concepts oillessly swing in winds from nowhere. It's not that our studies have lost their relevance to the spit and cough and curse of daily life. It is rather that they seek their rules, and find their justifications, elsewhere. Never fear. We can still break a leg with a logarithm.

The ambitions of fiction are greater, if not purer, than poetry's. But the function of both is the detachment of language from the fort. From, that is, the main body. One ought to hear the bones snap. It is as if our idea were to empty out the whole house onto a snowy figure so great and multifaceted and polymath that it could incorporate a grand piano, that string of fish which Uncle Schuyler caught, the portrait of Greatgrandfather Gass, in chalk, by several hands, an antique chamber pot, including a puddle of ancient pee, now like paint, and a needle-pointed divan, a glass of ale, a diaphragm; and at no time during the accumulation would we say: my god, you're getting snow between the black keys of our Steinway, but always, rather: ah! a snowman so inclusive as to be by Master François Rabelais himself, including the bathroom and eight rolls of saffron-flowered paper.

What a shame it will be when the monster melts, and returns all our goods to the world and themselves the way props are sometimes returned from the stage to those less real rooms in our homes.

What a pity, indeed. What a shame. What a loss.

The Ontology
of the Sentence,
or
How to Make
a World of Words

(For Max Black)

1
The Overture

It might at first seem difficult—to make a world of words—but actually nothing is easier. Think how Plato's Demiurge did it, or the Muse of Lucretius . . . not needing a syllable, only a little open space, a length or two of line, and perhaps a gentle push. We must try to be brave.

The right triangle, for instance, will suffice for a universe. Lean a few together like subway passengers at rush and soon triangles of varying slopes—homologues, conjugates, and other oddities—rectangles of many sizes, stars and flowers, the uninflated sides of soccer balls, diamonds and devious parallelograms, will appear—some weak in the crotch as anything aging is apt to be, some sharp, some fierce—spilling out as though we'd hit the jackpot with a nickel through the quarter slot: towers of triangles in the silhouette of Christmas trees or lengths reshaken into stairs or trampled flat like zipper tracks, and then eventually elbows of emptiness in the form of hollow squares, boring corridors of air, and shafts of endlessly reverberating vacancy. This rich shower of shape will be followed shortly by the cube, foursquare and nosy as an interested cop.

Stone needles next: the pyramid, the obelisk; then bird bath, pond, and garden bench . . . a walk made of hexagonal flags. Sniff, if you will, the pungent scent of this articulated air.

It might at first seem difficult, but if I swing my engendering figure around one side like a hinge, a cone comes into being —easily—the way a cylinder is configured by a door that's dervishing. The cone contains nearly everything of course— blessed being. It is a miracle of pure manufacture, a cornucopia of curves. The parabola, hyperbola, ellipse—each is native to it.

Then, if I on my imagination work, I can picture a uniformly expanding pinprick, and the cone it constructs as something the clock draws through the tiresome space of its ticks. Again, it is a stack of shrinking rings, a nest of spirals, a dense pack of upright triangles like an unshuffled deck of cards. If you fancy a sphere, merely pivot the base of the cone on any of its diameters; better yet, follow the suggestion of Nicholas of Cusa and conceive a fine point evenly enlarging itself to form a cone whose base has diameters outrageously infinite. The sides of this cone will progressively flatten without once altering their altitude; the peak will collapse into the center without moving a multimillimeter, and the cone by becoming so immense will return to the plane from which we can conjecture it originally erupted.

And do I hear you say now that these are only shapes? Merely lines loose like lightning in the frank resourcelessness of space? Were the atoms of Democritus or Lucretius anything else? uninvadable shapes in motion? and except for their resistance to intrusion, indistinguishable from the void itself? and did Descartes manage to make matter more interesting? If things are extensions, there is no difference between the unimpeachably full and the irreproachably empty. All are zeros enclosed by lines. And words, too—as notions and noises— words, too, are only signs.

Did you notice how neatly the full and the empty were

combined? There is a certain poetry to the logic of limits which tempts us to forgive it everything. Any segment of an infinite circumference seems straight; there is not a groat's worth of difference, as Bruno computed it, between the smallest possible chord and the smallest possible arc; and what could be more completely finite than the infinitely small?

Imagine two equal piles, one of heat and one of cold, as though you had a heap of coal and a heap of ice. Will not the least of each pile be the same? Of course. In general, the minutest pinch, the smidgiest smidgin of any pair of contraries will be alike as one pea. Think next of the least wet. Will it not be the same as the most dry? Indeed. Least light is deepest darkness, least evil greatest good. And Vico concluded from these arcane observations that not only were the maxima and minima of particular contraries identical, but because the mimima were also identical, the maxima had to be identical as well. Which is unquestionably the long and the short of it, inasmuch as God, for Bruno, is both the ultimate minimum (since everything is external to Him), and the ultimate maximum (since all things are contained in Him); and from this paradoxical point we and all our friends, environments, and artifices, flow like words from a writer's pen. We just saw how the triangle took in and propped up and became whatever is, so we shouldn't be surprised.

External to Him but contained . . . Is your fancy in fine fettle? God is a bubble of soap then—infinitely thin, infinitely large, infinitely hued. The outer rim of reality—its rubberous skin—is all that's real.

James Joyce decided that these metahistorical transformations were consequently circular (or square or pendular or corkscrew—we may now be allowed to wonder what's the diff), for it has become shamefully plain (hasn't Samuel Beckett argued so, throwing himself on top of this notable pile?), that the minimum of one contrary takes its motion from the maximum of another; that we die by living; that corruption is generation; that the Upward and Downward Paths (if we remember our Heraclitus) are the same; that the concave creates the convex, sin the saved, etcetera the series etcetera continues by concluding?

These processes, which we've lined up front to back and max to min (the way softness connives against the hard), have four loose ends now, and they provide us with poles terminal enough to substantiate a world (as earth, air, fire, and water), or to come from noble corners like the winds, or crouch above church porches like the four evangelists, although these theological companions are called, in Vico's case, Fate, Chance, Liberty, and Providence (or something else at other times when he had other aims), for names are names, and fours are fours, and one will do for the other.

Apollo is the sun, is fire, is heat, light, sight, life, soul surge, energy, understanding; so if least cold is greatest heat, utmost light is final mind. This is the analogical waltz, one of the diviner dances, and as we turn round and round through its music, we metaphysically rise, level upon level the way parking ramps spiral in the great garage, till lo! there is the roof and the twinkle of the town. The subject of music can afford us an example. The tendency a tone has to seek out, in a melody, other tones, becoming a kind of actively inclining agent, is described by Zuckerkandl thusly:

> We *hear* this state, we hear it clearly and directly, in the tone itself. What we hear in this way we can best designate as a state of disturbed equilibrium, as a tension, a tendency, almost a will.
>
> *(Sound and Symbol,* Princeton U. Press, 1956, p. 19)

Then the same steps are danced with the contrary partner:

> Instead of the disturbed equilibrium, the tension and dissatisfaction which we registered there, we here receive the impression of perfect equilibrium, of relaxation of ten-

sion and satisfaction, we might almost say of self-affirmation. (p. 20)

With the help of such sentences we can pass from Spinoza to Schopenhauer in nearly a single bound. Joyce also skips his thought like stones across his subject. The River Liffey swiftly overflows its banks to become Woman (i.e. History, i.e. Time), and shortly the cycle of evaporation, cloud formation, rain and run-off, is serving Vico's system of historical renewal and decay as if the world, and not the *Wake*, had been planned that way.

When one pair of Vico's extremities is allowed to coalesce (as min with min may), only three such terms remain: the Theocratic, Heroic, and Human Ages, for instance (though we could play in Bruno's ballpark just as well, or in many another); and if both ends fold like bad hands, they leave some basic binary confrontation behind, such as Dog with Cat, Night with Day, Dreaming with Waking, or Good with Bad. Then when finally, as it happens in Pythagoras's holy triangle, four and three and two disappear into one WHAM! like that last everlong thurrrrrrrrrump of thunder which, as we learn from Joyce, is a sign that the beginning has been whistled from the end of Being once again, and "by four hands of fourthought the first babe of reconcilement is laid in its last cradle of hume sweet hume"; we have reached the shovel-scraped bottom of our heaps of hot and cold, the hub and heart of all series, since no one now would dare deny that there are as many positive numbers as negative and that they run as far as they run as wide, and that when we match one against the other, scratch to scratch, zero is always left, the eternal conclusion of every equation, the pointless starting point, the divine remainder . . . that Nothingness, Meister Eckhart said, which is the negation of Negation itself (whereby Naught falls upon its own emptiness as some Caesar on his sword), though not so thoroughly a negation of Negation as to retain something you might imagine you'd just got rid of (not on your life!), since, as one can see upon the blindest inspection, 'no' takes 'thing' away, and then 'nothing' takes the 'no' away, so that literally nothing is left, not even the name or a letter to make one or spaces where you might write the damn word down.

Therefore, in the drawn-out wink of a giant's eye, or in less time than it takes to refold a road map and stow it away, we have created and destroyed a world—brought it from zero back to zip, dancing our Heideggerean reel; though not to the same nothing, notice, no siree! for who would want to claim that pasteurized displeasures were at all like truly tubular roll-calls, just because there's necessarily nowhere any one of either?

Every nullity has parents, husky sometimes too, and normal as napkins, even when the warp is square and the weft is round; and the absence of money in an empty purse, the annoying nothing of the nebbish, the missing number in an otherwise winning lottery ticket, a fellmonger who sells pans, the unavailable elevator's vertiginous shaft, the apparently adequate parking space, an inexplicable hiatus in some notorious continuum (puzzling as an armistice in peacetime), not to mention, as I nevertheless shall, those peculiar anomalies, the lady novelist, the vaginal orgasm, and the raisinless strawberry; or at bedtime that familiar dry wave dashing against the soft line of some snickering pillow: every one of these catacritical errors is as otherwise to the other as ostrich and angular are, prune and juice too, box and cox, *sic et non*, dear Mom and dearer Dad, and each erupts out of its own emptiness and with its own emptiness into its own emptiness like a cartoon volcano.

Into vacancy of one sort or other, but not always of the same sort, for the nothing of a nebbish is in the realm of values where the nothing of a blank bank balance also is (because you can overdraw on your account, but just try to get four more spoons of soup from an emptied bowl), while the hungry stomach is a chemical condition, the parking space an insured misjudgment, the raisinless strawberry a counterfactual innuendo, lady novelists merely amusing oddities like beauty marks or moles in indiscreet locations, and the losing lottery ticket an ordinary human disappointment; whereas many are made of consternations of an altogether different kind, since there have always been those who believed they might square the circle or defeat infinity in some way, while no one to my knowledge has attempted to pasteurize pain, or open a weather vane to bleed the sky, or warm cold comfort, or cast an ego like a fishing fly: crimes requiring a different punishment, a more discriminating blame—lashes across the bare bottom perhaps with a willowy metaphysical cane.

Plato complained that language falsified the Forms, and Aristotle warned everyone about the fix he would eventually be found in:

> Now some [reasonings and refutations] do not really achieve this, though they seem to do so . . . ; and of these the most prolific . . . is the argument that turns upon names only. It is impossible in a discussion to bring in the actual things discussed: we use their names as symbols instead of them; and therefore we suppose that what follows in the names, follows in the things as well, just as people who calculate suppose in regard to their counters. But the two cases [name and things] are not alike.
>
> *(De Sophisticis Elenchis* 164a4-10)

It is also impossible to replicate relations whenever they're wanted (I can father my firstborn but once), or refasten properties like trousers or stamps, or mimic postures, or picture places upon our ease and inclination. It is equally hard to reenact responses by making heartfelt promises, to restore the past like dry skin, or reproduce whatever qualities might be in question (2 pigs, 3 sisters, 30,000 kroner); so we must bring in our names and numbers, our scales and tables, glottals, grammars, our languages and all our computations, and *they*— what do they bring?—they bring along all of their private paraphernalia; they bring their freak shows and their friends, their camp followers, babies, baggage, dogs—the poets Plato warned us of, speechifiers, preachers, lectures like this one— their brassy bands, their quarrels, their ambiguities like dirty pots and pans; they attract the criminal element; they pitch their tents in our yards (and you can't bargain with King Zeno); they leave us the mess I've just made us wade through: a sodomous love of limits and a thirst for contradiction like a thirst for wine, a potpourri of worlds perceived by peering between subject and predicate like the shutters of a window (yet who can overcome the pronounced pushiness of the letter *p* or the pop of the pursed lip when producing it?); then in addition they encourage us to conceive the relations between material things as if they were elements in a valid argument, to imagine Perfect Beings and immaculate contraceptions, to confuse middle terms and causes, to entertain the quaint idea that the Universe is a grandfather's clock, or hold onto the monstrous notion that it's someone thinking, dreaming, screaming, or is the process of thought, dream, scream, itself, or tells a story, or exhibits a plan, or celebrates a value, or is fastened together by the mind the way words are clenched in the fist of any judgment, or that such judgments themselves may be logical pictures, or to believe that certain symbols may have the power— how amazing!—to represent their own representational skills, and in signs which are both other and the same as the signified, to picture the very act of that picturing itself.

But aren't we right to seek in language the imprint of reality? Doesn't it shape the syntax of our sentences? Surely the way we speak about the world is a response to it just as thoroughly as the world is a reflection of the way we speak? In a moment of uncustomary lucidity, Heidegger puts it this way:

> Is the structure of a simple propositional statement (the combination of subject and predicate) the mirror image of the structure of the thing (of the union of substance with

accidents)? Or could it be that even the structure of the thing as thus envisaged is a projection of the framework of the sentence?

What could be more obvious than that man transposes his propositional way of understanding things into the structure of the thing itself? Yet this view, seemingly critical yet actually rash and ill-considered, would have to explain first how such a transposition of propositional structure into the thing is supposed to be possible without the thing having already become visible. The question which comes first and functions as the standard, proposition structure or thing-structure, remains to this hour undecided. It even remains doubtful whether in this form the question is at all decidable.

("The Origin of the Work of Art,"
in Poetry, Language and Thought, trans. by Albert Hofstadter.
New York: Harper and Row, 1971, p. 24)

But if we were making a world rather than trying to render one, wouldn't all of our questions be answered? *Kennst du das Land* where all such tricks are fair? where the very sense of transcendence which is made possible by ontological projection and equivocation and type-token confusion and reification and hidden contradiction and rhetorical sleight-of-hand, is appropriate and functional; where Being, if it is so willed, can stick to things like glue or sprout like hair; where certain epistemologies are not merely possible but true; where the affective life is like the sea, only the peaks of the waves can be counted; where space and time are palpable and stored in sacks like sand; a realm where acts are truly caused or truly free or truly fated, and where certain values are happily realized or tragically lost; where the ancient dream of the rationalist—that somewhere in language there is a blueprint or a map of reality (where Eeyore's meadow's marked, and Piglet's tree, as well as where the Woozle wasn't)—that dream remains a dream because now language *is* the land—in fiction—where every fact has to have the structure of the sentence which states it, value too, and quality, and apprehension, since there is no out-of-doors in the world where language is the land, no bird in bush or grocery store—just think—no sex or motion, jail or war—just think of that!

2
A Five Finger Exercise

Let's make a hand. That seems simple enough. Nothing should be easier. A hand. Then we can have the hand do whatever else we want done. *The figure, in greeting, thrust forth a hand.* There—the work's complete. I told you nothing was easier. Well. The thrusting-forth of a hand, does that give us a hand? Your ear captured the word. You have it before you, and while the word is perfectly general regarding hands, you know it isn't your hand that was just thrust forth in greeting, or your neighbor's—no—or mine, or anyone's you know. Yet what was thrust forth was not the word, but a hand. Was it an imaginary hand then? a day-dreamed hand? the visual relic of a hand mounted in the memory like a snapshot in a photo album? Once again: no. And it's not a general blur made by the superimposure of countless uninteresting images. No. Yet it's not any specific hand, not the hand of a movie star whom you dream is fumbling with the buttons on your blouse, not Rodin's Praying Hands, not *Las Manos de Orlac con Peter Lorre* either.

The responses of epistemologists are too often irrelevant to reading, and we know they rarely listen. In this context, the word 'hand' doesn't even bring along its definition. A person could understand the sentence perfectly well without being able to say that a hand was that part of the human arm below the wrist. Many people must suppose that the hand is attached to the arm rather than being part of it. In any case, our own hands hang beside us. We need to know no more. All hands resemble our example because resemblance is not an issue.

We are aware that every actual hand has its own physiognomy, nevertheless these features have no function in the greeting in question. So we have fashioned a hand whose singularities are otherwise unspecified. If a rockslide kills my cat, who cares what kind of rocks they are?

It might be going too far to say that a noun *names* a network of possibilities, but it certainly involves one, activates one, makes one relevant. If you like you can argue that the word 'hand' is referring to what is common to all hands, but what is common to all hands is just this matrix, this set of slots: six cubbyholes called color, and within these many shades; at least five textures, not omitting slimy; a rich range of temperatures between the fever of sickness and the chill of death; several hundred sizes, equally many shapes, parts rather firmly attached and determined, including swollen knuckles; location of the member on the far hinge of the wrist, ditto; adornment from nail paint to gemwork, utility, behavior, expressiveness, cleanliness, beauty; in short, we are faced with a shoestore's filing system, and must suspect that the word 'shoe' designates the store.

Shall we fill up some of the blanks? color in, and so control, contours? try to find a shoe that will fit, or a pair of woolen gloves not too scratchy for our sensitive hands? Why? Do we need to know more about a hand than—there's one? The sentence which has been serving as our signal instance is entirely surrounded by logical space like parking lots around a bowling alley. In its case, *any* unspecified figure, *any* undeclared hand, although not just any greeting, will do (a wave won't, a loud hello, a reverential bow). The sentence, as it stands, does not permit us to fill up its emptiness with conjecture. On the contrary.

Still, we are supposed to be in charge here, and if we want to describe, we damn well will. Yet occasions are actually hard to come by. Yesterday I shook hands with the President. Hey! Wow! And what shape were his hands in? I don't like to shake hands with Fred. His hands are made of molasses. Myrtle's, though, make my thumb sweet as maple sugar for hours after. We now and then describe events in newspapers (snow fell heavily on the southern sections of the city and on houses where there were numerous pets and several chimneys), and once in a while in ordinary conversation (you should have seen what she wasn't wearing!), but by and large such descriptions, as well as sentences like *The figure, in greeting, thrust forth a hand,* are pretty well confined to fiction. And mail-order catalogues, of course. If you don't think this is so, try to imagine the circumstances in which our example would be in no way out of the ordinary. It is a written sentence, not a spoken one—plain as pie. "This strange guy stuck out his hand, so I figured he was friendly" . . . that's one conversational version. The point is that while God may have spoken the world like a cough or a curse, the hand we have here is as "all-in-print" as a ransom note.

And if we describe it, what parts shall we list? shall we mention the fingers of the hand? Not unless we want to find ourselves in ontological hot toddy. Consider the following examples: (1) the fingers of her hand were knuckled like bubbles in a pudding; (2) he received a loving letter of rejection; (3) the fleas of the dog fled; (4) the cock of the walk crowed; (5) the wife of the house felt unfulfilled; (6) the uniforms of the band were tacky. Each of these expressions has the same grammatical structure, but the kind of relation shown by the Noun-X of the Noun-Y form is different in each case. What then, exactly, does the structure *show?*

With the first—fingers—we have a standard case of part-to-whole, and in the second—that of loving rejection—we have another; however the message of a letter is not a part of the letter in the same coarsely physical fashion as its stamp. Anyway, there's not temptation to suppose that the fingers belong to the hand the way fleas do to a dog. Quantities pose another problem, for instance, in (7): all of the wrapper was eaten, but none of the candy. "None of the candy" is the kind of deeply puzzling expression Bruno might have pondered long and fondly. Then there are the disquieting formulas: "none of the following," and "none of the above." What are you doing today? I am visiting none of my relatives. Next, in "the rapture of the deep" (8), a causal relation is indicated, while in "the odor of the rose" (9), the rose is simply a source.

Now some of these phrases can be rewritten without too much trouble. We can say, "the band's uniforms," or "the hand's fingers," or "the dog's fleas," but are we ready for "the house's wife," or "the none's candy," or "the walk's cock"? Something is amiss. We can't similarly rebend a bee's knees or rejoint the Pope's nose, though some kinds of 'of' can suffer a complete verbal reversal. It was Abraham Mendelssohn who said: "Formerly I was known as the son of my father; now I am simply known as the father of my son."

Suppose we concluded that in every phrase of the form X-of-the-Y, the X was a poor relation to the Y which, in some vaguely menacing fashion, "possessed" it. Well, we would be wrong. It may be that the walk does indeed "have" the cock that's strutting up and down on it the way a hill or a road has a king, but it is also clear that the cock is in charge of the walk, the king the hill. In the case of the wife, it is not obvious who possesses whom. Certainly the dog wants nothing to do with his fleas and will rejoice to learn they are fleeing him. Should we say "the dog of the fleas" then, since they made the original decision about their doubtful room and board? Again, the uniforms of the band belong to the band, but not quite as fingers are fastened to palms, because we can imagine the Dukhobor Drum and Bugle Corps, naked as saints, giving concerts across Canada. With regard to my knowledge of French (10), the language is an object which certainly does not possess my nasalless ineptitudes, and when we call a donkey a beast of burden (11), our emphasis and interest, and presumably our sympathy, is yet another burden to the beast. In the face of this fickleness

(12)—of which (13) I have provided but a sliver-sized sample—
what in the name of grammar (14) does the word 'of' do?

The grammar of our sentences is generally disappointing
in this way, and if we wanted to build a world of words, perhaps
we would be wise not to use the word 'of'. However, is 'to' or
'on' or 'at' any better? Who was the ninnie who said it was
easy? Some writers believe that the notational inadequacies of
ordinary language have important philosophical consequences.
The sound and shapes of syllables, they say, their variable dis-
positions in sentences, are mere appearances, while behind or
beneath this phonetic din lies reality like trout asleep in a
sunny stream. Appearance beguiles and bamboozles. As Wittgenstein wrote:

> Language disguises thought. So much so, that from the
> outward form of the clothing it is impossible to infer the
> form of the thought beneath it, because the outward form
> of the clothing is not designed to reveal the form of the
> body, but for entirely different purposes.

So the expression X-of-the-Y is not the form of a thought, but
the form of a falsie.

To the same end, here are two mini-arguments offered us
by Jerrold Katz.[1]

A

There is a fire in my kitchen.
My kitchen is in my house.
There is a fire in my house.

B

There is a pain in my foot.
My foot is in my shoe.
There is a pain in my shoe.

---

[1] Jerrold Katz, *The Underlying Reality of Language* (New York: Harper and Row, 1971), p. 6.

Katz sharpens his own point by becoming beguiled himself.
Let me reformulate the argument:

C

The mice in my pantry give me a pain in the ass.
My pantry is in my house and my ass is in my pants.
So the mice in my house give me a pain in my pants.

We might at first imagine that the mistake we are making
is based upon the considerable differences between pains and
pantries, rumps and mice, but Katz goes wrong when he supposes that both fire and kitchen are in my house in exactly the
same way, just as my version assumes that the pantry and its
residents are part of the same whole. My house has 3½ baths,
not 8½ mice. If Katz had used mice in his example he might
have noticed this.

Given a more precise notation, we might be able to distinguish between the various senses of 'in' or the various senses
of 'of'; and in order that we shall no longer be deceived by the
ambiguities of surface and subsurface padding—the slit skirt
and the billowing blouse—I propose the following thirteen new
prepositions, spelled ob, oc, od, of, og, oj . . . and so on. Now,
quite confidently and unambiguously, we can say what we
mean:

(1) odor ob the rose   (7) fingers op her hand
(2) cock oc the walk   (8) beast os burden
(3) fleas od the dog   (9) face ot fickleness
(4) none og the candy   (10) letter ow rejection
(5) uniforms ol the band   (11) wife oy the house
(6) rapture om the deep   (12) knowledge oz French

with the original word 'of' left to insert between 'name' and
'grammar' where it belongs, and 'oj' to express the last relation
oj which we were speaking.

Why is such a sensible suggestion so absurd? There are, I think, two principal reasons: (1) if we were to introduce enough fresh symbols to articulate the relations already implicit in our speech, the increase in vocabulary would weigh so heavily upon our tongues we'd never wag them, since the alleged inefficiency of our language is in fact efficiency itself; and (2) it is simply not true that these relations are hidden or disguised and that we need some special equipment—a map or a set of plans—to find them. Our prepositions do not pretend to name a specific sort of conjunction. They refer to a rather motley group of relations, and the rest of the sentence, as well as the context in which it appears, enables us to choose the kind of connection meant. Nor does our language pretend that 'bank' refers only to financial institutions and then fool us with curves and rivers.

How do I know, for example, that the two expressions, "knowledge of French" and "knowledge of the French" are so very different? Because I know that my knowledge of the French language, and my knowledge of the French people are of distinctly different things. The presence of the 'the' will indicate a change, but it will not tell me what the change is or its degree. The phrase I just used (which was "the presence of the 'the' ") is not much altered if I omit the article and say "the presence of 'the' " instead.

It may be true that the form of the sentence and the form of some thought which we might metaphorically say was contained in the sentence are distinct, but they are distinct notationally, not notionally. My knowledge of kitchens, fires and feet, bums and shoes, pants, pains, panties, enables me immediately and effortlessly to interpret the preposition correctly. One may now strike a light to the suspicion that a form without meaning is formless, and that there can be no ontology to structures without interpretation. Although some forms inhibit or deny others (it isn't easy to see the circle as a square), nevertheless I can picture my cone in a lot of different ways—as a turning triangle, a stack of diminishing doughnuts, and so on. We must construe before we can construct, and so we might say, watching the fuse burn, that it may be semantics which makes syntax possible.

Our word 'of,' for instance, which I have accused of being so blatantly ambiguous, may be defended from the charge by adopting a Platonic view of predicates and prepositions. The difference between the beauty of boys and girls, women and men, of practices and actions, laws and regulations, sciences generally, and Beauty Absolute, lies not in Beauty itself, which is the same in every case and occurrence, but in the subject where it shyly shows its nature; for the harmony of laws and bodies discloses itself differently in different media, just as music does when it tracks the page or flattens itself in a disc of chilly plastic or delights the air with dancing.

'Of,' we could insist, stands for one and only one relation, but a relation which is compelled to refeature its features when forced to appear between a finger and its hand rather than between wife and house or between tunics and their band.

If Quine wants to talk this way, will syntax stop him? Is he encouraged by the common occurrence of the word to a belief in a common property?

> Why not say that chairs and questions, however unlike, are hard in a single inclusive sense of the word? There is an air of zeugma about 'The chair and question were hard' but is it not due merely to the dissimilarity of chairs and questions? Are we not in effect calling 'hard' ambiguous if at all, just because it is true of some very unlike things?
>
> (*Word and Object*, p. 130)

Chairs are hard because they are made of stiff compacted material, though some chairs are hard to sit in because they are low slung and made of canvas or are really heaps of beans. If the chair is firm, it may be uncomfortable to sit on, and if it is uncomfortable to sit on, it may be difficult to continue sitting in it . . . which is what we say if it has arms. A side chair one sits on, an armchair one sits in. Difficulty is the common denominator here. A question is hard because it is impenetrable, like the wood of the chair, or embarrassing, and therefore psychologically uncomfortable and bruising to the ego as the chair may be bruising to the bottom, or simply difficult to answer in a number of obvious ways. Quine is right about the presence of a common property, but 'difficulty' is itself a word hugely ambiguous. There are all *kinds* of difficulties, and Ryle is right in claiming that such expressions as "tides, hopes, and the average age of death, are rising," like many of the outrages I made up earlier, involve equivocation. In our example, there are four senses to the word 'hard' on the chair side alone. Children love both hot dogs and cats, but since you eat one and pet the other, children *must* love them differently. I love to murder and create. My two loves are only metaphorically the same. Most of our difficulties regarding chairs and questions are brought beneath the general term 'hard' metaphorically too. To say that a question is difficult is straightforward enough, but to say that it is difficult because it is hard to penetrate is not. To use the word 'exists' for both minds and bodies, numbers and bombast and building sites, is not the kind of automatic error Ryle so smoothly suggests it is, nor will Quine's sturdy Platonism do. Cases must be taken one by one, and the form of the expression will solve nothing for us.

Meanwhile that hand, which was to reach out and bring a world to life the way it's done in Michelangelo's fresco, has neither palms, nor, so far, any fingers of.

3

The sentences which we are about to consider constitute their world. They are everything that is. Each sound they make is a sound in this world; their lengths are its lengths, their places its places; their intonations are like weather, their stresses like storms, their rhythms are time dancing its grave way toward our demise. We must remember how wide the word 'Iowa' is. We must bear in mind how some words are closed at both ends like 'top' or are as open as 'easy' or as huffed as 'hush.' Some words click and others moan. Some grumble. Listen to the way the word 'sister' is put together. Can you feel the blow which chops off the end of 'clock'? Nothing can be forgiven or forgot, certainly not the weighing of clauses against phrases, or the long departure of qualifiers from the wheel they were supposed to turn, or rim they were to rubber.

Our number-one sentence is dominated by its verb: 'thrust.' In a context as tame as our specimen creates, a word like 'thrust' is like a drunk in a church. "The figure in greeting held out a hand." Nothing there. Flab from one end to the other. Yet you see how readily strangeness is lost. Normally we hold out pencils, beer mugs, hope, help, but to hold out a hand is surreal. We have forgotten. We forget. The phrase, 'in greeting,' serves as a pivot on which the sentence is nicely balanced, but 'thrust' disturbs the equilibrium, as does the double stress, 'thrust forth,' with its two *th*s like rind around it.

The sentence does not tell us that a gentleman, in greeting, thrust forth a hand. It speaks only of a figure. So there is fog, or muffle, or swaddle, or darkness. Whatever the reason, the initial word raises questions of knowledge and point of view, the way the word 'gentleman' brings up questions of class and value. The thrusting forth is all the more appropriate for a shadowy figure. Consider 1.1:

A hand emerged from his sleeve like a mouse from its hole.

You think you know how that is? You have observed many a mouse, and they always bolt out as if several small cats were after them? or do they creep out cautiously, look round and around, or saunter, whistling through their tiny teeth? The point is that the sentence suggests that the hand came out tim-

idly, warily; that it was far from *thrust*. The mouse we are referring to here is a cartoon mouse, a literary mouse, not a real
mouse. Neither author nor reader has watched mice—that's a
good bet—but they have read about them. Even if you were an
accomplished mouse-watcher and knew that mice first warily
peeked about before bolting, you would have to forget what
you'd seen and remember what you'd read: that mice creep until they're scared and then they scurry. So a literary convention
appears here in the guise of an observation. Just as we recognized that our model sentence was a written not a spoken one,
we must now acknowledge the wind-up nature of this particular mouse. We have had to invoke what is commonly called the
pragmatic dimension. A mouse that bolted like lettuce from its
hole would be, of course, another matter and another mouse.

Could we have sentence 1.2, now, please?

A gentleman, in the livery of a butler in a play or a count
in a comedy, thrust toward me what appeared to be a plate
of pickled worms, yet he did so with a smile so appropriate
to the serving of drinks or the offering of *hors d'oeuvres*
that I was quite at a loss as to how to receive them.

We are plainly in the mind of some mordant wit now, and
not in the physical world at all. Our initial sentence was ambiguous about that. It contained an interpretation (that the hand
was thrust forth in greeting, not in anger or pleading), and if
we were making a world without a mind, we couldn't include
it. Similarly, if we were imagining an unseen scene, or one observed only by a telescope, Robbe-Grillet, or a tree, then we
couldn't make any kind of comparison, because nature doesn't
make metaphors, metaphors must be made by a figure in the
fiction or by the author from without. If by an author from without, the sentence is still compatible with a world of dumb matter, though there will be above it, as in a satellite, a godlike
eye, or some of our astronauts crying wow! and golly! at the
moon.

Yet suppose we wish to be in the sort of world which Borges might imagine, the figment of some falsified encyclopedia, not just a world where there were no qualities and nouns, so that our expression, "The moon rose above the river," would have to be rendered, as he suggests, "Upward behind the onstreaming it mooned"; but a world which made metaphors the way we make babies or mistakes, a world filled with smoke from flaming cheeks and bedrooms frosted with icy looks, where the ground was littered with the rubbery remains of punctured hopes, and the milk of human kindness was spooned on wounds like sour cream on baked potato . . . well, it could be done, but only by altering the conventions concerning the literal, so that "she fairly flew into his arms" would be literal, while "she ran to meet him" would be an amusing metaphor involving the refusal of metamorphosis, as though a butterfly might refuse to relinquish its cocoon. Whether we're in Tlön or Toledo, the principle remains unchanged: the text must give us the clues for its own interpretation, and it is by means of that interpretation that the fictional world arises above its page, or "Inwardly over and through its typening it fairytaled."

If our funny gentleman is in the livery of a butler, and the butler is in a play, is the gentleman in a play? And if we shake his wormy hand, will we then be in a play as well? We must be brave, but careful too. This sentence undermines itself. It can't decide whether to advance a butler or a count, and the comparison of the hand to a plate of worms is so weird, we have to wonder about its description of the costume. It is, moreover, a sentence which calls attention to itself, reminding us that if we are in some man's mind, we are very definitely in the verbal part. In the rococo consciousness of our observer, the actual extension of a hand has been nearly lost. Let us try to recover it with sentence-set 2.

2. He held out his hand. It was plump, pale, stubby, damp.

2.1 It was a seamed and broken, dirty hand. He held it out.

2.2 He thrust out a threatening, greedy, malicious hand. I backed away.

2.3 Nails? bitten. Palm? small. Lifeline? early broken. Skin? dry and freckled. Cuticles? unkept. Condition? loose or limp. Condition? soft. Color? pale. Conditon: calm.

Our model sentence merely *noticed* its hand, nothing more, while 1.1 paid more attention to a mouse. A hand was noticed, but *what* was noticed was *displaced*. All of the sentences of set 2 *observe* the hand, they do not merely notice it. The lackey of 1.2 extended toward us an *imagined* hand, and then that gesture was compared to the offering of *hors d'oeuvres*. Since the number of things which might be observed is indefinitely large, each observation must select, but we can nevertheless classify some selections as *compatible*, others as incompatible. The plump, pale, stubby, damp hand of 2 might be the seamed and broken, dirty hand of 2.1, yet the qualities do not reinforce one another; they do not call to one another for confirmation. As a color, white is equally appropriate to snow, lard, or sugar, and the color is therefore equally compatible with sweet, cold, or greasy. Except to the careful reader (bless his moving lips), this would hardly matter, but a world made of merely compatible qualities is one which we experience quite differently from a world of constant reinforcement where, despite the danger of catching cliché, 'damp' and 'nervous' are inevitably found locked in an adjectival embrace, let alone a world in pieces like a torn-up letter, aflutter with clear calm muddy colors and quiet untroubled screams.

The first sentence of this series proceeds properly. A hand is held out, I notice it, then I commence my collection. Since I have not grasped the hand (that gnarled, almost fingerless, tree knob? not on your life), its dampness must be copious, and the light right. If the sentence said that the hand was plump, pale, damp, and scented, we might become suspicious. Thus my observations place me at a certain distance. The lifeline which was noted as broken in 2.3 suggests a closer approach than either 2 or 2.1. There is another sort of distance, and this one will add to our collection of hands (so far, noticed, imagined, and observed), because 2.4 ("He held out a hand so like the one which had struck me as a child I flinched without knowing why") contains a hand which, clearly, is being *recalled*.

The fictional quality of our sentences has little relation to their logical form. As we unfold our initial set-2 sentence so as to articulate fully the nature of its structure, the character of the original simply disappears, meaning changes, and what is more important, the actual manufacture of the hand exhibits different principles. We are in another world. Listen as we become more logically explicit:

2. He held out his hand. It was plump, pale, stubby, damp.
2a. He held out his hand. It was plump, and pale, and stubby, and damp.
2b. He held out his hand. It was plump, and it was pale, and it was stubby, and it was damp.

Our original was not a hand made up of four equal and merely conjoined facts, because, if it were, any order of properties would, like numbers, reach the same sum.

2c. He held out his hand. It was damp, stubby, pale, plump.

Anyone for whom that is the same sentence has a thumb in their ear. The more logically naked version is also the more breathlessly adolescent. It is no longer a hand observed, but one noticed so emotionally that it appears cut apart like a chicken: to be just one thing—wing, thigh, neck, breast,

pope's nose, beak, feet—on seven different occasions. I saw
a dragon, and it was breathing fire, and it was all covered with
green scales, and it had a tail which reached a thousand miles,
and breath bad enough to poison Poland. Nor can we hope to
insert a few *if*s, *or*s, and *and*s, like UN Observers along a dis-
puted strip, and expect them to remain semantically neutral.
Every *and*, every *it*, every *was*, will wear a number: the third
it, the second *was*, the first *and*. Fiction is like garbage
washed to sea on Heraclitus' river. As the famous chef said:
you can't take the same bite twice, especially if you swallow.

It is the multiplied *p* and *b* sounds; it is the dum dum dum
de dump; it is *ump* and *ubb* and *amp*, which makes this hand.
A hand that's damp, stubby, pale, plump, is a hand which
doesn't hang together. The sounds of any sentence are its
bones. This is all skin like an empty glove. The rhythm is dependent on that sound, the sound on the order of ideas, the
ideas on the Early English bluntness of the words, that bluntness then on the notions it hardens and rounds, those notions
in turn on the order and nature of their noises, and these noises
again on good old dum dum dum de dump. Fictional form is
wholly up front like the body of a woman. It is surface, like
sculpture. It fills the ear with the moist eager mouth of the
speaker—worse luck.

In contrast, consider the hand that is threatening, greedy,
and malicious. It is a completely subjective hand. It has
neither palm nor fingers, it has only meaning. On the other
hand, if I dare to say so, 2.3 has the ring of an autopsy report.
Nails? it inquires. Bitten, is the answer. Or a pilot's checklist.
Palm? small. And it drops over its description a rhetorical
form drawn from another realm. We have already had hands
which were noticed, observed, remembered, and imagined.
Now we see that we can have hands which are rhetorically observed, as this one is, or rhetorically remembered or imagined.
However, in this particular example, even that form is askew,
because no checklist, no interrogation, would repeat the same

question and expect different answers: Condition? loose or limp. Condition? soft. Condition: calm.

May not grammar dictate metaphysics here: one of substances and their qualities? All are adjectives, and doesn't an adjective modify a noun? Yet is it the way we modify an engine in order to run it faster, or a request in order to con a boss? If I understand my metaphysics, qualities don't modify substances, whose entire business it is to remain as constant as concrete, but sprawl about on them like bathers on hot rocks. Besides, do we want to call plumpness and stubbiness qualities? Aristotle would surely classify them as states or conditions. No. Subjects are subjects, not substances, and there is no quality or relation I can't turn into a noun if that's what I want to talk about, and if I am a student of stubbiness in hands and pencils, torn tickets, checks, or pen ends, I shall have no great difficulty, like Quine, in thinking of the quality as swinging into its substance like a wrecker's ball, for you may recall that it was his suggestion that subjects, in effect, modified their predicates, rather than the usual other way.

3.   I should say that the hand he held out to me was not above seven inches from wristwatch to tip of middle finger, and its breadth couldn't have been more than four inches, even while receiving change.

3.1 All his fingers were the same size.

I described that greedy threatening hand as subjective because it recorded a reaction rather than an action, but the first hand here is even more withdrawn, and the description tells us far more about its anally compulsive composer than its alleged object, because held-out hands are normally never noted this way. Seven inches? Is that a large hand or a small one? We carry a file on penises but not on hands, and so we would most likely have to stop and think, if the sentence didn't imply hand-size in other ways. "Not above seven," it says. "With a breadth which couldn't have been more than four," it goes on, even when stretched to its greediest width. This is false precision, useless accuracy, and if it means to define a hand for us, it fails. Of course, it has no such intention. It aims at an epiphany of the observer's character.

3.1 is equally deceptive. It is written in the grammar of assertion, but are we likely to believe that every finger is the same size unless we're looking at a drawing by Dr. Seuss? It is a metaphor of appearance, an *als ob* observation. In short, some such thing as a threatening hand is thrust out. All the fingers seem to be the same size. It is a hand anyone might respond to by drawing back. Our hand, however, held out like a filing card perhaps, has only the observer's character written on it, and the hand which grasps such a hand is unique, and no doubt dangerously odd.

Four properties are listed. There might have been three. Why these, and this many, rather than that many, and those? And how are these properties laid on: like paint and wallpaper? If I see a damp palm, it is open to me to construe the relation as that of dew to grass or pond to its basin, but in fiction the matter is decided. Right after the hand is stubby, it is damp, and the simple unassuming 'is' we've used allows only the most unadorned conjunction: there is dampness upon the hand, but dampness in this case does not wrap the hand as water does a diver.

Real things connect, function, act, and a hand which does nothing, however grandly introduced, will soon have no more substance than a damp and stubby shadow. Let's take hold of this hand, then, and see what happens.

4. His hand shook me, and I knew I'd be his friend.
4.1 She gave me her left hand, and I gently shook something upside down.
4.2 Our hands shook while our eyes locked and our smiles curled like wet hair.

Let this set serve us with examples of defeated expectation. One cannot stress too much the function of those standard normal forms which either shade the extraordinary ones or fall beneath them like a shadow. "His hand shook mine," is certainly the customary usage; "his hand shook me," is not, and forces us to call in a second meaning, the one which refers to emotional upheaval, in order to grasp the sense. In fact, he may have laid his hand upon my arm, or clapped my back, or issued an amorous invitation.

4.1, the next sentence in the sequence, is clearly incomplete. Don't you feel it? "She gave me her left hand, and I gently shook something upside down." That's how shaking the left hand feels—it's true—not like shaking a hand, but like vaguely shaking something; nevertheless, the dish is weakly spiced, and needs . . . what?

> 4.1a She gave me her left hand, and I gently shook something upside down as one shakes freshly cut blossoms to release the dew.
>
> 4.1b She gave me her left hand, and I gently shook something upside down the way I shake my penis where it overhangs the john.

Sentences like these create a world in which you very well may turn a corner in a marble hall and find yourself in a shack; in which every custom is a cover for novelty, and novelty is normal; where you learn to proceed with caution because a wave of meaning may flow back over you and alter everything; that it's you and not your husband who is leading a double life. They are unfun houses, these Shandys, but they do introduce us to a new element in the sentence—the reader, the listener— there you are!—for these sentences don't fool themselves, shock themselves, the verb does not cry "surprise!" at the noun. They fool us. We, and our response, are their object. We must be prepared. Remember, only a little wet hair curls. Most wet hair is as straight as the white line on the highway. Yet just how straight is that?

Sterne's famous sentence: "A cow broke in tomorrow morning to my Uncle Toby's fortifications," carries its surprise inside itself like a pregnant woman, for if 'tomorrow morning' hadn't disturbed its lines, the sentence would have reported how a cow had broken into Uncle Toby's fortifications, information only ordinarily odd; yet by using the 'to' from 'morrow' as an entry, this derelict date erases the normal like a spelling error, and we hear how a cow has broken into morrow morning, a fortification more difficult to breach, and forever amazing; because however familiar we are with this sentence's sublime disjunctions, as we may be with Haydn's surprises, or the great sea chase in *Moby Dick*, or the eloquence of Sir Thomas Browne, these features will remain as if engraven, wholly unworn by repeated use, for not even a bored eye can rob a Rembrandt of its greatness, alter a Piero by a jot.

5. Her hand felt like a mouth with twenty tongues.

5.1 My hand suddenly seemed smothered by a steaming towel. Then her nails scraped my palm like a razor.

5.2 She had a hand like a potholder of quilted cotton, the kind made in missions, one that has a yellow chicken on it, clucks in the kitchen, and runs in the wash.

If we are building a world by beginning with a hand, and if neither the logical nor grammatical form of our sentences is going to help us very much; if the total presentation is what counts, and if the structures we believe we find there are already interpreted like laws; if we must know that only barbers use steaming towels, or that the scratched palm is a sexual invitation; then we may be inclined to suppose that the sentences of fiction reflect a world more than make one; that they rely too fully on the life we presume we lead to be other than commentary; that we haven't made a hand, a nail, a finger even, but merely mirrored a few of the billions which weave expressive paths every hour through some human, inhuman, or holy space—millions of Hindu hands, the workers' fists, a dancer's like a sailing leaf, the uncountable gimme-gimmes, as cease-less and self-absorbed as waves; yet it must be this data we draw on, because the flow of the world, which often deposits itself in words like silt, is all we have; but after that, after we know what our *ofs* are, we can fasten fingers to the hand like strings on a guitar; we can use the old to create the new, make as we imagine; for what are the forms of the facts, and what are the facts, in the sentences we have been fabricating?

In 5.2 it is hand as potholder we have hold of, not a rectangle which we can pretend is a window or a door, fenced backyard, or tennis court, or wall, or vinyl floor; not a line which is some path of motion, the measure of a distance, or the edge of an infinite abyss; it is the hand of a dime-store mother, a hand that does not advertise its toil, the pieties which it has served with such simple wrinkled redness, or soft fat care, but which instantly occupies the center of a system of social relations, a quilted wad of love and vulgarity, of *Küche, Kirche, Kinder*, and constitutes a fact which is the coalescence of a milieu and a life, not the way a pudding hardens, but like the splash of a risen fish: both sudden and determinate.

Here are four more which refine on the relation of hand-shaker to shaken, as of subject and active verb to object:

6. He doused my hand in his.
6.1 His huge hands, rough with toil and stained by leather, held mine as if mine were the flanks of a skittish horse.
6.2 With a smirk, he inserted his hand into mine.
6.3 What could I tell from his hand? It was the hand of a missionary. Its calm persistent skin would soon grow over and conceal mine.

Earlier we had examples enough of "nothing." Try to catch a glimpse of these two hands, neither of which exists:

7. Where were his hands? He hadn't eyes either, or shirts in his suitcase.

7.1 Here, try this on for size, he said, giving me a hand.

You have of course heard of the tail which wagged the dog, just like that tale did which invented its author. How's this?

8. It was a hand so huge and prepossessing, it cast him like a shadow on the wall behind it.

8.1 He held his hands before his face, yet there seemed to be no change in his features.

Hands may be hidden in gloves, in muffs, in trouser pockets. We can live in a world of microbes, complicated crimes, and distant stars, of inferred or suspected objects like magnetic fields and islands like Atlantis. From finger to nail and nail to scratch and scratch to . . .

9. She lifted toward me a tray of diamonds. I mumbled something and kissed a carat.

9.1 The ring said something in Latin and rose from his finger like a boil.

We must take our sentences seriously, which means we must understand them philosophically, and the odd thing is that the few who do, who take them with utter sober seriousness, the utter sober seriousness of right-wing parsons and political saviors, the owners of Pomeranians, are the liars who want to be believed, the novelists and poets, who know that the creatures they imagine have no other being than the sounding syllables which the reader will speak into his own weary and distracted head. There are no magic words. To say the words is magical enough.

10. Out of his hands fell irregular white wads of fisted air.

To understand a sentence philosophically (which is as far from understanding a philosophical sentence as Bayonne is from Butte on bad roads) is to project its entire structure into an imaginary world, but this projection, which is in effect an ontological interpretation of the structure, can only be accomplished by the most careful consideration of the entire meaning of the sentence (and its neighbors of course, if there are any). Logical and grammatical forms appear to have minimal, and, at most, limiting effect on literary ones, and even these are unreasonably noncommittal about reality. The most important measure is something we might vaguely call "normal form." Out of his hands fell irregular white wads of crumpled Kleenex, for instance—normal enough if you are clumsy and careless and have a cold.

> 10.1 Our bargain struck, we separated. I wiped my right hand carefully on your leather sleeve, but my sweat was indelible like dye. In an hour your bones would be as stained as a crazed plate, while my hands would be pure enough to play pinochle on the piano and Chopin on the drums.

Perhaps all we have left now is a hand—my pure palm and your dirty brown bones—but perhaps it is better to end with a hand than a whole world. How much applause, after all, has God got for all His trouble over the years?

Notes & Acknowledgments

*The selections in the present work
have appeared previously in the following publications,
although in many cases in a considerably different form:*

"The Doomed in Their Sinking"
A review of *The Savage God* by A. Alvarez and *Suicide* by Jacques Choron, in
The New York Review of Books, May 18, 1972.

"Malcolm Lowry"
A review of *Malcolm Lowry: A Biography* by Douglas Day, in *The New York
Review of Books* as "Malcolm Lowry's Inferno: I," November 29, 1973, and
"Malcolm Lowry's Inferno: II," December 13, 1973.

"Wisconsin Death Trip"
A review of *Wisconsin Death Trip* by Michael Lesy, in *The New York Times
Book Review,* June 24, 1973.

"Mr. Blotner, Mr. Feaster, and Mr. Faulkner"
A review of *Faulkner: A Biography* by Joseph Blotner, in *The New York
Review of Books* as "Facts on Faulkner," June 27, 1974.

"Gertrude Stein and the Geography of the Sentence"
Parts I and III first appeared in *The New York Review of Books* as "Gertrude
Stein, Geographer, I," May 3, 1973, and "Gertrude Stein, Geographer, II,"
May 17, 1973, and these two parts were reprinted as an "Introduction" to
Stein's *Geographical History of America*, New York, Vintage Books, 1973.

"Three Photos of Colette"

A review of *The Complete Claudine* by Colette, in *The New York Review of Books*, April 14, 1977.

"Proust at 100"

The New York Times Book Review, July 11, 1971.

"Paul Valéry"

A review of the *Collected Works of Paul Valéry*, in *The New York Times Book Review* as "Paul Valéry: Crisis and Resolution," August 20, 1972, and "Paul Valéry: The Later Poems and Prose," August 27, 1972.

"Sartre on Theater"

A review of *Sartre on Theater*, edited by Michel Contat and Michel Rybalka, in *The New York Review of Books*, October 14, 1976, as "Theatrical Sartre."

"Upright Among Staring Fish"

A memoir of Nabokov occasioned by the publication of *Transparent Things*, in *Saturday Review of the Arts*, January 6, 1973.

"The Anatomy of Mind"

A review of *Freud and His Followers*, by Paul Roazen, and *Social Amnesia*, by Russell Jacoby, in *The New York Review of Books* as "The Anatomy of Mind," April 17, 1975, "The Scientific Psychology of Sigmund Freud," May 1, 1975, and "The Battered, Triumphant Sage," May 15, 1975.

"Food and Beast Language"

A review of *Genius and Lust: A Journey Through the Major Writings of Henry Miller*, by Norman Mailer, in *The New York Times Book Review*, October 24, 1976.

"Groping for Trouts"

As "Metaphor and Measurement," in *Salmagundi*, No. 24, Fall, 1973.

"Carrots, Noses, Snow, Rose, Roses"

The Levy Lecture at Princeton, spring of 1976; approximately half of the essay was published in *The Journal of Philosophy* for November 4, 1976, with comments by David Hills and Patrick Maynard.

"The Ontology of the Sentence, or How to Make a World of Words"

Lecture given at Cornell University in honor of the retirement of Max Black as Professor of Philosophy. Published in *The Cornell Review*, No. 2, Fall, 1977.

A Note on the Type

This book was set in film in Bodoni Book, so called after Giambattista Bodoni (1740–1813), son of a printer of Piedmont. After gaining experience and fame as superintendent of the Press of the Propaganda in Rome, Bodoni became in 1768 the head of the ducal printing house at Parma, which he soon made the foremost of its kind in Europe. His Manuale Tipografico, *completed by his widow in 1818, contains 279 pages of specimens of types, including alphabets of about thirty languages. His editions of Greek, Latin, Italian, and French classics are celebrated for their typography. In type-designing he was an innovator, making his new faces rounder, wider, and lighter, with greater openness and delicacy, and with sharper contrast between the thick and thin lines.*

This book was designed by Betty Anderson and was composed by Precision Typographers, New Hyde Park, New York.